Alcohol Problems Among Adolescents: Current Directions in Prevention Research

Alcohol Problems Among Adolescents: Current Directions in Prevention Research

Edited by

Gayle M. Boyd
Jan Howard
National Institute on
Alcohol Abuse and Alcoholism

Robert A. Zucker
Michigan State University

LAWRENCE ERLBAUM ASSOCIATES, PUBLISHERS

1995   Hillsdale, NJ   Hove, UK

Lawrence Erlbaum Associates, Inc., Publishers
365 Broadway
Hillsdale, New Jersey 07642

Cover design by Kate Dusza

Library of Congress Cataloging-in-Publication Data

Alcohol problems among adolescents : current directions in prevention research / edited by Gayle M. Boyd, Jan Howard, Robert A.
Zucker.
    p. cm.
Includes bibliographical references and index.
ISBN 0-8058-1915-0 (acid-free paper)
    1. Teenagers—Alcohol use—United States. 2. Alcohol-
ism—United States—Prevention. I. Boyd, Gayle M. II. Howard, Jan. III. Zucker, Robert A.
HV5135.A413 1995
362.29'2'0835—dc20
    94-45216
    CIP

Printed in the United States of America
10 9 8 7 6 5 4 3 2 1

Contents

Foreword

Enoch Gordis
Director, National Institute on
Alcohol Abuse and Alcoholism

Alcohol misuse presents a major risk for health and well-being throughout the life span, but youth have a special vulnerability. Alcohol is the most widely used drug by adolescents. The vast majority of junior and senior high school students have already had some experience with drinking. For some this may be one or two isolated occasions of youthful experimentation. But for others alcohol use is excessive, placing the individual in danger of immediate adverse consequences such as accidental injury and alcohol poisoning; and drinking may occur within a constellation of other high-risk behaviors, including unprotected sex. Moreover, for some youth a pattern of heavy drinking established in adolescence and young adulthood will continue into an adult pattern of alcohol abuse.

Concerned communities and institutions across the nation are tackling the problem of alcohol use and abuse by young people. Research-based knowledge is urgently needed to inform these efforts and to ensure that limited prevention resources are used as effectively as possible. The origins of youthful alcohol use and abuse are found within the complex interplay of individual characteristics, family and peer influences, the larger societal context for alcohol use, environmental conditions, and maturational processes that accompany adolescence. The challenge to researchers who seek to disentangle the key determinants of risk and to develop effective interventions is tremendous.

As is well documented by the findings presented in this volume, alcohol prevention researchers have met the challenge. Steady progress is being made in understanding the risk for alcohol-related problems among our youth and in developing and testing effective interventions. Key sources of influence on youthful alcohol use are described, ranging from individual expectancies about alcohol effects and cognitive decision processes to parenting practices, peer influences, social environments, and economic factors; and a corresponding range of prevention interventions is described. The information presented in this book can serve as a primer to those with an interest in developing and improving effective programs and activities to reduce alcohol-related problems among our young people. And for those engaged in prevention research, this book provides useful reviews and current findings that should aid in directing future research activities.

Preface

Most of the chapters in this volume first appeared as articles in a special issue of the *Journal of Research on Adolescence* entitled: "Preventing Alcohol Abuse Among Adolescents: Preintervention and Intervention Research," published in June 1994. When Lawrence Erlbaum Associates expressed interest in incorporating these articles into a book, the editors of the special issue decided to add two new chapters and to expand the introductory overview. In addition, certain sections of the other eight original articles were also expanded where space constraints of the journal had restricted discussion. One of the entirely new chapters focuses on decision making among adolescents, with particular consideration of risky alcohol-related situations. The other examines a harm-reduction intervention for preventing alcohol abuse among heavy-drinking college students.

In most instances, the original research conducted by the authors of chapters in this volume has been funded by the National Institute of Alcohol Abuse and Alcoholism. Other contributors have included the National Institute on Drug Abuse, the National Science Foundation, the Carnegie Council on Adolescent Development, the Eli Lilly Endowment, the Robert Wood Johnson Foundation, and the Michigan Department of Mental Health and Michigan Department of Public Health.

Gayle M. Boyd

1

An Overview of Issues

Jan Howard
Gayle M. Boyd
*National Institute on
Alcohol Abuse and Alcoholism*

Robert A. Zucker
Michigan State University

Although the minimum legal drinking age in all 50 states is 21 years, alcohol use and attendant problems are commonplace among American adolescents. Recent surveys indicate that by the eighth grade, 70% of students have tried alcohol, 25% have used it during the preceding 30 days, and 13% report consuming five or more drinks on a single occasion during the previous 2 weeks (Johnston, O'Malley, & Bachman, 1992a). These figures increase with age: In 1991, 30% of high-school seniors and 43% of college students indicated that they had engaged in binge drinking within the past 2 weeks (Johnston, O'Malley, & Bachman, 1992b).

Alcohol use and abuse among adolescents are associated with a broad range of high-risk behaviors that can have profound health, economic, and social consequences. These behaviors include drinking and driving, participation in deviant peer groups, abuse of other drugs, unprotected sexual intercourse, interpersonal violence, destruction of private property, and poor school performance.

Trend data suggest that most measures of alcohol consumption by youth and young adults have decreased during the past decade (Johnston et al., 1992a, 1992b). Current rates of consumption and alcohol-related problems still remain alarmingly high, however. For example, recent data from the Fatal Accident Reporting System (FARS) indicate that 33% of fatally injured drivers 16 to 20 years of age had a blood alcohol concentration (BAC) level of 0.10 or higher (National Transportation Safety Board [NTSB], 1993). In 1990, drivers 15 to 20 years accounted for only 7.1% of all licensed drivers, but they were involved in 14.9% of all driver fatalities (NTSB, 1993). Research suggests that younger drivers are more susceptible to impairment from alcohol at moderate BAC levels than are older drivers. Although younger drivers have higher relative risks of fatal crash involvement than other drivers regardless of their BAC levels, that risk is particularly notable at BAC levels in the .05–.09 range (Zador, 1991).

The consumption of alcoholic beverages is embedded in the social fabric of the nation and, for many youths, learning to drink has become a rite of passage and a signal of emergent independence. For these reasons, studying youth drinking behavior has helped developmentally focused researchers understand the causal matrix of cognitive, emotional, and social development underlying the transition from childhood to adolescence, and thereafter to adulthood (Jessor & Jessor, 1977; Kandel, 1980). At the same time, alcohol researchers have focused very heavily on this developmental period to understand the emergence of drinking-related behaviors, including how patterns of alcohol use are acquired and maintained, how expectancies about drug taking are formed, how social pressures and individual differences shape the development of different drinking patterns, and how environmental factors influence use.

Research on the use of alcohol by adolescents and its prevention is necessarily driven by a public-health concern. Alcohol is implicated in the behavior disorder of greatest prevalence in the U.S. population: alcohol abuse/dependence (Regier et al., 1990). Because for most individuals, drinking practices are initiated during adolescence and because the prevalence of problem drinking is very high in this age group, the potential gains from intervention activities that target adolescents are also especially great.

The urgency of the problems associated with adolescent use and misuse of alcohol impels lawmakers, educators, parents, and communities to take action. Intervention efforts instituted in response to public demand, however, are often not informed by research, and it is seldom clear whether the interventions are effective. In this environment, researchers are challenged to develop theoretically grounded, well-tested, effective preventive interventions. At the same time, they are frequently asked to provide immediate practical guidance for incipient or ongoing community-driven intervention activities and policy decision making. The ubiquitous presence of alcohol prevention programs and the variety of relevant legal sanctions can expand the prevention-research laboratory to communities, states, and the nation as a whole, and sometimes provide opportunities to "test" interventions that would be too costly to institute for the sake of research alone.

PREVENTION STRATEGIES

To address alcohol-related problems among youth, a wide range of prevention policies has been adopted and implemented at national, state, and local levels. These strategies include the adoption by all 50 states and the District of Columbia of the minimum legal drinking age of 21 years for the sale of alcohol. All but one state and the District of Columbia also prohibit public possession of alcohol by minors, and all but five states and the District prohibit purchase of alcohol by minors (NTSB, 1993).

A number of states have enacted lower BAC limits for young drivers, ranging from limits of 0.00 to 0.06. Studies have shown such constraints to be effective in reducing alcohol-related crashes, especially when the restrictions are adequately publicized and combined with administrative license revocation (Hingson, 1993; NTSB, 1993; U.S. Department of Transportation, 1992).

The NTSB concluded that several other legislative and policy actions can also be effective in reducing alcohol-related automobile crashes among youth: more vigorously enforcing minimum purchase age laws, enacting laws that establish a provisional license system that is combined with nighttime driving restrictions for young novice drivers, and developing carefully targeted multimedia information and education campaigns directed at youth (NTSB, 1993).

Although drinking and driving by youth is a major concern, prevention efforts are not limited to the area of drunk driving. The Drug-Free Schools and Communities Act and its amendments required institutions of higher education and state and local educational agencies to certify to the Department of Education by October 1, 1990 that they had adopted and implemented a program to prevent the illicit use of drugs and the abuse of alcohol by students and employees (Drug-Free Schools and Communities Act Amendment of 1989). At a minimum, the program must include the annual distribution to each student and employee of: standards of conduct that prohibit the unlawful possession, use, or distribution of drugs and alcohol at the institution or its activities; a description of relevant legal sanctions, health risks, and available counseling, treatment, or rehabilitation programs; and a clear statement that the institution will impose described sanctions on students and employees for violations of the standards of conduct, including expulsion or termination of employment and referral for prosecution. Elementary and secondary schools are also required to provide age-appropriate, developmentally based drug and alcohol education and prevention programs for all students and grades. Receipt of federal funds by educational institutions and agencies is contingent on their compliance with the Act.

Throughout the United States, communities as a whole and organized constituencies within them have designed and implemented a variety of interventions for the prevention of alcohol-related problems among youth. In rare instances, these interventions have been developed for the specific purpose of testing their effectiveness. In other instances, "naturally occurring" prevention programs, initiated by public and private organizations, have provided opportunities for researchers to study their effectiveness by conducting "natural experiments."

The number of prevention strategies worthy of being studied, singly and in combination, taxes the imagination. However, the resources available for research are finite, and their judicious expenditure requires difficult choices. Researchers have therefore suggested various theoretical and pragmatic schemes for classifying the broad array of interventions (Howard, 1993). For example, interventions have been distinguished in terms of whether they target individuals (through processes of socialization) or the larger environment (through mechanisms of social control). Attempts have also been made to structure prevention research in terms of a continuum of systematic research phases.

PHASES OF PREVENTION RESEARCH

In several fields of health research, models of research phases have been set forth that establish frameworks for the logical progression of research from more basic to more applied studies. The National Cancer Institute uses a five-phase model to guide research on the prevention of cancer and consequent morbidity and mortality. The five-phase sequence includes hypothesis development, methods development, controlled intervention trials, defined population studies, and demonstration and implementation studies (Greenwald, Cullen, & McKenna, 1987). Similarly, the National Heart, Lung, and Blood Institute has a five-phase sequence, but only the last category is specifically concerned with prevention—testing the effectiveness of interventions "designed to promote healthful behaviors and to prevent or ameliorate disease in defined populations" (National Heart, Lung, and Blood Institute, 1987, p. 2).

The most widely known model of research phases is the Food and Drug Administration (FDA) sequence that involves three phases of drug testing in human or clinical populations: safety or toxicity studies, efficacy studies, and more extensive clinical trials that assess drug effectiveness and monitor adverse reactions among larger groups of patients under realistic conditions (Flieger, 1990; Young, 1990).

Staff from the National Institute on Alcohol Abuse and Alcoholism (NIAAA) and a select group of extramural researchers have been considering components of a phases model for alcohol prevention research. The specific dimensions of the model and its accompanying sequence of methods are still being developed. Suffice it to say here that the model recognizes that intervention research (i.e., the testing of strategies believed to have the potential of preventing or reducing alcohol-related problems) must be based on a foundation of more basic preintervention research, generally in the social and behavioral sciences.

Depending on the prevention strategy of interest, preintervention studies might focus on: (a) examining risk and protective factors; (b) identifying appropriate target groups and endpoint or outcome variables; (c) developing feasible intervention approaches aimed at the individual (i.e., host), the agent (i.e., alcohol), and/or the social, economic, political, and cultural environment; (d) identifying potential mechanisms for cost-effective delivery of interventions; and (e) selecting, adapting (or constructing), and pretesting appropriate measuring instruments.

STRUCTURE AND THEMES

This volume is organized in terms of an implicit phases model. It begins with two analyses of risk and protective factors that influence adolescent drinking patterns over time without the intrusion of deliberate intervention. These can be considered preintervention studies. The third chapter also falls into the preintervention category. It examines decision-making processes among adolescents, with particular consideration of choices concerning risky alcohol-related situations. Although the author suggests possible approaches for making health communications more relevant to adolescents and reducing the likelihood of harmful decisions, he has not reached the stage of testing these interventions. Chapter 4 explores the role that alcohol expectancies play in teenage problem drinking; but it goes beyond the boundary of preintervention studies by including laboratory research on the experimental manipulation of expectancies as a means of reducing alcohol abuse.

The next six chapters focus almost entirely on intervention research—studies that test or evaluate intervention strategies in terms of their impact or potential impact on alcohol use and abuse by adolescents. The chapters are organized in terms of a micro/macro environmental perspective, moving from the smaller microcosm of the family through school and university settings, communities, and large governmental jurisdictions. In five of the six chapters, the intervention being discussed was originally initiated and implemented by the investigators for research purposes. However, the final chapter evaluates the effects of taxation policies (natural events) that are beyond the control of the investigator and were implemented for reasons extraneous to research.

THEMES AND CONCLUSIONS

In the first chapter, Barnes and her colleagues examine risk and protective factors influencing the development of drinking patterns among Black and White adolescents in Buffalo, New York. The ongoing longitudinal study includes a large representative sample of adolescents and their parents. Of particular interest is the impact of family influences as predictors of alcohol abuse among adolescents. Regardless of race or other sociodemographic factors, the quality of parenting has proven to be a critically important influence on adolescent drinking behavior. "High levels of parental support and monitoring as well as positive adolescent–parent communication" serve as "key elements in the prevention of alcohol abuse and other deviant behaviors."

Peterson and her colleagues also examine the effects of several family influences (parent alcohol consumption patterns, family management practices, and parental alcohol norms) on alcohol use among African-American and European-American adolescents. The initial study population consisted of a large sample of fifth-grade students from Seattle and one of their parents, generally the mother. Students were followed over time through the ninth grade. Those from high crime neighborhoods were overrepresented in the sample. Among both ethnic groups, current alcohol use by the adolescents was strongly and inversely associated with proactive family management practices. Moreover, the influence of parent drinking on adolescent alcohol use appeared to be mediated by family management practices and by parental norms regarding alcohol use. According to the authors, these findings have important implications for the design and implementation of preventive interventions.

Fischhoff and Quadrel describe a cognitive framework for decision making theory and show how this theoretical perspective may be applied to adolescents' decisions about alcohol use. For illustrative purposes, they focus some of their discussion on a single decision: whether to ride with a friend who has been drinking. To indicate how decision theorists would study this type of choice, the authors consider both normative and descriptive approaches to the question. Normative analysis attempts to show how decisions should be made if decision makers are to choose wisely, whereas descriptive analysis attempts to show how people actually make decisions. Using data from their own studies, the authors report similarities between teenagers and adults in perceived vulnerability to alcohol-related risks. Their discussion highlights methodological challenges in applying decision theory to adolescent drinking behavior.

Smith and Goldman provide strong empirical support for their thesis that alcohol expectancies play a causal-mediational role in teenage problem drinking. They argue that these expectancies predict the future onset of problem drinking among teenagers and mediate family influences on such behavior, and that experimental manipulation of alcohol expectancies can significantly reduce heavy drinking among college students. The authors also contend that assessments of expectancies may contribute to the identification of high-risk adolescents before they actually begin to drink. Thus, alcohol expectancies have the potential of being an important index in the early identification of high-risk youth and an object of challenge or manipulation for the purpose of preventing or reducing alcohol abuse.

Maguin and his colleagues describe and evaluate their family-based approach to arresting conduct problems among high-risk preschool children as a means of deterring later onset of alcohol abuse and alcoholism. The intervention combined parent training with a marital issues component, and was focused on families with preschool-aged boys in which the father had been convicted of drunk driving. Compared to their controls, boys in the intervention group showed a sustained increase over time in their prosocial behavior. Significant decreases in overt negative behavior and increases in affectionate behavior were also observed, although these changes may not have been lasting. Evidence suggests that the involvement of both parents in the intervention program was more effective than involving mothers only. These data indicate that moderating effects can be produced with very high-risk families on behaviors believed to be prodromal to later alcohol problems. However, longer term follow-up is essential to demonstrate the efficacy of this family-based approach for moderating later alcohol use.

Teddy Dielman reviews the history and progression of school-based strategies for the prevention of adolescent alcohol use and misuse. He argues that the new generation of school-based prevention research uses promising theoretical approaches that recognize the deterrent value of social norms and social (or refusal) skills. To illustrate his thesis, Dielman summarizes findings from his own research on adolescents. His data establish or confirm that school-based prevention programs can reduce the rate of increase of adolescent alcohol use and misuse; that these effects can endure over time; that intervention is most effective among adolescents who have already started to experiment with alcohol in settings without adult supervision; that there may be an optimal age for intervention; that the degree of adolescent susceptibility to peer pressure is an important mediating variable; and that parental influences are important independent of the effects of peer influences.

Alan Marlatt and his colleagues believe that college students represent a unique population of adolescents and young adults at risk for alcohol problems. And these researchers have been testing a harm-reduction approach to the prevention of alcohol abuse among a sample of heavy-drinking college students. Findings indicate that the intervention program, which involves motivational enhancement, has resulted in meaningful risk reduction among the exposed group compared to randomly selected heavy-drinking controls. The authors also describe a new prevention project targeted at students who belong to fraternities and sororities (the Greek system), because studies show them to be particularly vulnerable to heavy drinking and attendant problems. According to the authors, results of the Greek project will indicate whether the motivational approach for individuals used in the earlier project is effective when administered to an entire high-risk group.

Using a select set of data from the Midwest Prevention Program in Indianapolis, Rohrbach and her associates discuss relationships between parental participation in the multifaceted community program and adolescent alcohol use. Their findings indicate that parental involvement in the program protects against alcohol use by their children, after controlling for other important covariates. The data also suggest that parental participation in the prevention program may serve as a mediating influence on their children's selection of non-drug-using friends. On the basis of their findings, the authors consider implications for the future development and adaptation of alcohol prevention programs for adolescents.

Wagenaar and Perry review a wide range of theories concerning underage drinking and integrate core concepts and propositions into a single theory of drinking behavior. The resulting model emphasizes the centrality of social interaction in influencing drinking practices, and "the critical importance of changing broader socio-environmental conditions to achieve long-term reductions" in the use and abuse of alcohol by youth. To implement and test this perspective, the authors are currently directing two large-scale randomized community trials in regions of Minnesota and Wisconsin. Their interventions focus on the broad social environment that encourages drinking by youth.

Grossman and his colleagues summarize studies of the effects of alcoholic beverage prices and excise taxes on a variety of alcohol-related outcomes for youth. These include consumption patterns, mortality from motor vehicle crashes, and college completion rates. The research perspective involves natural experiments, that is, studies of naturally occurring preventive interventions, which are beyond the control of the investigator. Moreover, in this case the focal natural intervention (taxes on alcohol) is policy driven. The research summarized by the authors suggests that "if reductions in youth alcohol consumption, heavy alcohol consumption, and alcohol-related injuries and deaths are desired, an increase in federal taxes on alcoholic beverages is an effective policy to accomplish these goals."

RESEARCH AGENDAS

The articles in this volume lay the foundation for future avenues of inquiry and highlight some very important emergent research themes. It is clear that family systems are attracting attention as potential environments for preventive interventions. Historically, families have been perceived as sources of alcohol problems and targets of treatment. Now they are being viewed as possible protective systems and settings for deliberate intervention before alcohol-related problems actually occur.

Community-based research that tests multiple prevention strategies as an integrated intervention system is also gaining prominence. These types of studies are very expensive, so they must be built on sound scientific theories and methodologies. The same can be said for school- and college-based studies. Sophisticated investigators appreciate the need to distinguish between subgroups of students at varying risk and the importance of peer, family, and community influences.

As Grossman and his colleagues point out, natural experiments offer valuable opportunities to evaluate the effects of prevention policies on alcohol use and abuse among youth. Other investigators, experienced in conducting cross-sectional and time series analyses, are continuing this line of inquiry. NIAAA is attempting to increase interest in policy-oriented research so that government bodies can learn whether their efforts are effective and how their preventive strategies might be improved. In the area of drinking and driving, a wide range of interventions is ripe for evaluation; this is also true for programs implementing the Drug-Free Schools and Communities Act.

There is obviously a need to stimulate further studies of ethnic-minority youth. The two chapters on risk and protective factors among Black families are illustrative, but this work falls into the category of preintervention research. In the intervention area, there is an extreme paucity of scientifically grounded studies of minority youth.

It is also important to note the absence of research on primary health-care systems as instruments for preventing alcohol-related problems among youth. NIAAA is trying to encourage researchers to develop and test special "anticipatory guidance" modules to be used by health professionals in advising and counseling adolescents before alcohol problems occur. Such studies would appropriately broaden the domain of health services research, which NIAAA considers to be of high priority.

Clearly, prevention research on alcohol-related problems profits from the contribution of investigators from a broad range of disciplines, who work independently and in close collaboration with other researchers. The authors of the chapters in this volume were trained in a variety of disciplines including psychology, sociology, health behavior, education, economics, and various subspecialties within these larger scientific fields. Although their research perspectives and approaches differ, all of these investigators are working toward the ultimate objective of reducing morbidity and mortality from the use and abuse of alcohol.

As indicated earlier, prevention research embraces preintervention studies as well as tests of actual intervention strategies. Thus, it is important to study and understand the causal role of risk and protective factors, the influence of alcohol expectancies, and the processes by which adolescents and adults make decisions regarding risky and nonrisky alcohol-related behaviors. These kinds of studies help lay the foundation for the development, testing, and fine tuning of effective preventive interventions.

REFERENCES

Drug-Free School and Communities Act Amendment of 1989 (Public Law 101–226). (1990). *Federal Register, 55* (159), 33580–33601.

Flieger, K. (1990). Testing in "real people." In *From test tube to patient: New drug development in the United States* (DHHS Publication No. FDA 90-3168; pp. 11–12, 15). Food and Drug Administration.

Greenwald, P., Cullen, J. W., & McKenna, J. W. (1987). Cancer prevention and control: From research through applications. *Journal of the National Cancer Institute, 79,* 389–400.

Hingson, R. (1993). Prevention of alcohol-impaired driving. *Alcohol Health Research World, 17,* 28–34.

Howard, J. (1993). Alcohol prevention research: Concepts, phases, and tasks at hand. *Alcohol Health Research World, 17,* 5–9.

Jessor, R., & Jessor, S. L. (1977). *Problem behavior and psychosocial development: A longitudinal study of youth.* New York: Academic.

Johnston, L. D., O'Malley, P. M., & Bachman, J. G. (1992a). *Smoking, drinking, and illicit drug use among American secondary school students, college students, and young adults, 1975–1991: Volume 1. Secondary school students* (NIH Publication No. 93–3480). Rockville, MD: National Institute on Drug Abuse.

Johnston, L. D., O'Malley, P. M., & Bachman, J. G. (1992b). *Smoking, drinking, and illicit drug use among American secondary school students, college students, and young adults, 1975–1991: Volume 2. College students and young adults* (NIH Publication No. 93–3481). Rockville, MD: National Institute on Drug Abuse.

Kandel, D. B. (1980). Drug and drinking behavior among youth. In J. Coleman, A. Inkeles, & N. Smelser (Eds.), *Annual review of sociology* (Vol. 6, pp. 235–285). Palo Alto, CA: Annual Reviews, Inc.

National Heart, Lung, and Blood Institute. (1987). *Guidelines for Demonstration and Education Research Grants.* Washington, DC: U.S. Government Printing Office.

National Transportation Safety Board. (1993). *Safety recommendation.* Washington, DC: Author.

Regier, D. A., Farmer, M. E., Rae, D. S., Locke, B. Z., Keith, S. J., Judd, L. L., & Goodwin, F. K. (1990). Comorbidity of mental disorders with alcohol and other drug abuse. *Journal of the American Medical Association, 264,* 2511–2518.

U.S. Department of Transportation: National Highway Traffic Safety Administration. (1992). *Lower BAC limits for youth: Evaluation of the Maryland .02 law.* (Traffic Tech, NHTSA Technology Transfer Series No. 26)

Young, F. E. (1990). Experimental drugs for the desperately ill. In *From test tube to patient: New drug development in the United States* (DHHS Publication No. FDA 90-3168; pp. 22–23). Food and Drug Administration.

Zador, P. L. (1991). Alcohol-related risk of fatal driver injuries in relation to driver age and sex. *Journal of Studies on Alcohol, 52,* 302–310.

2

Family Influences on Alcohol Abuse and Other Problem Behaviors Among Black and White Adolescents in a General Population Sample

Grace M. Barnes
Research Institute on Addictions
New York State Office of
Alcoholism and Substance Abuse Services

Michael P. Farrell
State University of New York at Buffalo

Sarbani Banerjee
State University of New York at Buffalo

As the largest minority group in the United States, Blacks account for 12% of the total population and nearly one third of the population in various urban areas, such as Buffalo, New York (31%), and New York City (29%; U.S. Bureau of the Census, 1991). Although population surveys provide rates of substance use among Black adolescents, the available data are largely descriptive in nature. Relatively little is known about whether the predictors of alcohol and other drug use, observed primarily in White samples, predict in the same or different ways among Black adolescents. As Gillmore et al. (1990) noted:

> Because of a lack of such information, prevention efforts aimed at or including minority youths have had to assume that the risk factors identified for the general population are relevant for members of racial minor-

ities as well. If patterns and predictors of substance use differ across race … , such an assumption may not be warranted. (p. 186)

Samples of only Black adolescents also do not allow for a determination of whether processes are different because of racial factors or whether they can be attributed to other variables, such as socioeconomic status. There is therefore a serious lack of empirical research systematically comparing family and peer processes as predictors of alcohol use and related behaviors in representative samples of Black and White adolescents. Furthermore, it has been noted that there are virtually no longitudinal studies of Blacks included in the alcohol research literature (National Institute on Alcohol Abuse and Alcoholism [NIAAA], 1989).

Another fundamental shortcoming in the research literature is the lack of appreciation for the wide diversity of Black youth and families. Recent critical reviews of Black adolescents and families (e.g., Jackson, 1991; McAdoo, 1988; Taylor, Chatters, Tucker, & Lewis, 1990) note that Black adolescents have been monolithically portrayed as low income, afflicted with a host of social problems, and lacking in resources and support from others. Research focusing only on groups of Black "problem" adolescents limits our understanding of those family and peer processes that lead to effective socialization of young people for nonproblem behaviors.

The present longitudinal study represents the full range of diversity of demographic and family factors among a representative sample of Black and White adolescents. In this chapter, the following central research question is addressed: Are sociodemographic, family, and peer influences on adolescent problem behaviors the same or different for Black and White adolescents? For instance, because low-income minority neighborhoods are often associated with drug-related crime, does family income show a different relationship to problem behaviors among Black and White adolescents? Because many Black churches are fundamental Protestant denominations that have clear abstinence policies, is religion a greater protective factor for Black adolescents than for Whites? This study assesses adolescent problem behaviors at Time 2, using a series of Time 1 independent sociodemographic, family, and peer predictor variables as well as interaction terms between independent variables and race.

METHOD

Sampling

A representative household sample of 699 adolescents and their families in Buffalo, New York, and its ring suburbs and towns was obtained by means of random-digit-dial (RDD) telephone procedures on a computer-assisted telephone interviewing (CATI) network. The criteria for inclusion in the sample were that the household have at least one adolescent between 13 and 16 years of age at Time 1 and at least one parent (biological or surrogate). Black families were oversampled (N = 210) to allow a sufficient subsample for meaningful analysis.

After eligibility was determined, the study was described to a parent, and this explanation was often followed by a more detailed information letter. Appointments were made with families to carry out face-to-face interviewing. Both mothers and fathers (biological and surrogate) of the target adolescents were included in the study, depending on family composition. Interviews were carried out by a trained, two-person interviewing team in the respondents' homes. Using stringent follow-up procedures, the Wave 1 completion rate was 71% of eligible families and 77% for Black families. Additional information on the methodology and detailed sociodemographic characteristics of the Black and White samples have been presented elsewhere (see Barnes & Farrell, 1992; Barnes, Farrell, Welch, Uhteg, & Dintcheff, 1991).

Retention. Six hundred fifty-eight (658) of the original 699 adolescents and their families (94%) were retained in the sample 1 year later at Time 2. A dichotomous variable was created that was coded *1* if the adolescent continued in the study at Time 2, or *2* if the adolescent and family dropped out at Time 2. Biserial correlations were run with this attrition variable and sex, age, race, family income, adolescent drinking, deviance, and parenting variables. All of these relationships except mother support had nonsignificant correlations. Although adolescents reporting higher mother support were less likely to drop out at Time 2, the strength of the correlation was weak (−.11).

Measures

Dependent Measures for Adolescents

For this multivariate analysis, three Time 2 dependent measures were derived for adolescents. (Although substantial parent report data were obtained from both parents, and are presented in other publications [e.g., Barnes & Farrell, 1992], current analyses use adolescent reports on all variables, with two exceptions: parental substance abuse [see following section] and family demographic information.)

Frequent Heavy Drinking (Past Year).   Frequent heavy drinking was derived from questions about the frequency of having five or more drinks of beer, wine, or liquor. Frequent heavy drinking represents the number of days in the past year that the adolescent drank five or more drinks of an alcoholic beverage (based on the beverage consumed most often).

Drunkenness (Past Year).   This variable represents the number of times the adolescent reported having gotten drunk or very high from alcohol in the past 12 months.

Number of Deviant Acts (Past Year).   This measure is based on a 20-item scale including a range of relatively minor acts, such as arguing with mother (or father) and staying out later than parents allow, as well as more serious deviance. These include having sexual relations; assault; breaking into a house, business, or car; and running away from home. Two items regarding the use of marijuana and other illicit drugs are also included in this deviance scale. An item asking about consuming large amounts of alcohol was omitted from this scale, however, so there would be no overlap with the other alcohol-abuse dependent variables. The reliability analysis on the deviance scale revealed an alpha of 0.75.

Independent Measures for Parents

Key parental socialization variables[1] include the following independent variables measured at Time 1. These variables have been operationalized on the basis of previous theory and empirical research (e.g., Barnes, 1990; Barnes & Farrell, 1992; Rollins & Thomas, 1979).

Support.   The support construct is defined as behaviors toward the adolescent indicating that he or she is valued and loved. An 8-item scale was used, with items such as: "When you do something well, how often does your mother give you praise or encouragement for what you do?"; "How much do you rely on your mother for advice

---

[1]Two of the parental socialization variables included in this analysis—support and communication—are for mothers only. Information was obtained about fathers' socialization, and in general, the correlations between respective mother and father variables are significant. The father variables result in more missing data, however, because of the prevalence of single-parent households. Because family structure is of theoretical importance to this analysis, the maximum sample size was preserved by using mother variables.

and guidance?"; and "How often does your mother give you a hug, a kiss, or a pat on the back?" (The alpha for the adolescent report of mother's support was 0.80.)

Monitoring.   This two-item scale represents an aspect of parental control. The items were: "How often do you tell your parents where you're going to be after school?" and "How often do you tell your parents where you're really going when you go out evenings and weekends?" There were five response choices, ranging from *always* (4) to *never* (0; $\alpha = .64$).

Positive Communication with Mother.   Barnes and Olson's (1982) 20-item communication scale was used to measure parent–adolescent interaction. Examples of the items are: "I am very satisfied with how my mother and I talk together" and "If I were in trouble, I could tell my mother." Response choices ranged along a 5-point Likert scale from *strongly disagree* (1) to *strongly agree* (5). Negatively worded items were reversed to form a scale representing positive adolescent–mother communication ($\alpha = .87$).

Peer Variables

Peer variables, as reported by the adolescent, include the following independent variables.

Peer (Versus Parent) Orientation.   Two items are included for this scale: "If you had a serious decision to make, like whether or not to continue in school, or whether or not to get married, whose opinion would you value most ... ?" and "With regard to your present outlook on life ... whose views have had a greater impact on you ... ?" Response choices were: "parents most," "parents and friends equally," and "friends most" ($\alpha = .68$).

Closest Friend's Drinking.   This variable represents the average number of ounces of absolute alcohol consumed per day. It is based on adolescent responses to two questions involving the frequency of the closest friend drinking any kind of alcohol beverage and the average number of drinks consumed per sitting.

Closest Friend's Deviance (Past 12 Months).   This scale is a condensed version (12 items) of the adolescent deviance scale just described. The major difference is in the response categories. For their friend's deviance, adolescents responded to more general frequency choices (i.e., "never," "seldom," "sometimes," and "frequently") because they could not be expected to know the precise number of occurrences in the past year for various behaviors of their friend ($\alpha = .79$).

Other Independent Variables

In addition to the self-explanatory demographic factors, other Time 1 independent variables included in the analysis are as follows.

Mother or Father's Substance Abuse.   A dichotomous variable (0, 1) was constructed representing a negative or positive indication of substance abuse in either the adolescent's father or mother. The adolescent's father was classified as having evidence of substance abuse if either of the following conditions were reported at Time 1: He reported three or more alcohol problems in the past year or an average daily consumption over three drinks per day. Because the number of single-parent households was not known at Time 1, there was a considerable amount of missing data for fathers who were not interviewed at Time 1. At Time 2, mothers were asked whether the adolescent's father had a problem with alcohol or substance abuse. This information was used to complete Time 1 information on father's abuse.

Mother's abuse was derived similarly in that the adolescent's mother was classified as having evidence of substance abuse if either of the following conditions were reported at Time 1: She reported three or more alcohol problems in the past year or an alcohol consumption level of over an average of two drinks per day. (This variable is not intended to represent a clinical diagnosis of alcohol abuse or dependence, but rather the upper end of the drinking and alcohol problem continuum, as in other general population surveys of adults [cf. Barnes, Welte, & Dintcheff, 1991; Hilton, 1988]. Although we have chosen to use a composite variable characterizing substance abuse by either parent, the separate mother and father abuse variables were entered independently in other analyses. Neither variable showed a significant relationship to adolescent problem behaviors.)

Religiosity.   A religiosity scale was derived from adolescent responses to four questions dealing with the importance of belonging to religious youth programs, getting religious counsel when facing a problem, believing in God, and praying when facing a personal problem. Four response choices ranged from *not important at all* (1) to *very important* (4; $\alpha = .77$).

RESULTS

Descriptive Analyses

Table 2.1 shows comparison mean levels for Black and White adolescents on sociodemographic factors, adolescent behaviors, and parent and peer factors at Times 1 and 2.

Sociodemographic Factors.   The age and gender breakdowns were exactly the same for Black and White adolescents at Time 1 and, 1 year later, at Time 2. The remaining sociodemographic factors do show significant differences between Black and White adolescent families at both waves of data collection. Family structure was strikingly different for Black and White families: 24% of Black families had two biological parents in the household; 62% of White families with adolescents had two biological parents living in the household. This finding is consistent with data from the U.S. Census Bureau's studies of trends in household and family characteristics (U.S. Bureau of the Census, 1992).[2] Similarly, family income was considerably lower for Black families in the sample than for White families. Mothers of Black adolescents had somewhat lower mean educational levels (12.8 years) than did mothers of White adolescents (13.4 years), although this difference was not as strong as family income.

There are highly significant differences between Black and White adolescents with regard to religious factors, which were consistent across both waves of data. The vast majority of Black adolescents (79%) reported belonging to Protestant denominations, whereas only about one third of White adolescents (31%) indicated belonging to Protestant denominations. In contrast, 52% of the White adolescents reported being Roman Catholic and 3% reported being Jewish, whereas less than 1% of Black adolescents reported being Roman Catholic and none reported being Jewish. According to White and Black adolescents, 6% and 9%, respectively, reported no religious

---

[2]The latest U.S census data for family groups with children under 18 show that 77% of White families and 37% of Black families comprise two-parent family groups (U.S. Bureau of the Census, 1992). For this analysis, we classified families as "two-biological" versus "other." In our more detailed breakdowns, which include stepfamilies (Barnes, Farrell, Welch Uhteg, & Dintcheff, 1991), we have shown for the present family study that 71% of White families and 35% of Black families with adolescents consist of two-parent groups.

TABLE 2.1
Selected Mean Comparisons of Sociodemographic Factors, Adolescent Behaviors, and Parent and Peer Factors for Black and White Adolescents at Times 1 and 2

Item	Time 1[b]			Time 2[e]		
	Black[c]	White[d]	F	Black[f]	White[g]	F
Sociodemographic factors[a]						
Proportion female	.54	.54	ns	.55	.55	ns
Adolescent age (years)	14.5	14.5	ns	15.5	15.5	ns
Proportion with two biological						
parents in household	.24	.62	***	.24	.63	***
Mother's education (years)	12.8	13.4	**	12.8	13.5	**
Family income (in thousands)	21.3	37.5	***	21.7	40.2	***
Proportion Protestant	.79	.31	***	.80	.30	***
Religiosity (4–16)	12.8	10.8	***	12.6	10.5	***
Adolescent behaviors						
Proportion drinkers	.22	.54	***	.32	.70	***
Number of days drank more than						
five alcoholic drinks (past year)	1.4	7.8	***	3.5	10.2	***
Times drunk (past year)	1.0	3.3	***	1.6	5.8	***
Deviant acts (in past year)	17.4	28.1	***	23.2	31.3	***
Expanded deviance scale (Time 2 only)	–	–	–	36.0	49.3	***
Parent and peer factors[a]						
Mother support (8–40)	27.3	27.3	ns	26.4	27.3	ns
Parental monitoring (0–8)	6.0	6.2	ns	5.6	5.8	ns
Positive communication with mother						
(20–100)	65.7	65.0	ns	63.8	63.3	ns
Proportion with a parent postive						
for substance abuse	.49	.41	*	–	–	–
Peer orientation (2–6)	3.1	3.7	***	3.4	3.7	***
Proportion whose closest friend						
is a drinker	.22	.43	***	.25	.63	***
Closest friend's absolute alcohol (oz./day)	.05	.10	*	.12	.18	ns
Closest friend's deviance (0–36)	6.3	7.3	*	6.0	8.5	***

[a]Numbers in parentheses next to variable names represent the ranges on the respective scales. [b]$N = 699$. [c]$n = 210$. [d]$n = 489$. [e]$N = 658$. [f]$n = 197$. [g]$n = 461$.
*$p \le .05$. **$p \le .01$. ***$p \le .001$.

affiliation, and similar proportions of both groups did not answer the question (5% for Whites and 3% for Blacks). As shown in Table 2.1, Black adolescents reported significantly higher levels of religiosity than did Whites.

Adolescent Behaviors.   Contrary to some popular notions, Black adolescents reported significantly lower levels of overall drinking, frequent heavy drinking, drunkenness, and overall deviant behavior than did White adolescents ($p < .001$ for all variables for both Time 1 and Time 2 surveys).

Parent and Peer Factors. Although there were highly significant differences between Blacks and Whites in sociodemographic characteristics and adolescent behaviors, there were no significant differences between Black and White adolescents with regard to mother support, parental monitoring, and positive communication with mother. Again, these findings hold for both waves of data collected.

Black families, as compared with White families, had a slightly higher proportion of parents who were classified as having indications of substance abuse. An important methodological caution should be noted in interpreting this slight difference. Because there are proportionately more single mothers in Black households, the ratings for father's substance abuse are therefore disproportionately based on mother's reports as opposed to self-reports.

With regard to peer influences, White adolescents had higher levels of peer orientation and reported more drinking and deviance on the part of their closest friend than did Black adolescents.

Multivariate Analyses

A multivariate analysis of variance (MANOVA; Norusis, 1990) was designed to examine the effect of Time 1 sociodemographic, parent, and peer variables on adolescent alcohol abuse and other problem behaviors at Time 2.[3] Multiple dependent variables were used because the behaviors of interest are significantly correlated. Correlations between deviance and frequent heavy drinking and deviance and drunkenness are 0.40 and 0.46, respectively, and the correlation between the two alcohol abuse variables is 0.67. Furthermore, it has been demonstrated repeatedly that alcohol abuse and other problem behaviors in adolescence constitute a problem behavior syndrome (Donovan & Jessor, 1985) and are likely to have common antecedents in the family/peer socialization process (Barnes & Welte, 1986).

Table 2.2 MANOVA results are analogous to a cross-sectional analysis, with the added advantage of Time 2 dependent variables that were

---

[3]The MANOVA permits us to test the three dependent variables taken together (Multivariate F) with the independent variables in Table 2.2 entered sequentially in the order listed. The MANOVA program also provides a univariate analysis for each of the dependent variables separately using the same sequence of independent variables. Unlike path modeling techniques, MANOVA allows us to easily examine various interaction effects, particularly between each independent variable and race for this investigation. Although we have not strictly adhered to the assumptions of normality in carrying out the analysis, ANOVA has been shown to be robust under such conditions.

TABLE 2.2

Multivariate Analysis of Variance (MANOVA) With Time 1 Sociodemographic and Socialization Predictors of Time 2 Adolescent Frequent Heavy Drinking, Drunkenness, and Deviance (Unweighted Analysis, Sequential Method)

Time 1 Independent Variables	Multivariate F — Three Dependent Variables Taken Together	Univariate F — Frequent Heavy Drinking (Time 2)	Drunkenness (Time 2)	Deviance (Time 2)	Interpretation of Effect
Race White and other Black	15.5***	12.8***	25.9***	34.9***	Blacks have less heavy drinking, drunkenness, and deviance than Whites.
Gender Male Female	7.7***	20.4***	7.8**	7.2**	Females are lower on all three indicators than males.
Adolescent age (13–16 years)	9.5***	10.4***	16.8***	19.9***	As adolescents get older, problem behaviors increase.
Mother/father substance abuse Negative Positive	3.3*	ns	ns	9.1**	If a parent is classified as having a substance abuse problem, the adolscent shows an increased level of deviance. (No effect is observed for the adolescent alcohol abuse indicators.)
Family structure Two biological parents Single parent and other	ns	ns	ns	ns	Family structure has no observed main effect on adolescent problem behaviors.
Mother's education (years)	ns	ns	ns	ns	Mother's education has no observed effect on adolescent problem behaviors.

Family income ($3,500–$80,000)	3.3*	ns	ns	8.7**	Higher family income is associated with somewhat more adolescent deviance. No observed effect of income on alcohol abuse indicators.
Religion Catholic and other Protestant	ns	ns	ns	ns	No observed main effect of religion on adolescent problem behaviors.
Religiosity (4–16)	6.3***	5.6*	3.9*	17.1***	Higher levels of religiosity predict lower levels of all problem behaviors.
Mother support (8–40) Parental monitoring (0–8) Positive communication with mother (20–100)	11.5*** 22.1*** 5.4**	ns 20.9*** 3.7*	4.4* 16.4*** ns	33.5*** 58.7*** 15.1***	Higher levels of mother support, parental monitoring, and positive mother communication are associated with fewer problem behaviors in adolescents.
Peer orientation (2–6) Closest friend's drinking (oz. per day) Closest friend's deviance (number in past year)	4.3** 26.7*** 15.0***	4.9* 79.3*** 4.0*	6.2** 22.1*** 7.9**	9.9** 6.7** 44.6***	The greater the peer orientation, and the higher the levels of drinking and deviance in the closest friends, the greater are the levels of adolescent problem behaviors.
Significant interactions with race Religion × Race	3.1*	4.3*	ns	ns	Although religion does not show a main effect on problem indicators, there is a significant interaction with race. Blacks who are Protestant are therefore less likely to be frequent heavy drinkers than Blacks of other religions.
Closest Friend's Drinking × Race	4.8**	10.7***	ns	4.8*	Friend's drinking has a stronger effect on heavy drinking and deviance among White adolescents than Black adolescents.

$*p \leq .05. **p \leq .01. ***p \leq .001.$

23

measured 1 year later than the predictor variables. Predictor variables were entered into the analysis sequentially, taking into account race and other sociodemographic factors first, followed by family factors and peer variables.

As indicated earlier, race was a significant predictor of alcohol abuse and other deviant behavior, with Blacks evidencing less heavy drinking, drunkenness, and deviance than Whites. After taking into account race, gender and age remained strong predictors of problem behaviors, with females being lower on all indicators than males, and problem behaviors increasing with age throughout adolescence.

Interestingly, parental alcohol or other substance abuse did not have a significant effect on the two adolescent alcohol abuse variables; however, parental substance abuse did predict increased levels of overall adolescent deviance. The effects of parental alcohol abuse might be manifested later in adolescence or into young adulthood or in the context of other risk factors. Family structure and mother's education had no significant effects on any of the adolescent dependent variables. Family income similarly showed no effect on adolescent alcohol abuse, but it did show somewhat of an effect on deviance—the effect, however, was positive such that higher family income was associated with somewhat more adolescent deviance.

As a main effect, being Protestant was not predictive of less alcohol abuse or related problem behavior. Religiosity was, however, negatively related to all of the problem variables.

After controlling for these demographic/family variables, Time 1 parental support, monitoring, and communication were significant determinants of Time 2 problem behaviors. (For example, if support and monitoring were each split at the median, forming high and low groups, adolescents with high parental support and monitoring at Time 1 had an average of 3.5 days in which they consumed five or more drinks at a sitting at Time 2, whereas adolescents with both low support and monitoring had an average of 13.5 days in which they consumed five or more drinks at a time; see Barnes & Farrell, 1992, for a more detailed breakdown of adolescent outcomes according to specific aspects of parental support and control in the overall sample.) Peer orientation and closest friend's drinking and deviance were also significant predictors of Time 2 problem behaviors after all other variables were taken into account.

To evaluate whether these main effects were equally important for Black and White adolescents, interaction terms for all independent variables and race were entered into the analysis after the main effects. Only two interactions were significant: Religion × Race, and Closest Friend's Drinking × Race. Although religion did not show a significant main effect on adolescent problem behavior, Black adolescents who were Protestant were less likely to be frequent heavy drinkers than Blacks who belonged to another (or no) religion. This religion effect did not hold true for White adolescents. In addition, friend's drinking had a stronger effect on heavy drinking and deviance in Whites, as compared with Black adolescents. In addition to these two differential effects, parenting and peer influences held equally important for Black and White adolescents.

A second similar MANOVA analysis was performed with the three comparable Time 1 dependent variables entered as independent variables after the demographic factors and before the parental and peer factors (table not shown). This analysis was designed to evaluate the effect of parent and peer factors as predictors of change in problem behaviors. For each of the three respective Time 1 and Time 2 pairs of dependent variables, the correlations were strong, ranging from .56 for Time 1 and Time 2 heavy drinking to .61 for both the drunkenness and deviance pairs. Nonetheless, there were increases in the mean levels for each of the dependent variables from Time 1 to Time 2 (see Table 2.1). This is consistent with past survey research showing increases in drinking and related problem behaviors with advancing age throughout adolescence (Barnes & Welte, 1986). Therefore, after controlling for Time 1 dependent variables, perceived parental support and monitoring were significant predictors of the change in adolescent problem behaviors. Friend's drinking at Time 1 was also predictive of the change in frequent heavy drinking. The "protective" effect of being Protestant for Black adolescents also remained significant in this second analysis.

DISCUSSION

Contrary to commonly held stereotypes, this study of early-to-middle adolescents in the general population shows alcohol abuse and other problem behaviors to be significantly lower among Blacks than Whites. This finding, however, is consistent with other general population surveys (Bachman et al., 1991; Barnes, Welte, & Dintcheff, 1991; Harford & Lowman, 1989; Herd, 1989; Welte & Barnes, 1987). It has also been found, however, that Black adults have higher alcohol-related morbidity than Whites and that the alcohol problems reach a peak at a later age for Blacks than for Whites (Herd, 1989). There was no observed interaction of age and race in our study, but the adolescents ranged from only 13 to 17 years old throughout the two waves of data collection. As these respondents are followed into young adulthood, the development of alcohol abuse according to age can be examined for Blacks and Whites.

Because the research literature notes this pattern of polarization of alcohol use among Blacks—disproportionate rates of both abstention and alcohol-related problems—our study was developed to investigate protective factors leading to nonproblem adolescent behaviors, as well as risk factors leading to alcohol abuse and other deviant behaviors. Two of the 14 interactions with race were significant, indicating that most of the same processes influence the development of adolescent problem behaviors for both Black and White adolescents. The interaction between religion and race, however, which was significant in both MANOVA analyses, indicates that being Protestant may well serve as a protective factor against alcohol abuse for Black adolescents. This empirical finding is consistent with accounts showing that historically, the Black church has been among the most important and influential social institutions in Black family life (Poole, 1990). In national surveys of Black Americans, overwhelmingly, respondents were Protestant, primarily Baptist or Methodist—denominations known to advocate abstention from alcohol and other substances. In these same studies it has been noted that church members provide a critical source of support among Black Americans; they also provide guidelines for moral behavior (Taylor & Chatters, 1989; Taylor, Chatters, Tucker, & Lewis, 1990). Therefore, strong proscriptions against the use of substances in the context of high levels of supportive church relations would understandably contribute to a stronger influence on drinking behavior for Black adolescents than for White adolescents.

The second significant interaction shows a different pattern in the relationship between closest friend's drinking and frequent heavy drinking for Black and White adolescents. Peer drinking appears to have a stronger influence on problem behaviors for White adolescents than for Black adolescents. Very little research exists on race differences in peer influences. Although some studies indicate that influence is consistent across racial groups, there are some suggestions that Black adolescents are less susceptible to peer influence than White youths (see Gillmore et al., 1990). This study lends some support to this latter position in that friend's drinking had a stronger effect on problem behaviors for White adolescents than for Blacks. Related to this finding, Windle, Miller-Tutzauer, Barnes, and Welte (1991) examined differences in sources for seeking help for substance abuse problems among adolescents in a large statewide survey. Blacks had a higher proportion of social isolates (i.e., those who would not use any resource for help) and more use of parents and other family members, whereas White adolescents disproportionately indicated they would go to peers for help. Similarly, Jackson (1991) found that Blacks use fewer resources for psychological help, relying more on family members. A major limitation of the present study, as well as other studies examining peer influences, is that they have relied on the adolescent for reports of peer behaviors. Adolescents might well report peer behaviors as more similar to their own than would be determined through independent reports. Future studies should include a peer for self-report of behaviors as well as for observation of joint interactions.

The central message from our study is that the quality of parenting is critically important for adolescent outcomes regardless of race or other sociodemographic considerations. High levels of parental support and monitoring, as well as positive adolescent–parent communication, are therefore key elements in the prevention of alcohol abuse and other deviant behaviors. It is important to note that the parenting variables used in this analysis are adolescents' perceptions of their parents' behaviors. Using cross-sectional data from Wave 1, we have reported elsewhere that mothers' reports on the quality of parenting are generally higher than adolescents' reports—that is, mothers' mean levels of support and control are higher than adolescents' mean levels. Nonetheless, both adolescents' reports and mothers' reports show the same significant impact on adolescent behaviors (see Barnes & Farrell, 1992).

Although family structure (two parent vs. single parent) varies significantly for Black and White families, this factor per se does not predict any of the three adolescent outcomes. Family structure is related to socioeconomic status and, undoubtedly, to other aspects of the quality of family life; nonetheless, it is not the key element in the development of adolescent alcohol abuse and other deviance. Rather, the quality of parental socialization is the important predictor of adolescent outcomes—namely, nurturing parents who monitor the whereabouts of their children and have open lines of communication are more likely to have adolescents with fewer problem behaviors than other families, regardless of sociodemographic and family structural conditions.

The lack of difference in parenting practices between Blacks and Whites goes against stereotypical notions, but there is no systematic body of recent research comparing parenting by race in general population samples. This is a contribution of our study. As discussed earlier, most studies of parenting among Blacks have relied on convenience samples of low-income groups. Such research does not accurately reflect the diversity of minority families in general populations.

Consistent with control theory (e.g., Hirschi, 1969), family factors may influence the choice of peers, and together these factors influence the development of adolescent drinking, deviance, and related behaviors. When parent–child interaction is problematic, adolescents are likely to withdraw from the family and rely more heavily on the influence of peer subcultures. Consistent with previous work (Barnes, Farrell, & Windle, 1987; Barnes & Windle, 1987), our study shows that adolescents who value peer opinions—as opposed to those of their parents—for important life decisions and values are at a high risk for alcohol abuse and other problem behaviors. Similarly, other scientists have shown that parental closeness discourages drug use, both directly and through its impact on peer-related variables, especially the choice of nondrug-using friends (Brook, Brook, Gordon, Whiteman, & Cohen, 1990; Jacob & Leonard, 1991; Kandel & Andrews, 1987). Kumpfer (1989) noted the critical lack of risk factor research in the field of alcohol and other drug abuse prevention. She pointed out the lack of empirically derived and statistically tested causal models, the lack of specificity for different types of youth (e.g., according to race, age, and gender), and the lack of longitudinal studies. This study is a step toward addressing this need. Nevertheless, in spite of strong evidence that family factors are critical in the development of children's substance abuse patterns, there are very few family-oriented substance abuse prevention programs (Kumpfer, 1989; Moskowitz, 1989). Kumpfer and DeMarsh's Strengthening Families Program, involving parental training and the development of parenting skills, is one notable exception. The program's concepts of monitoring the child's behavior and enhancing parent–child communication in a nurturing environment is entirely consistent with our research findings here. This type of prevention program has shown promise in decreasing alcohol and drug use in older children (DeMarsh & Kumpfer, 1986; Kumpfer, 1989). In further recognition of the importance of parenting in preventing substance abuse, the Office of Substance Abuse Prevention (OSAP) has developed parent training materials to help communities identify and implement programs designed specifically for parents (OSAP, 1991). Most prevention efforts with adolescents are school based, outside of the family context; but, given the primary importance of family influences on adolescent alcohol abuse and other problem behaviors, there is a critical need to link research with the development of creative family-based prevention programs.

ACKNOWLEDGMENTS

An earlier version of this chapter was presented at the annual meeting of the Research Society on Alcoholism, San Diego, June, 1992. This research was supported by NIAAA Grant R01–AA06925, awarded to Grace M. Barnes.

We gratefully acknowledge the contributions of Lois Uhteg and the interviewing staff for careful and complete data collection. The contribution of Barbara Dintcheff to data file management is acknowledged with appreciation. We also thank Audrey Topinko for her excellent work in preparing this chapter for publication.

REFERENCES

Bachman, J. G., Wallace, J. M. Jr., O'Malley, P. M., Johnston, L. D., Kurth, C. L., & Neighbors, H. W. (1991). Racial/ethnic differences in smoking, drinking, and illicit drug use among American high-school seniors, 1976–1989. *American Journal of Public Health, 81*(3), 372–377.

Barnes, G. M. (1990). Impact of the family on adolescent drinking patterns. In R. L. Collins, K. E. Leonard, & J. S. Searles (Eds.), *Alcohol and the family: Research and clinical perspectives* (pp. 137–161). New York: Guilford.

Barnes, G. M., & Farrell, M. P. (1992). Parental support and control as predictors of adolescent drinking, delinquency, and related problem behaviors. *Journal of Marriage and the Family, 54,* 763–776.

Barnes, G. M., Farrell, M. P., Welch, K. W., Uhteg, L., & Dintcheff, B. (1991). *Description and analysis of methods used in the family and adolescent study.* Buffalo, NY: Research Institute on Alcoholism.

Barnes, G. M., Farrell, M. P., & Windle, M. (1987). Parent–adolescent interactions in the development of alcohol abuse and other deviant behaviors. *Family Perspectives, 21*(4), 321–335.

Barnes, G. M., & Welte, J. W. (1986). Adolescent alcohol abuse: Subgroup differences and relationships to other problem behaviors. *Journal of Adolescent Research, 1,* 79–94.

Barnes, G. M., Welte, J. W., & Dintcheff, B. (1991) Drinking among subgroups in the adult population of New York State: A classification analysis using CART. *Journal of Studies on Alcohol, 52,* 338–344.

Barnes, G. M., & Windle, M. (1987). Family factors in adolescent alcohol and drug abuse. *Pediatrician: International Journal of Child and Adolescent Health, 14,* 13–18.

Barnes, H., & Olson, D. H. (1982). Parent–adolescent communication. In D. H. Olson, H. I. McCubbin, H. Barnes, A. Larsen, M. Muxen, & M. Wilson (Eds.), *Family inventories* (pp. 33–48). St. Paul: University of Minnesota, Family Social Science.

Brook, J. S., Brook, D. W., Gordon, A. S., Whiteman, M., & Cohen, P. (1990). The psychosocial etiology of adolescent drug use: A family interactional approach. *Genetic, Social, and General Psychology Monographs, 116*(2).

DeMarsh, J., & Kumpfer, K. L. (1986). Family-oriented interventions for the prevention of chemical dependency in children and adolescents. In S. Griswold-Ezekoye, K. L. Kumpfer, & W. J. Bukowski (Eds.), *Childhood and chemical abuse: Prevention and intervention* (pp. 117–151). Binghamton, NY: Haworth.

Donovan, J. E., & Jessor, R. (1985). Structure of problem behavior in adolescence and young adulthood. *Journal of Consulting and Clinical Psychology, 53*(6), 890–904.

Gillmore, M. R., Catalano, R. F., Morrison, D. M., Wells, E. A., Iritani, B., & Hawkins, J. D. (1990). Racial differences in acceptability and availability of drugs and early initiation of substance use. *American Journal of Drug and Alcohol Abuse, 16,* 185–206.

Harford, T., & Lowman, C. (1989). Alcohol use among black and white teenagers. In NIAAA, *Alcohol use among U.S. ethnic minorities* (DHHS Publication No. ADM 89–1435, pp. 51–61). Washington, DC: U.S. Government Printing Office.

Herd, D. (1989). The epidemiology of drinking patterns and alcohol-related problems among U.S. Blacks. In NIAAA, *Alcohol use among U.S. ethnic minorities* (DHHS Publication No. ADM 89–1435, pp. 3–50). Washington, DC: U.S. Government Printing Office.

Hilton, M. E. (1988). Trends in U.S. drinking patterns: Further evidence from the past 20 years. *British Journal of Addiction, 83,* 269–278.

Hirschi, T. (1969). *Causes of delinquency.* Berkeley: University of California Press.

Jackson, J. S. (Ed.). (1991). *Life in Black America.* Newbury Park, CA: Sage.

Jacob, T., & Leonard, K. E. (1991, November). *Family and peer influences in the development of adolescent alcohol abuse.* Paper presented at NIAAA conference, "Working group on the development of alcohol-related problems in high-risk youth: Establishing linkages across biogenetic and psychosocial domains," Washington, DC.

Kandel, D. B., & Andrews, K. (1987). Processes of adolescent socialization by parents and peers. *The International Journal of the Addictions, 22,* 319–342.

Kumpfer, K. L. (1989). Prevention of alcohol and drug abuse: A critical review of risk factors and prevention strategies. In D. Shaffer, I. Philips, & N. B. Enzer (Eds.), *Prevention of mental disorders, alcohol, and other drug use in children and adolescents* (DHHS Publication No. ADM 90–1646, pp. 309–371). Rockville, MD: National Clearinghouse for Alcohol and Drug Information.

McAdoo, H. P. (Ed.). (1988). *Black families* (2nd ed.). Newbury Park, CA: Sage.

Moskowitz, J.M. (1989). The primary prevention of alcohol problems: A critical review of the research literature. *Journal of Studies on Alcohol, 50,* 54–88.

National Institute on Alcohol Abuse and Alcoholism. (1989). *Alcohol use among U.S. ethnic minorities* (DHHS Publication No. ADM 89–1435, p. 467). Washington, DC: U.S. Government Printing Office.

Norusis, M. J. (1990). *SPSS advanced statistics user's guide.* Chicago: SPSS.

Office of Substance Abuse Prevention, U.S. Dept. of Health and Human Services (1991). *Parent training is prevention: Preventing alcohol and other drug problems among youth in the family* (DHHS Publication No. ADM 91–1715). Rockville, MD: Author.

Poole, T. G. (1990). Black families and the black church: A sociohistorical perspective. In H. E. Cheatham & J. B. Stewart (Eds.), *Black families* (pp. 33–48). New Brunswick, NJ: Transaction.

Rollins, B. C., & Thomas, D. L. (1979). Parental support, power, and control techniques in the socialization of children. In W. R. Burr, R. Hill, F. I. Nye, & I. L. Reiss (Eds.), *Contemporary theories about the family* (Vol. 1, pp. 317–364). New York: Free Press.

Taylor, R. J., & Chatters, L. M. (1989). Family, friend, and church support networks of black Americans. In R. L. Jones (Ed.), *Black adult development and aging* (pp. 245–271). Berkeley, CA: Cobb & Henry.

Taylor, R. J., Chatters, L. M., Tucker, M. B., & Lewis, E. (1990). Developments in research on black families: A decade review. *Journal of Marriage and the Family, 52,* 993–1014.

U.S. Bureau of the Census. (1991). *Selected population and housing characteristics for New York: 1990*. Washington, DC: Author.

U.S. Bureau of the Census. (1992). *Household and family characteristics: 1991* (Current Population Reports, Series P–20, No. 458). Washington, DC: U.S. Government Printing Office.

Welte, J. W., & Barnes, G. M. (1987). Alcohol use among adolescent minority groups. *Journal of Studies on Alcohol, 48*(4), 329–336.

Windle, M., Miller-Tutzauer, C., Barnes, G. M., & Welte, J. (1991). Adolescent perceptions of help-seeking resources for substance abuse. *Child Development, 62*, 179–189.

3

Disentangling the Effects of Parental Drinking, Family Management, and Parental Alcohol Norms on Current Drinking by Black and White Adolescents

Peggy L. Peterson
J. David Hawkins
Robert D. Abbott
Richard F. Catalano
University of Washington

Preventing initiation of alcohol use during childhood and adolescence has been an important prevention goal. Nevertheless, most teenagers in the United States do try alcohol. In 1991, approximately 54% of 8th-grade students, 72% of 10th-grade students, and 78% of high-school seniors had used alcohol in the past year; approximately 25% of 8th-grade students, 43% of 10th-grade students, and 54% of high-school seniors had used alcohol in the past month (Johnston, O'Malley, & Bachman, 1992). Although the majority of youths who have initiated alcohol do not become "problem" drinkers or alcoholics, early initiation of alcohol use is one of the strongest predictors of subsequent problem use (Robins & Przybeck, 1985). Furthermore, alcohol use during adolescence directly increases risk for other adverse outcomes, including accidents and homicides, which are the leading causes of death among adolescents (National Center for Health Statistics, 1990), and sexually transmitted diseases, including AIDS (Gillmore, Butler, Lohr, & Gilchrist, 1991; Hingson & Strunin, 1992; Leigh, 1990). Alcohol use may also interfere with the development of a young person's sense of self-identity and social competence, skills acquisition, and fulfillment of social roles (Baumrind & Moselle, 1985; Jessor, 1991; Newcomb & Bentler, 1988; Newcomb, Bentler, & Collins, 1986).

Because most teenagers have at least tried alcohol, their continuing use of alcohol during adolescence may be a more relevant indicator of increased risk for alcohol-related problems than initiation per se. Understanding the etiology of continuing alcohol use during adolescence is an important research goal for alcohol abuse prevention in that malleable factors predictive of this behavior can be addressed. Researchers have identified several factors within the domains of community, family, school, peers, and the individual that predict alcohol and other drug use during adolescence (Hawkins, Catalano, & Miller, 1992; Jessor, 1991; Simcha-Fagan, Gersten, & Langner, 1986). Within the family, the factors of parental alcohol consumption, poor family management practices, and permissive parental attitudes and norms toward adolescent alcohol use have been identified as increasing risk for adolescent alcohol use, although the strength of association and consistency of their relationship to adolescent alcohol use has varied among studies. In this article, we examine the relative independence of these parental factors in the etiology of adolescent alcohol use in Black and White adolescents. We also examine whether the pattern of prediction for these factors is similar or different for the two ethnic groups, with the objective of contributing to the development of culturally appropriate preventive interventions.

PARENTAL INFLUENCES ON ADOLESCENT ALCOHOL USE

Parental Alcohol Consumption

Although its observed effects have often been small or indirect, parental alcohol consumption has been associated with adolescent alcohol initiation (Andrews, Hops, Ary, Tildesley, & Harris, 1993; Kandel, Kessler, & Margulies, 1978), current use (Ary, Tildesley, Hops, & Andrews, in press; Biddle, Bank, & Marlin, 1980; McDermott, 1984), and anticipated future use (Ahmed, Bush, Davidson, & Iannotti, 1984; Biddle et al., 1980). Direct effects are explained primarily by social learning theory's behavioral modeling (Bandura, 1977), in which adolescents learn to drink by observing their parents drink (Kandel & Andrews, 1987). Indirect effects of parental alcohol consumption may operate on attitudes and normative standards (Ary et al., in press; Biddle et al., 1980) or on family management practices (Dishion & Loeber, 1985).

Family Management

Poor family management practices were initially identified as an important predictor of delinquent behavior (Bank, Patterson, & Reid, 1987; Loeber & Dishion, 1983; McCord, 1979; Patterson & Dishion, 1985; Patterson & Stouthamer-Loeber, 1984). These practices have since been found to predict other forms of adolescent problem behavior, including alcohol use. Unclear expectations for behavior, poor monitoring of behavior, few and inconsistent rewards for positive behavior, and excessively severe or inconsistent punishment for unwanted behavior are among the family management practices that increase risk of problem behavior in adolescence (Baumrind, 1985; Hawkins et al., 1992; Penning & Barnes, 1982; Simcha-Fagan et al., 1986). In earlier work, we found that the proactive family management practices of setting clear expectations for children's behavior, monitoring children, and reinforcing children's prosocial behavior were inversely associated with substance use among children ages 10 to 11 (Catalano et al., 1992).

Parental Alcohol Attitudes and Norms

Parental attitudes and normative standards favorable toward alcohol use have been associated with adolescent alcohol initiation, escalation, and continued use (Andrews et al., 1993; Ary et al., in press; Brook, Gordon, Whiteman, & Cohen, 1986; McDermott, 1984). Parental norms about alcohol use can be communicated directly—when parents explicitly state their views on adolescent alcohol use and specific expectations for their child's use or nonuse—or indirectly—through behavior. When parents involve children in their own alcohol use by allowing them to pour or serve drinks, they may be contributing to a normative context conducive to alcohol use by the children. In a study of children in elementary grades, the degree of children's involvement in parental alcohol use was found to predict both the children's expectations that they would eventually use alcohol and their actual alcohol use (Ahmed et al., 1984).

Relative Influence of Family Factors

The relative influence of parental alcohol use, basic family management practices, and parental attitudes and norms regarding adolescent alcohol use are of theoretical and practical importance in determining adolescent alcohol use. Extant data are inconsistent. Some data indicate parental modeling effects on alcohol initiation or use (Kandel & Andrews, 1987; Thompson & Wilsnack, 1984); other studies suggest that "permissive" parental attitudes exert a stronger influence than do actual parental alcohol use behaviors (Andrews et al., 1993; Ary et al., in press; Barnes & Welte, 1986; Brook et al., 1986; McDermott, 1984).

Poor family management practices have consistently been strongly associated with adolescent problem behavior (Loeber & Dishion, 1983) and have been found to exert a stronger influence on adolescent alcohol use than does parental drinking behavior (Dishion & Loeber, 1985). Dishion, Patterson, and Reid (1988) conceptualized parental drinking practices as influencing adolescent drinking directly through modeling drinking behavior and indirectly through disrupting family management practices, the latter increasing the likelihood of adolescents' involvement with antisocial peers. Some support was provided for these hypotheses, although composite measures of alcohol and other drugs were used for both parents and adolescents and the results were not entirely replicated in their study's two cohorts.

Do parental attitudes and normative standards specific to alcohol use have an influence on adolescent alcohol use over and above the effects of parental drinking and family management practices? To our knowledge, no studies have examined this question. Studies investigating the effects of parental norms and attitudes towards alcohol use on children's alcohol use have not examined the effects of family management practices. Conversely, studies examining the effects of family management practices have not explicitly examined parental alcohol attitudes and normative standards for alcohol use.

ETHNIC DIFFERENCES IN ALCOHOL USE

Consistent empirical findings have revealed that in the United States, despite the fact that Blacks experience more drug-related arrests and higher rates of cirrhosis mortality in adulthood than Whites, Black youths generally initiate alcohol use later than White youths (Bachman et al., 1991; Barnes & Welte, 1986; Gillmore et al., 1990; Harford, 1985;

Headen, Bauman, Deane, & Koch, 1991; Newcomb & Bentler, 1988); and Black youths are also less likely to be current users of alcohol during early and mid-adolescence (Rachal et al., 1980).

There are several possible explanations for these ethnic differences in initiation and adolescent use of alcohol (Catalano et al., in press). One explanation is that Black youths are exposed to lower levels of risk factors or higher levels of protective factors associated with adolescent alcohol use; another is that the etiological processes leading to alcohol use among Black youths are different from those at work among White youths. Family management practices and parental norms and attitudes have been explored for possible ethnic differences in exposure and importance in influencing alcohol initiation and adolescent use. Black families, for example, may use more proactive family management techniques or family management practices may exert a stronger influence on alcohol use behavior in Black families. In earlier analyses, Black elementary school children in our study (ages 10 to 11) reported significantly more proactive family management practices in their families than did White youths, although the magnitude of the difference was small (Catalano et al., 1992). There was, however, no evidence at that age that proactive family management practices themselves had differential effects on Black and White youths' initiation of drug use (Catalano et al., in press). With regard to parental alcohol attitudes and norms, in earlier analyses we found ethnic differences in youths' perceptions of parental tolerance of their alcohol use at ages 10 to 11 (Catalano et al., 1992; Gillmore et al., 1990). Black 10- and 11-year-olds reported more negative parental attitudes toward youth alcohol use than did White children of the same age. Normative influences may also operate differently within ethnic groups. Biddle et al. (1980) found no effect of parental drug use norms on adolescent alcohol use for White youths; Black youths' attitudes toward alcohol use, however, were influenced by parental norms, which in turn influenced the youths' own alcohol use. Other researchers have also found that Black adolescents considered parents to be more important influences regarding drug use than did White adolescents (Headen et al., 1991; Ringwalt & Palmer, 1990).

In these analyses, we investigated the separate contributions of parental alcohol use, proactive family management practices, and parental normative standards and attitudes about alcohol use longitudinally across an important developmental period of increased alcohol use: the transition between middle school and high school (Johnston et al., 1992; Kandel & Logan, 1984). Parental variables from 1988, when youths in the sample were ages 12 to 13, and most were in seventh grade, were used to predict current adolescent alcohol use in 1989 and 1990, when youths in the sample were ages 14 to 15, and most were in ninth grade. In this article, we address (a) the extent to which family management and parental norms have additive effects on current alcohol use of teenagers over and above the effects of parental drinking per se, (b) whether parental norms and attitudes regarding teenage alcohol use predict current adolescent alcohol use beyond the effects of parental drinking frequency and family management practices, and (c) possible ethnic differences in relative exposure and importance of family management practices and parental alcohol norms among Black and White adolescents. We hypothesized that the effects of parental alcohol consumption would be mediated through family management practices and parental alcohol attitudes and norms. Good family management practices were expected to be directly and inversely related to adolescent alcohol use, and parental alcohol attitudes and norms were expected to have an independent effect on adolescent alcohol use beyond that of parental alcohol consumption and family management practices.

METHOD

Procedures

The sample was from the Seattle Social Development Project (SSDP), a longitudinal drug prevention study of youth. Initial data were collected in Fall 1985, when students were in fifth grade. Annual spring follow-up surveys were conducted with the youths and one parent or adult caretaker. Parent interviews were conducted by phone; youth interviews were conducted in person. Mothers were designated as the priority target for parent interviews, and 88% of parent respondents were mothers or female caregivers.

Sample Characteristics

The initial sample comprised all fifth grade students in 18 public elementary schools in Seattle, Washington. These schools were sampled to overrepresent students from high-crime neighborhoods. A total of 919 out of a possible 1,050 (87.5%) students completed the fifth-grade student survey. Approximately 25% (n = 228) were Black, 46% (n = 422) were White, 21% (n = 191) were Asian American, and 3% (n = 28) were of other ethnic backgrounds. This is consistent with the school district population fifth-grade students, comprising 25% Blacks, 46% Whites, and 17% Asian Americans.

This report is restricted to a longitudinal sample of Black and White youths for whom complete data were available for all 3 years from 1988 to 1990 (when the majority of youths progressed from Grade 7 to Grade 9), and parents who were interviewed in 1988. This longitudinal sample of 142 Black youths and 308 White youths represents 69% of the initial sample of youths from these ethnic groups ($n = 650$). The Asian-American sample included several different cultural groups, each of which was too small to allow meaningful ethnic group comparisons. Asian Americans were therefore not included in these analyses.

The longitudinal sample is equally divided by gender. White youths accounted for 69.1% of the sample ($n = 308$), and Black youths accounted for 31.5% ($n = 142$). Black and White youths differed on sociodemographic characteristics. Parents of White youths had higher levels of education than Black parents. Approximately 91% of White parents, compared to 81% of Black parents, had completed high school. Approximately 65% of the White parents, compared with 50% of the Black parents, had attended college. Public-school records indicating eligibility for free lunch were used as an indicator of low economic status. Black youths in this sample generally were from families of lower socioeconomic status than White youths. Approximately 71% of Black youths in the sample, compared with 25% of the White youths, were eligible for the free lunch program. Approximately 36% of the Black youths were from two-parent families, compared with 72% of the White youths.

Attrition

To investigate whether the longitudinal sample systematically differed in demographic and drug use characteristics from the initial sample, attrition analyses were conducted using chi-square statistics or analyses of variance (ANOVA). In the ANOVA analyses, independent variables included attrition group status, ethnic group, and ethnic group by attrition group interactions; dependent variables consisted of demographic characteristics plus alcohol, cigarette smoking, and marijuana use at baseline.

The results indicated some overall differential attrition by ethnic group. Approximately 27% of White youths and 38% of Black youths were not included in the longitudinal sample, $\chi^2(1, N = 650) = 8.34, p < .004$. As is often found in longitudinal studies, however, attriters in *both* ethnic groups were more likely to have lower socioeconomic status and higher levels of risk behavior (Ary & Biglan, 1988; Biglan et al., 1991; Hansen, Collins, Malotte, Johnson, & Fielding, 1985; Snow, Tebes, & Arthur, 1992; Tebes, Snow, & Arthur, 1992). For the attrition analyses, effects significant at p < .20 were examined. Youths not included in the longitudinal sample because of missing data during any year from 1988 to 1990 were more likely: (a) to be from low-income families (F = 5.58, p < .02), (b) to be from non-two-parent households (F = 5.20, p < .03), (c) to have lower mother education level (F = 11.276, p < .001), (d) to have initiated alcohol use (F = 5.46, p < .02), and (e) to have initiated smoking (F = 2.02, p < .16). These findings suggest that the external validity may be somewhat constrained by these differences. Although there was no baseline survey for parents by which to compare parental alcohol-related variables for attriters and non-attriters, there was no differential parental response rate by ethnic group. Importantly, there were also no significant ethnic-group-by-attrition interactions, indicating that the internal validity of conclusions about differential effects of explanatory variables was not compromised.

MEASUREMENT

Family Management

Proactive family management was based on the average of six items from the student interview, each rated on a 4-point scale. The items measured degree of parental monitoring, clarity of family rules, and parental positive reinforcement. A higher score reflected greater proactive family management. Items were: "When you are away from home, do your parents know where you are and who you are with?," "The rules in my family are clear," "When you have misbehaved do your parents talk to you about what you have done?," "My parents say good things to me when I do well in school," "My parents notice when I am doing a good job and let me know about it," and "My parents put me down." (reverse coded). Internal reliability alpha coefficient was .66.

Parental Alcohol Norms and Attitudes

Three types of measures were used to assess different aspects of parental normative influences: parental alcohol attitudes, parental normative standards, and child's involvement in family alcohol use. All three were assessed in the parent interview.

Parental alcohol attitudes (perceived harm) is a 2-item scale from the parent interview assessing perceived harm from alcohol use. Items were rated on a 5-point scale ranging from *no risk* (1) to *very great risk* (5). Items were: "How much do you think people risk harming themselves (physically or in other ways) if they: drink alcohol occasionally; drink alcohol nearly every day?" ($r = .43$).

Parental alcohol normative standards were assessed through 4 single-item measures:

1. *Parental norms* was measured by the item, "How would you feel about your child using alcohol before graduating from high school?" The item was originally rated on a 5-point scale but was then collapsed into a 3-point scale from *I would prefer child not use/experimentation is okay* (1), to *I would discourage use as best I could* (2), to *I would absolutely forbid my child's use* (3).

2. *Alcohol situations* consisted of two individual items. Parents were read hypothetical situations in which teenagers might drink alcoholic beverages and were asked to rate the acceptability of the parental response on a 4-point scale ranging from *quite acceptable* (1) to *quite unacceptable* (4). The situations were *use carefully* ("A father finds out his teenage son has been drinking alcohol; he tells his son that he would use alcohol carefully and not let it interfere with his school work") and *use with parents* ("Parents offer their teenage child an alcoholic beverage to drink with them if she or he wants to experience it, saying that they prefer she or he use it with them than learn about it elsewhere"). Results indicated that parents' ratings on the two items were not strongly correlated, so responses to each of the items were treated separately in the analyses.

3. *Child's involvement in family alcohol use* was a single item coded as a binary response. Parents were asked, "Has your child ever brought, opened, or poured a drink containing alcohol for a family member?"

Parental Alcohol Use

Parent respondents were asked how often they drank beer, wine, or liquor, and how often their spouse or partner drank beer, wine, or liquor. This was originally asked with six response categories but, because of distributional considerations, the response was collapsed into a 4-category scale ranging from *never* (0), to *less than once a week* (1), to *about once a week* (2), to *several times a week or more* (3). The parent with the higher frequency of alcohol consumption was used in the analyses.

Alcohol Use by Youth

Cumulative lifetime initiation was assessed with the question "Have you ever drunk beer, wine, wine coolers, whiskey, gin or other liquor?" In 1990, this question was modified to specify alcohol use as meaning more than having drunk a sip or two. Once youths reported use, they were coded as initiators at all subsequent measurement points.[1]

Current use was defined as alcohol use within the last month, ranging from *no use* (0) to *used in the past month* (1).

ANALYSIS

The goal of these analyses was to understand relative parental influences on current adolescent alcohol use. At the age addressed (14 to 15 years old), frequent drinking or even binge drinking was not prevalent. Current use was selected for these analyses as indicating a risk for early problem alcohol involvement, and a standard definition of adolescent current use—alcohol use in the past month—was applied (Bachman, Johnston, & O'Malley, 1981). We compared students who had not initiated alcohol by ages 14 to 15 (ninth grade) to current alcohol users by ages 14 to 15. Focusing on this comparison, and excluding youths who had initiated use but used only in the past, provides a clear separation of alcohol use groups for this investigation of parental influences. In these analyses, students who reported alcohol use in the preceding month in either 1989 (eighth grade) or 1990 (ninth grade) were considered current alcohol users. Approximately 35% of both Black and White youths had initiated alcohol use at an earlier time but were not current alcohol users and were excluded from the analyses.

Results from univariate analyses are presented first, to address the question of whether there are ethnic differences in parental alcohol use, family management practices, and parental alcohol attitudes and norma-

---

[1]We examined the data of students who responded in ninth grade that they had only a sip or two of alcohol in their lifetime. If youths reported for 2 or more years that they had drunk alcohol in their lifetime, or if in any year they reported having used alcohol in the past month, they were still coded as having initiated alcohol. If there was only 1 study year from fifth grade through eighth grade in which they reported having drunk alcohol (and there was no monthly use reported at that time), but they reported in ninth grade that they had only a sip or two, they were coded as not having initiated. There were 5 subjects for whom the former condition applied and 5 for whom the latter condition applied.

tive standards for alcohol use. Correlations among the parent measures are then presented as an aid to interpreting the multivariate results. Hierarchical logistic regression analyses were performed to assess the unique contribution of parental drinking frequency, family management practices, parental alcohol norms assessed attitudinally, and parental alcohol norms measured behaviorally. The order of variable entry was chosen to answer specific theoretical questions. Because the central question of this study was whether parental alcohol attitudes and normative standards contributed uniquely to the prediction of current alcohol use, these variables were entered last. Results from hierarchical logistic regression analyses address the question of whether parental alcohol attitudes and norms, assessed in 1988, added to the prediction of current alcohol use during years 1989 to 1990, once the effects of demographic characteristics, parental drinking frequency, and proactive family management were taken into account. This analysis also addressed the question of whether there are moderating effects of ethnicity on the influence of family management and parental alcohol attitudes and norms concerning adolescent alcohol use on current alcohol use.

RESULTS

Prevalence of Alcohol Use

Prevalence of alcohol initiation by ethnicity during years 1988 to 1990, when the majority of youths were in seventh through ninth grades, are presented in Table 3.1. White youths were more likely to have initiated alcohol use than were Black youths at ages 12 to 13 and 13 to 14. By ages 14 to 15, there was no longer a significant ethnic difference in prevalence of alcohol initiation. The prevalence of initiation found in this sample is consistent with that found in national samples. Johnston

TABLE 3.1
Longitudinal Sample: Percentage Alcohol Initiation

Group	1988 (12–13 Years of Age)		1989 (13–14 Years of Age)		1990 (14–15 Years of Age)	
	%	Chi-Square	%	Chi-Square	%	Chi-Square
Black[a]	56.3	10.43**	65.5	6.22*	73.2	2.27
White[b]	71.8	–	76.7	–	79.6	–

[a]$n = 142$. [b]$n = 308$.
*$p \leq .05$. **$p \leq .005$.

TABLE 3.2
Percentage Current Alcohol Users Versus Noninitiators of Alcohol by 1990
(14–15 Years of Age)

Group	% Current Users	Chi-Square
Black[a],*	56.6	2.61
White[b]	67.2	—

[a]$n = 76.$ [b]$n = 174.$
*$p = .11.$

et al. (1992) reported that 70.1% of 8th-grade students and 83.8% of
10th-grade students had reported use of alcohol in 1991. The percentage of initiators at eighth grade for the combined ethnic groups in this sample was 75%. Table 3.2, which compares the prevalence of current users versus noninitiators for the two ethnic groups, shows that although a smaller percentage of Black youths are current users at ages 14 to 15 years than White youths, this difference is not statistically significant at $p < .05$.

Ethnic Comparison of Parental Influences

Ethnic differences in parental drinking, family management, and parental norms regarding drug use were analyzed next. Ethnic differences in parental drinking and family management were examined using t tests. Multivariate analyses of variance (MANOVA) were used to compare parental alcohol attitudes and norms, with ethnic group as the independent variable and the five measures of parental alcohol attitudes and norms as dependent variables. Univariate F tests were then used to examine differences for the individual variables. All of the parental attitude and norms scales were coded so that a higher score indicated stronger parental norms *against* drug use. Similarly, child involvement was coded to reflect the percentage of children *not* involved in family alcohol use. Results from these analyses are shown in Table 3.3.

Levels of proactive family management were no different between Black and White families. Ethnic differences were found, however, in the drinking frequency of parents and mean levels of parental alcohol attitudes and norms. Parents of Black youths drank less frequently than did parents of White youths, and they had stronger norms against alcohol use. All but one of the variables assessing parent alcohol norms (*use carefully*) were significantly different for the two ethnic groups. The means for the parental alcohol attitudes and norms for both groups were high, indicating that, in general, parents held norms against adolescent drug use. The largest ethnic difference was found for children's involvement in family alcohol use. About 20% more White youths than Black youths were involved in the alcohol use of family members through such activities as getting or pouring drinks. Parents of Black youths were also more likely to hold stronger norms against adolescent use and to perceive drug use generally as harmful than were parents of White youths. Furthermore, in analyses not shown here, these ethnic differences in parental alcohol attitudes and normative standards were consistent over the 3 years covered by the current analyses. Although the magnitude of the ethnic differences in parental attitudes and norms was not large, the consistency of the differences across the measures and across the years is striking and suggests that this finding is reliable.

Bivariate Relationships Among Predictor Variables

Before multivariate effects were considered, the correlations among the predictor variables were examined separately by ethnic group and the

TABLE 3.3
Ethnic Differences in Parental Drinking Frequency, Family Management, and Parental Alcohol Attitudes and Norms

| | | | 1988 (Ages 12–13) | | | |
| | | | Black | | White | |
Variable Name	t Test	df	M	SD	M	SD
Parental drinking	4.04***	447	1.14	1.10	1.59	1.08
Proactive family management[a]	.72	220.23	3.64	.46	3.68	.35

| | Parental Alcohol Attitudes and Norms | | | | | | |
| | Approximate Multivariate | | Univariate | Black | | White | |
Variable	F	df	F	M	SD	M	SD
All variables	4.75***	5,400					
Parental norms			6.22*	2.28	.66	2.13	.55
Perceived harm			8.95**	4.07	1.05	3.70	.75
Use with parents			8.02**	3.05	1.13	2.77	1.03
Use carefully			.48	3.47	.94	3.44	.89
Child involvement			13.92***	.67	.47	.49	.50

[a]Variances were not equivalent for the two groups. Separate variance estimates were used for this t test.
*p ≤ .05. **p ≤ .005. ***p ≤ .001.

TABLE 3.4

Intercorrelations Among Predictor Variables by Ethnic Group:[a] Frequency of Parent Drinking, Family Management, and Parent Alcohol Attitudes and Norms for Longitudinal Samples

Variable	1	2	3	4	5	6	7
1. Parent drinking		-.07	-.19	-.25	-.19	-.13	-.22
2. Family management	-.02		-.01	.05	-.03	-.05	.09
3. Parent norms	-.09	-.06		.11	.19	.11	.20
4. Perceived harm	-.39	-.01	.06		.23	.29	.27
5. Use with parents	-.22	.02	.29	.31		.43	.19
6. Use with care	-.18	-.05	.34	.18	.34		.18
7. Child's involvement	-.39	.04	.12	.32	.25	.14	

Note. $n = 124$ for Black youth; $n = 281$ for White youth. Only people with valid data for all variables are included in the table.

[a]Values for parents of Black youth are above the diagonal, and parents of White youth are below the diagonal.

TABLE 3.5

Intercorrelations Among Family Management and Parent Norm Variables, Noninitiators Versus Current Users Only

Variable	1	2	3	4	5	6	7
1. Parent drinking		.03	-.14	-.26	-.24	-.21	-.12
2. Family management	-.03		-.10	.01	-.22	-.08	.02
3. Parent norms	-.03	.01		.17	.20	.17	.27
4. Perceived harm	-.29	-.04	-.01		.27	.39	.24
5. Use with parents	-.27	.04	.21	.32		.45	.19
6. Use with care	-.15	-.03	.37	.17	.34		.23
7. Child's involvement	-.37	.06	.10	.28	.32	.13	

Note. $n = 76$ for Black youth, $n = 174$ for White youth. Only people with valid data for all variables are included in the table.

[a]Values for parents of Black youth are above the diagonal, and parents of White youth are below the diagonal.

entire longitudinal sample and for the noninitiator versus current user longitudinal subsample. Table 3.4 presents the intercorrelations for the longitudinal sample and Table 3.5 presents the intercorrelations for the subsample of noninitiators and current users.

The patterns in the two tables are substantially the same. In Table 3.4, proactive family management is uncorrelated with all the variables assessing parental drug attitudes and norms. One specific item from the parent survey that assessed parent monitoring was also uncorrelated with parent alcohol use norms, indicating that the lack of correlation between family management and parent norms is not simply a methodological artifact. As seen in Table 3.4, the correlations among the parental alcohol attitude and norm variables are low to moderate. The degree of correlation should not produce multicollinearity problems for multivariate analyses. As a further check for multicollinearity, regression analyses of the independent variables on each other were conducted and evidence of multicollinearity was not found. Correlations were transformed using the z transformation (Cohen & Cohen, 1983) to test whether correlation coefficients were significantly different between the two ethnic groups. There were no significant differences at $p < .05$ (two-tailed tests) for any pair of the corresponding correlations for either Table 3.4 or 3.5. The overall pattern and magnitude of correlations in Table 3.5 is consistent with those found in Table 3.4; thus the generalizability from the subsample of noninitiators and current users to the longitudinal sample should not be substantially compromised.

Hierarchical Logistic Regression

Hierarchical logistic regression was used to examine the independent effects of parental alcohol use, family management practices, and parental alcohol attitudes and norms on current adolescent alcohol use. All of the parental predictor variables were from 1988 surveys, when most youths were in seventh grade (ages 12 to 13). The dependent variable, noninitiator versus current user, was based on drinking status in 1989 and 1990, when youths were between the ages of 13 to 14 and 14 to 15.

In the hierarchical logistic regression analyses, each of the variable subsets was entered as a step, and the order of variables was based on theoretical considerations. Demographic variables (i.e., gender, percentage two-parent households, and mother's education) were treated as control variables and entered in Step 1.[2] Youth's ethnic background was entered in Step 2 to examine whether current alcohol use was associated with ethnicity when demographic variables were controlled. Parental drinking frequency was entered in Step 3 to examine whether there was any evidence of parental alcohol consumption on adolescent current use and, if so, whether the effects subsequently remained once family management and parental attitudes and norms were considered. Family management was entered in Step 4, before

---

[2]The analyses were also run controlling for eligibility for free lunch as an indicator of poverty. This variable was obtained from public-school records and was therefore not available for all students. It was not a significant predictor, and the results were virtually the same as those reported in Table 3.2. To maximize the sample size, free-lunch eligibility was not included in the models shown here.

parental alcohol attitudes and norms, to assess to what extent parental alcohol attitudes and norms made a unique contribution to the prediction of current adolescent alcohol use beyond demographics, parental alcohol consumption, and proactive family management. On the basis of prior studies, it was expected that there would be a strong direct effect of family management.

The variables assessing parental alcohol normative standards were entered in two steps to investigate the independent contribution of norms assessed attitudinally and norms assessed behaviorally. Attitudinal measures of parental alcohol norms (four variables) were entered as Step 5. Child's involvement in parental alcohol use, defined as a behaviorally expressed norm, was entered as Step 6. Interactions between ethnicity and parental alcohol consumption frequency, ethnicity and family management, and ethnicity and parental alcohol attitudes and norms were entered in the final step to investigate whether parental influences were moderated by ethnicity.

Table 3.6 presents the results of this analysis. The upper part of the table presents the chi-square tests of the fit of the model. The −2 log likelihood chi-square statistic evaluates the goodness of fit of the model. A small (i.e., insignificant) −2 log likelihood indicates a high likelihood of the observed results given the parameter estimates, and it indicates a better model fit. The "improvement chi-square" indicates whether the variables added in each step improved the fit of the model, and a significant chi-square indicates a better fit. This statistic is analogous to the F-change test in multiple regression. In the lower part of the table, the columns present the parameter estimates and significance at each successive step. The parameter estimates for the demographic variables are not shown in this table but are controlled throughout the analyses.

As seen in Table 3.6, youth's ethnicity was significant in the Step 2, but once parental drinking was entered, it no longer had a significant direct effect. Both parental drinking frequency and proactive family management improved the model fit in Steps 3 and 4, respectively. More-frequent parental drinking was associated with current adolescent drinking. The use of proactive family management techniques reduced the likelihood that an adolescent would be a current user of alcohol. Contrary to expectations, the results from Step 5 show that parental alcohol attitudes and normative standards did not significantly improve the model fit. However, parental drinking was no longer a significant predictor of current alcohol use. The results from Step 6 show that child's involvement in family alcohol use was associated with current use, even with family management and parental drinking frequency controlled. Parental drinking frequency was still

TABLE 3.6

Hierarchical Logistic Regression: Parent Drinking, Family Management, and Parental Alcohol Attitudes and Norms Predicting Current Alcohol Use, With Demographic Variables Controlled[a]

Step	Model df	−2 log likelihood Chi-Square	p	Step df	Improvement Chi-Square	p
1. Demographics	246	321.30	.001	3	5.41	.15
2. Youth's race (percent Black)	245	316.52	.002	1	4.78	.03
3. Parental drinking	244	310.06	.003	1	6.46	.02
4. Family management	243	275.81	.08	1	34.25	.001
5. Parental alcohol attitudes and norms	239	271.12	.08	4	4.69	.33
6. Child's involvement	238	263.38	.13	1	7.74	.006
7. Interactions: Race × Parental Drinking, Family Management, Parental Alcohol Attitudes and Norms	231	249.25	.23	7	16.13	.03

Variable	Results Step 2			Results Step 3			Results Step 4			Results Step 5			Results Step 6			Results Step 7		
	β	SE	p	β	SE	p	β	SE	p	β	SE	p	β	SE	p	β	SE	p
Youth's race	−.65	.30	.03	−.57	.31	.07	−.48	.33	.15	−.43	.34	.21	−.29	.35	.40	−1.54	.67	.03
Parental drinking				.36	.14	.02	.36	.15	.02	.28	.16	.09	.19	.17	.25	−.06	.22	.79
Family management							−1.03	.21	.002	−1.05	.21	.001	−1.10	.22	.001	−1.34	.30	.001
Parental norms										−.07	.16	.67	−.005	.16	.98	.04	.23	.87
Perceived harm										−.13	.19	.50	−.06	.20	.76	.15	.25	.57
Use with parents										−.05	.18	.78	.03	.18	.88	−.33	.24	.17
Use carefully										−.24	.18	.18	−.27	.18	.15	−.18	.23	.44
Child's involvement													−.96	.35	.007	−1.47	.44	.001
Race × Parent Drinking																.70	.37	.06
Race × Family Management																.63	.43	.15
Race × Parental Norms																−.10	.34	.78
Race × Perceived Harm																−.43	.43	.32
Race × Use With Parents																1.18	.45	.009
Race × Use Carefully																−.45	.45	.32
Race × Child's Involvement																1.53	.82	.07

aThe following demographic variables are controlled and not shown in this table: gender, two-parent households, and mother's education.

not significant, suggesting that its influence on current use was indirect, possibly operating through normative influences. Family management remained strongly and directly associated with current alcohol use.

The results from the final step, testing interactions with ethnic group, suggest that frequency of parental drinking and family management practices do not operate differently for the two ethnic groups. The interaction of parental drinking frequency by ethnicity has a p value of less than or equal to .06, and in analyses in which it was entered in a step prior to the interactions between parental norm and ethnic background, it did not improve the model fit. The interaction between family management practices and ethnic group was also not significant. This latter finding is consistent with Catalano et al. (in press) and Barnes, Farrell, and Banerjee (this issue), who reported that proactive family management practices appear to inhibit adolescent alcohol use in a similar way for both Black and White youths.

The findings provide some evidence, however, that parental normative standards about alcohol use may operate differently for the two ethnic groups. There was a significant interaction between ethnicity and *use with parents* (i.e., the endorsement of alcohol use at home, supervised by the parents). Endorsement of this practice by parents was more strongly predictive of current alcohol use among White youths than Black youths. Approximately 57% of the children of Black parents who endorsed this item had not initiated alcohol use. In contrast, only 20% of White youths whose parents endorsed this practice had not initiated alcohol use. These findings are based on small sample sizes and therefore should be interpreted cautiously; only 21 parents of Black youths (28%) and 74 parents of White youths (42%) endorsed use with parents. Nevertheless, the pattern seems worthy of further investigation. There were no other significant interactions of predictors with ethnic group at $p < .05$, although the interaction between child's involvement in the alcohol use of family members and ethnic group was in the direction suggesting that child's involvement is a stronger influence on current use for White youths than for Black youths. The analyses were also conducted using only mothers as the parental respondent. The pattern of results was the same, suggesting that heterogeneity of parent respondents did not compromise internal validity.

To clarify group membership, the analysis strategy chosen here explicitly excluded youths who had initiated alcohol use at some point but were not current users. Assuming, however, that current use is an indicator of more frequent or regular use, excluding this middle group who had not escalated to more regular use of alcohol potentially introduces a confound between initiation and escalation. To examine this

possibility, logistic regressions were conducted that combined "experimenters" (i.e., those who had initiated alcohol use but who were not
current alcohol users by ages 14 to 15) with current users and compared them to noninitiators. This analysis thus compared people who
had initiated alcohol use to those who had not. The pattern of results
remained the same as reported in Table 3.6, suggesting that family
factors influence initiation. A logistic regression was then conducted,
combining noninitiators and experimenters and comparing this group
to current users. The same family factors were significant as in Table
3.6. Two additional significant interactions, however, ethnic group by
parental drinking and ethnic group by child's involvement in family
alcohol use, were also significant. A larger percentage of current users
among Black youths had at least one parent who drank more than once
per week more than the combined group of noninitiators and experimenters (27% vs. 12%), whereas for Whites the difference was not
significant (28% vs. 30%). Again, this interaction should be interpreted
cautiously because of the small numbers of Black current users present.
There was no significant difference between the percentage of current
users and the combined group of noninitiators and experimenters who
were involved in family alcohol use (25% vs. 35%) for Black youth,
whereas significantly more White current users were involved in family alcohol use than the combined group of noninitiators and experimenters (61% vs. 46%).

DISCUSSION

Previous research has identified poor family management practices as
an important risk factor for adolescent alcohol and other drug use. In
separate research literature, parental drinking behavior and parental
alcohol norms favoring alcohol use have been identified as increasing
risk for adolescent alcohol use. Our analyses expands on the prior
research in these areas to address two important gaps in knowledge:
(a) the independent effects of family management, parental drinking,
and parental norms and (b) ethnic differences in the levels of family
risk factors, and their relationship to current alcohol use by adolescents.

As expected, current alcohol use was strongly and inversely associated with proactive family management practices in both ethnic
groups. Those parents who had monitored their children, communicated clear expectations for their children's behavior, and provided
positive reinforcement for desired behavior when their children were
ages 12 to 13 had teenage children who were less likely to be current

users of alcohol by ages 14 to 15. Good family management was therefore an important protective factor against current alcohol use in both
ethnic groups studied here. No ethnic differences were found in either
mean level of proactive family management or in strength of association with alcohol use. This conclusion is consistent with earlier findings from this sample when youths were in fifth grade (Catalano et al.,
in press) and with the findings reported in this volume by Barnes et al.

The influences of parental drinking frequency on current alcohol use
by adolescents appeared to be mediated by family management practices and parental alcohol use norms. When considered alone, parental
drinking frequency when adolescents were ages 12 to 13 was associated with current adolescent alcohol use at ages 14 to 15. When parental drinking occurred in the context of good family management
practices and parental norms unfavorable to adolescent alcohol use,
however, and when parents did not involve adolescents in their own
alcohol use, frequency of parental drinking was no longer predictive of
current adolescent alcohol use. An area for future investigation is the
influence of parental drinking on such patterns of drinking among
adolescents as binge drinking.

The findings provide limited support for the hypothesis that parental alcohol attitudes and norms have a unique and additive effect in
predicting current use beyond the effects of parental drinking frequency and family management practices. Parents' normative standards, assessed as attitudes about their teenagers using alcohol and
about the harmfulness of alcohol, were not significantly associated
with current alcohol use. Alcohol norms measured behaviorally, however, through children's involvement in the alcohol use of family members, were associated with current adolescent use. This result is
consistent with that of Ahmed et al. (1984). Children's involvement in
family alcohol use was measured in this study by a single item indicator. Future investigations of this construct would be strengthened by
assessing the behavioral involvement more comprehensively, with
such items as frequency of involvement, specific ways in which youths
are involved, and how family members' involvement occurs.

Ethnic differences were found in parental alcohol attitudes and
norms. Black parents held stronger norms against adolescent alcohol
use, perceived alcohol use as more harmful, and involved their children less in adult alcohol use in the family than did White parents.
These differences should be viewed cautiously, remembering that a
higher percentage of Black youths than Whites were lost to follow-up.
This might bias the sample toward Black parents with more favorable
norms. Attrition analyses, however, revealed no ethnic differences in
parental response rate and no higher risk in terms of demographic

characteristics and alcohol or other drug use among Black youths lost to follow-up compared with White youths lost to follow-up. These findings diminish the likelihood of bias due to differential selection on parental norms. The observed ethnic differences in parental normative standards regarding adolescent alcohol use should be studied further.

The findings suggest that Black parents in this sample provided a strong normative context against alcohol use that reduced the likelihood of current adolescent alcohol involvement. White youths may thus be exposed to higher risk within the family than Black youths because of more permissive parental alcohol norms. Although Black adolescents in this sample initiated alcohol use later than did White youths, however, by ages 14 to 15 there were no significant ethnic differences in the prevalence of alcohol initiators or current alcohol users. This suggests that the rate of initiation during this time of transition between middle school and high school is higher among Black youths. Although this is an important risk period for initiation for all youths, it may be even more critical for Black youths. It appears that family factors were not responsible for this increased prevalence in current alcohol use among young Blacks in this sample. Therefore, although the strong normative context within the family of Black youths appeared to inhibit current adolescent alcohol use, factors that explain the more rapid rate of increase in the prevalence of alcohol use among Blacks during this critical period should be sought in other domains, including the school, peer group, and community.

The results indicate that parents who manage their families proactively and who communicate through their alcohol use behaviors that alcohol use is inappropriate for teenagers appear to reduce significantly their children's risk of alcohol use at ages 14 to 15. These results also suggest that moderate parental alcohol consumption in the context of good family management practices, clear norms against adolescent alcohol use, and not involving children in family alcohol use does not significantly increase the risk of current adolescent alcohol use.

One important limitation of this study is the measurement of alcohol use. Lifetime prevalence of use and use in the past month were obtained, but frequency of alcohol use in the past year was not measured. This is an important omission for assessing adolescent alcohol use behavior given that it may occur sporadically. All of those identified as current users in this study were appropriately identified, but some of those who were not included as current users may have used alcohol recently, although not in the past month. Excluding the "experimenters" from the analysis to obtain groups whose membership criterion was clear caused the loss of subjects from these analyses whose behavior will be important to understand in the future. The post hoc analyses to distinguish between predictors of initiation and predictors of current use suggest that there may be different etiological pathways for initiation of alcohol use than for escalation or continuation of use, a finding consistent with other studies (Bailey, Flewelling, & Rachal, 1992; Ellickson & Hays, 1991); also, these pathways may differ by ethnic group. In particular, although parents of Black youths tended to drink less frequently than did parents of White youths, parental drinking frequency may exert a stronger influence on current drinking, although not on alcohol initiation, for Black youths than for Whites, whereas child's involvement in family alcohol use appeared to be more strongly associated with current drinking for White youths than for Black youths.

In this study, we focused on family factors. A future step is to build on these findings and examine family influences within the context of individual risk factors, such as aggression or antisocial behavior and youth's alcohol attitudes and norms, and peer influences. By examining the parental influences in this broader context, indirect and direct influences can be identified, and the underlying processes governing adolescent alcohol use behavior can be illuminated.

The results of this study have important implications for preventive interventions. First, family management skills are important for parents of children ages 12 to 13, not only in preventing alcohol initiation but in preventing current alcohol use by ages 14 to 15. Interventions that help parents improve skills in monitoring their children, setting clear expectations, and reinforcing prosocial behaviors should reduce the risk of adolescent alcohol use. Second, parents' involving their children in their own use, even with family management practices controlled, increases the chances that their children will use alcohol as adolescents. Educating parents not to involve their children in their use of alcohol can provide an important mechanism to reduce risk for adolescent alcohol involvement. Interventions that help parents create a strong normative environment against alcohol use may be particularly important for White parents, primarily because they appear less consistent than Black parents in behaviorally asserting norms unfavorable to alcohol use among adolescents. If this finding is replicated in other studies, it further suggests that preventive interventions for Black parents should reinforce and help support existing parental norms against adolescent alcohol use and perhaps focus on ways to reduce risk external to the family, such as school, peer, or other community influences. In summary, our data suggest that good family management practices and avoiding children's involvement in the alcohol use of other family members can protect against adolescent alcohol use in both Black and White families.

ACKNOWLEDGMENTS

The research and preparation of this chapter were supported by National Institute on Drug Abuse Grants DA 04506 and DA 03721 and by a grant from the Robert Wood Johnson Foundation.
We thank Gloria Liu, for her help with data analysis and Patricia Huling, for her editorial assistance.

REFERENCES

Ahmed, S. W., Bush, P. J., Davidson, F. R., & Iannotti, R. J. (1984, November). *Predicting children's use and intentions to use abusable substances.* Paper presented at the annual meeting of the American Public Health Association, Anaheim, CA.

Andrews, J. A., Hops, H., Ary, D., Tildesley, E., & Harris, J. (1993). *Parent influence on adolescent use: Specific and nonspecific effects.* Unpublished manuscript, Oregon Research Institute, Eugene.

Ary, D. V., & Biglan, A. (1988). Longitudinal changes in adolescent cigarette smoking behavior: Onset and cessation. *Journal of Behavioral Medicine, 11,* 361–382.

Ary, D. V., Tildesley, E., Hops, H., & Andrews, J. (in press). The influence of parent, sibling, and peer modeling and attitudes on adolescent use of alcohol. *The International Journal of the Addictions.*

Bachman, J. G., Johnston, L. D., & O'Malley, P. M. (1981). Smoking, drinking, and drug use among American high school students: Correlates and trends, 1975–1979. *American Journal of Public Health, 71,* 59–69.

Bachman, J. G., Wallace, J. M., Jr., O'Malley, P. M., Johnston, L. D., Kurth, C. L., & Neighbors, H. W. (1991). Racial/ethnic differences in smoking, drinking, and illicit drug use among American high school seniors, 1976–1989. *American Journal of Public Health, 81,* 372–377.

Bailey, S. L., Flewelling, R. L., & Rachal, J. V. (1992). Predicting continued use of marijuana among adolescents: The relative influence of drug-specific and social context factors. *Journal of Health and Social Behavior, 33,* 51–66.

Bandura, A. (1977). Self-efficacy: Toward a unifying theory of behavioral change. *Psychological Review, 84,* 191–215.

Bank, L., Patterson, G. R., & Reid, J. B. (1987). Delinquency prevention through training parents in family management. *The Behavior Analyst, 10,* 75–82.

Barnes, G. M., & Welte, J. W. (1986). Patterns and predictors of alcohol use among 7–12th grade students in New York State. *Journal of Studies on Alcohol, 47,* 53–62.

Baumrind, D. (1985). Familial antecedents of adolescent drug use: A developmental perspective. In C. L. Jones & R. J. Battjes (Eds.), *Etiology of drug abuse: Implications for prevention.* (DHHS Publication No. ADM 85–1335, pp. 13–14). Washington, DC: U.S. Government Printing Office.

Baumrind, D., & Moselle, K. A. (1985). A developmental perspective on adolescent drug use. *Advances in Alcohol and Substance Use, 5,* 41–67.

Biddle, B. J., Bank, B. J., & Marlin, M. M. (1980). Social determinants of adolescent drinking: What they think, what they do, and what I think and do. *Journal of Studies on Alcohol, 41,* 215–241.

Biglan, A., Hood, D., Brozovsky, P., Ochs, L., Ary, D., & Black, C. (1991). Subject attrition in prevention research. In C. G. Leukfield & W. Bukowski (Eds.), *Drug abuse prevention intervention research: Methodological issues* (NIDA Research Monograph No. 107, pp. 213–234). Washington, DC: U.S. Government Printing Office.

Brook, J. S., Gordon, A. S., Whiteman, M., & Cohen, P. (1986). Some models and mechanisms for explaining the impact of maternal and adolescent characteristics on adolescent stage of drug use. *Developmental Psychology, 22*, 460–467.

Catalano, R. F., Hawkins, J. D., Krenz, C., Gillmore, M., Morrison, D., Wells, E., & Abbott, R. (1993). Using research to guide culturally appropriate drug abuse prevention. *Journal of Consulting and Clinical Psychology, 61*, 804–811.

Catalano, R. F., Morrison, D. M., Wells, E. A., Gillmore, M. R., Iritani, B., & Hawkins, J. D. (1992). Ethnic differences in family factors related to early drug initiation. *Journal of Studies on Alcohol, 53*, 208–217.

Cohen, J., & Cohen, P. (1983). *Applied multiple regression/correlation analysis for the behavioral sciences.* Hillsdale, NJ: Lawrence Erlbaum Associates.

Dishion, T. J., & Loeber, R. (1985). Adolescent marijuana and alcohol use: The role of parents and peers revisited. *American Journal of Drug and Alcohol Abuse, 11*, 11–25.

Dishion, T. J., Patterson, G. R., & Reid, J. R. (1988). Parent and peer factors associated with drug sampling in early adolescence: Implications for treatment. In E. R. Rahdert & J. Grabowski, (Eds.), *Adolescent drug abuse: Analyses of treatment research* (DHHS Publication No. ADM 88–1523, pp. 69–93). Washington, DC: U.S. Government Printing Office.

Ellickson, P. L., & Hays, R. D. (1991). Antecedents of drinking among young adolescents with different alcohol use histories. *Journal of Studies on Alcohol, 52*, 398–408.

Gillmore, M. R., Butler, S., Lohr, M. J., & Gilchrist, L. (1991). *Substance use and other factors associated with risky sexual behavior in a sample of pregnant adolescents.* Unpublished manuscript, University of Washington, School of Social Work, Seattle, WA.

Gillmore, M. R., Catalano, R. F., Morrison, D. M., Wells, E. A., Iritani, B., & Hawkins, J. D. (1990). Racial differences in acceptability and availability of drugs and early initiation of substance abuse. *American Journal of Drug and Alcohol Abuse, 16*, 185–206.

Hansen, W. B., Collins, L. M., Malotte, C. K., Johnson, C. A., & Fielding, J. E. (1985). Attrition in prevention research. *Journal of Behavioral Medicine, 8*, 261–275.

Harford, T. C. (1985). Drinking patterns among Black and non-Black adolescents: Results of a national survey. In R. Wright & T. D. Watts (Eds.), *Prevention of Black alcoholism: Issues and strategies* (pp. 122–139). Springfield, IL: Thomas.

Hawkins, J. D., Catalano, R. F, & Miller, J. Y. (1992). Risk and protective factors for alcohol and other drug problems in adolescence and early adulthood: Implications for substance abuse prevention. *Psychological Bulletin, 112*, 64–105.

Headen, S. W., Bauman, K. E., Deane, G. D., & Koch, G. G. (1991). Are the correlates of cigarette smoking initiation different for black and white adolescents? *American Journal of Public Health, 81*, 854–857.

Hingson, R. W., & Strunin, L. (1992). Monitoring adolescents' response to the AIDS epidemic: Changes in knowledge, attitudes, beliefs, and behaviors. In R. J. DiClemente (Ed.), *Adolescents and AIDS: A generation in jeopardy* (pp. 17–33). Newbury Park, CA: Sage.

Jessor, R. (1991). Risk behavior in adolescence: A psychosocial framework for understanding action. *Journal of Adolescent Health, 12*, 1–9.

Johnston, L. D., O'Malley, P. M., & Bachman, J. G. (1992, January 25). *Most forms of drug use decline among American high school and college students, U–M survey reports. Smoking remains stable. Steroid use down. Rates are high in 8th and 10th grades.* News release, The University of Michigan News and Information Service, Ann Arbor, MI.

Kandel, D. B., & Andrews, K. (1987). Processes of adolescent socialization by parents and peers. *The International Journal of the Addictions, 22*, 319–342.

Kandel, D. B., Kessler, R. C., & Margulies, R. Z. (1978). Antecedents of adolescent initiation into stages of drug use: A developmental analysis. *Journal of Youth and Adolescence, 7*, 13–40.

Kandel, D. B., & Logan, J. A. (1984). Patterns of drug use from adolescence to young adulthood: I. Periods of risk for initiation, continued use, and discontinuation. *American Journal of Public Health, 74*, 660–666.

Leigh, B. (1990). Alcohol and unsafe sex: An overview of research and theory. In D. Seminara, A. Pawlowski, & R. Watson (Eds.), *Alcohol, immunosuppression, and AIDS* (pp. 35–46). New York: Alan R. Liss.

Loeber, R. T., & Dishion, T. (1983). Early predictors of male delinquency: A review. *Psychological Bulletin, 93*, 68–99.

McCord, J. (1979). Some child-rearing antecedents of criminal behavior in adult men. *Journal of Personality and Social Disorder, 37*, 1477–1481.

McDermott, D. (1984). The relationship of parental drug use and parent's attitude concerning adolescent drug use to adolescent drug use. *Adolescence, 19*, 89–97.

National Center for Health Statistics. (1990). Advance report of final mortality statistics, 1988. *Monthly Vital Statistics Report, 39(7)*.

Newcomb, M. D., & Bentler, P. M. (1988). Impact of adolescent drug use and social support on problems of young adults: A longitudinal study. *Journal of Abnormal Psychology, 97*, 64–75.

Newcomb, M. D., Bentler, P. M., & Collins, C. (1986). Alcohol use and dissatisfaction with self and life: A longitudinal analysis of young adults. *The Journal of Drug Issues, 16*, 479–494.

Patterson, G. R., & Dishion, T. J. (1985). Contributions of families and peers to delinquency. *Criminology, 23*, 63–79.

Patterson, G. R., & Stouthamer-Loeber, M. (1984). The correlation of family management practices and delinquency. *Child Development, 55*, 1299–1307.

Penning, M., & Barnes, G. E. (1982). Adolescent marijuana use: A review. *The International Journal of the Addictions, 17*, 749–791.

Rachel, J. V., Guess, L. L., Hubbard, R. L., Maisto, S. A., Cavanaugh, E. R., Waddell, R., & Benrud, C. D. (1980). *Adolescent drinking behavior: Vol. 1. The extent and nature of adolescent alcohol and drug use: The 1974 and 1978 national sample studies.* Research Triangle Park, NC: Research Triangle Institute.

Ringwalt, C. L., & Palmer, J. H. (1990). Differences between white and black youth who drink heavily. *Addictive Behaviors, 15*, 455–460.

Robins, L. N., & Przybeck, T. R. (1985). Age of onset of drug use as a factor in drug and other disorders. In C. L. Jones & R. J. Battjes (Eds.), *Etiology of drug abuse: Implications for prevention* (DHHS Publication No. ADM 85–1335, pp. 178–192). Washington, DC: U.S. Government Printing Office.

Simcha-Fagan, O., Gersten, J. C., & Langner, T. (1986). Early precursors and concurrent correlates of illicit drug use in adolescents. *Journal of Drug Issues, 16*, 7–28.

Snow, D. L., Tebes, J. K., & Arthur, M. W. (1992). Panel attrition and external validity in adolescent substance use research. *Journal of Consulting and Clinical Psychology, 60*, 804–807.

Tebes, J. K., Snow, D. L., & Arthur, M. W. (1992). Panel attrition and external validity in the short-term follow-up study of adolescent substance use. *Evaluation Review, 16*, 151–170.

Thompson, K., & Wilsnack, R. (1984). Drinking problems among female adolescents: Patterns and influences. In S. Wilsnack & L. Beckman (Eds.), *Alcohol problems in women* (pp. 37–65). New York: Guilford.

4

Adolescent Alcohol Decisions

Baruch Fischhoff
Carnegie Mellon University

Marilyn Jacobs Quadrel
Battelle, PNL

Alcohol consumption involves a wide variety of decisions. Some are *strategic*, setting commitments for future behavior (e.g., "Should I begin drinking?" "Should I drive with people who have been drinking?" "Should I look for friends who drink less?"). Others are more *tactical*, responding to immediate situations (e.g., "Should I have this beer now?" "Should I call my parents to take me home, instead of going with my date who has had three beers in the last hour?"). Some decisions involve drinking itself, whereas others involve managing its consequences. Some are made alone, whereas others are made in social settings. Some are made while sober, whereas others are made while under the influence.

To make these decisions well, people must balance the risks and perceived benefits of alcohol use in ways that are in their own best interest. There is ample reason to believe, however, that these decisions are not being made well. Indeed, many of our society's responses to alcohol involve efforts to change how people, especially young people, make such decisions (Dryfoos, 1990; Feldman & Elliot, 1990, Millstein, Peterson, & Nightingale, 1993). These efforts include public service announcements (PSAs), warning labels, high school health classes, and self-help groups. Other societal responses reflect a belief that people's decision-making processes are not to be trusted. These include legal restrictions on consuming and serving alcohol. In May 1989, the outcome of a widely publicized court case hinged on whether a pregnant woman had been adequately informed about the risks that drinking posed to her fetus.

Although the substance of each alcohol-related decision is unique, people bring to it the same basic cognitive skills that they have for other kinds of decision making. These skills include some ability to judge the extent of their own knowledge, to evaluate the relevance of other people's experiences to their own circumstances, to estimate the cumulative risk from repeated exposure to a hazard, to generate alternative courses of action, to determine what is important to them, and to consider how good their previous decisions have been.

All of these processes have been studied extensively, both as general cognitive processes and in the context of many specific decisions. These studies have revealed complex but recurrent patterns of strengths and weaknesses (Fischhoff, 1988; Kahneman, Slovic, & Tversky, 1982; Yates 1990, 1992). For example, people are fairly good at remembering how frequently they have seen or heard about various events (e.g., crashes attributed to drunk drivers). However, they are much less able to detect (and correct for) systematic biases in their exposure to information about risks. As a result, people tend to underestimate the frequency of events that are hard to observe and to overestimate the likelihood of more observable ones. Thus, for example, because blood alcohol concentrations cannot be observed directly, people might not realize how often drinking is related to diminished driving ability or poor schoolwork.

THE DECISION-THEORETIC APPROACH TO DECISION MAKING

The common tie in these studies is decision theory's notion of decision making. It conceptualizes decisions as choices among alternative courses of action (including, perhaps, inaction). Decisions can be characterized qualitatively by:

- a set of actions (or options), describing what a person can do;
- a set of possible consequences of those actions, describing what might happen (in terms of desirable and undesirable effects); and
- a set of sources of uncertainty, describing the obstacles predicting the connection between actions and consequences.

Decisions can be characterized quantitatively by:

- value trade-offs among consequences, describing their relative importance; and
- beliefs describing the probability that the consequences will actually be obtained.

This basic conceptual scheme has been used by investigators to describe a wide variety of choices, including decisions about whether to go to war (Jervis, 1976; Lebow & Stein, 1987), have children (Beach, Townes, Campbell, & Keating, 1976), operate on the basis of x-rays (Eddy 1982), and guess which of two sequentially presented lights is brighter (Coombs, Dawes, & Tversky, 1970). In some cases, the usage has been descriptive, attempting to show how people actually make decisions in these situations. In other cases, the usage has been normative, attempting to show how decisions should be made—if decision makers are to choose wisely. In some cases, both approaches are used, in order to show the differences between how well people actually make decisions and how well they might. Often, there is also a prescriptive purpose, attempting to bridge that gap by showing people how to make better decisions (Raiffa, 1968; von Winterfeldt & Edwards, 1986; Watson & Buede, 1988).

Decision theory offers a number of potential advantages. First, its basic concepts are well understood and widely accepted, in a community of scholars stretching across parts of several disciplines (e.g., psychology, economics, philosophy, political science). This commonality allows a degree of comparability and coordination among investigators that is unusual in the social sciences. Second, decision theory provides a systematic way of identifying discrepancies between optimal and actual behavior, pointing to where help may be needed. Third, such discrepancies often prove theoretically useful: There may be many explanations for appropriate behavior (e.g., instruction, modeling, conditioning), but only one for a particular pattern of errors (e.g., the estimates based on the observation of risks differing in their visibility). Fourth, decision theory helps ensure comprehensiveness when attempting to account for or guide actual decision making.

As a result, decision theory provides a point of departure for studying any decisions, including those made by adolescents regarding alcohol. The formal tools of decision theory provide a way to describe decisions. Its measurement procedures provide ways to elicit people's perceptions of the decisions facing them. Its theories provide a possible account of decision making in any particular area. This chapter provides guideposts to the literature, along with illustrative results.

As a device for introducing this perspective, we focus on a single alcohol decision, whether to ride with a friend who has been drinking. To illustrate how decision theorists would study this decision, we consider first a normative and then a descriptive approach. Our discussion draws on relevant existing research where possible. Typically, however, we refer to decision research on other topics, given the limited literature on applications to alcohol-related decisions.

The next two sections consider the normative and descriptive components of decision theory, respectively. The third section considers structured approaches to eliciting risk perceptions. The difficulties encountered by these studies sometimes require the use of more open-ended approaches, described briefly in the next section. The concluding section considers some strengths and limits of decision theory, as well as some possibilities for extending it to alcohol-related decisions.

NORMATIVE ANALYSIS

Purposes

As noted, normative analysis attempts to show how decisions should be made, if decision makers are to choose wisely. The first step in studying a decision is to describe it as accurately as possible. Figure 4.1 shows a decision tree, a common way of summarizing such a description. It includes the available options, the possible consequences (with some measure of their attractiveness), and the critical intervening events (and their probabilities). This particular example is fairly rudimentary. It could be refined in a number of ways, such as including different ways of declining the ride. A second refinement would distinguish accidents of different severity. A third would refine the consequence evaluations. A fourth would assess the probabilities of those consequences occurring.

Such a representation is *objective*, in the sense of trying to capture the actual options, uncertainties, and consequences facing the decision maker. Any discrepancy between that representation and the decision maker's perceptions threatens the optimality of the pending choice, that is, the extent to which the choice is in the decision maker's best interest. Such "gaps" also suggest opportunities for interventions (e.g., refining beliefs, identifying overlooked options).

The representation is inherently *subjective* in the sense of reflecting the individual's evaluations of the attractiveness (or aversiveness) of the consequences. In this sense, it respects decision makers' sovereignty in determining what is important to them. Deciding that someone has the wrong values would indicate another gap that might be closed through intervention. However, there is a fundamental difference between telling people, "you do not know how disabling paraplegia would be" and telling them, "you shouldn't value the high of binge drinking so much."

Even the rudimentary analysis in Fig. 4.1 suggests some potentially significant features of the decision facing an adolescent offered a ride

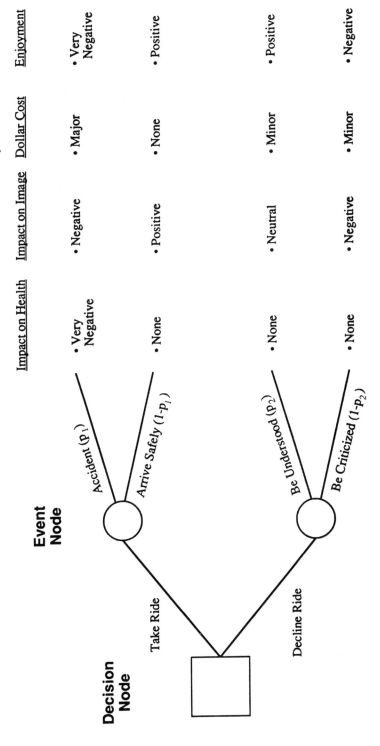

FIG. 4.1. Decision tree for whether to take or decline a ride from friends who have been drinking.

63

by a friend who has been drinking. Initially, the decision seems fairly simple, insofar as it involves only two options. However, both options have many variants, each with its own profile of consequences. On the plus side, this means that an adolescent facing this situation might be able to design more satisfactory ways to accept or decline the ride; there might also be better ways to take a ride from someone who has been drinking (e.g., sit in the back seat, wear a seatbelt, ask to be dropped off first). On the negative side, this increases the number of options requiring analysis. In a study of sexual assault decisions, Fischhoff, Furby, and Morgan (1987) identified more than 1,100 options, each sufficiently different from the others that it might be expected to have a different profile of consequences. Unless they can be combined somehow, such arrays of options defy systematic analysis, even by trained investigators (Fischhoff, 1992a).

Another feature of this decision is that it involves a very small probability, about which there are some relevant scientific data (the chance that such a trip will end in an accident), and a much larger probability, about which the adolescent is as close to being an expert as anyone (the chance of being criticized for declining the ride). A third feature of the decision is that the set of central consequences is small, but contains elements that are very hard to compare (e.g., the trade-off between enjoyment and bodily injury). Unless an adolescent has strong, clear, and relevant values, these are difficult trade-offs, of the sort that might cause frustration and prompt abrupt choices.

Once a decision has been described, one can study its sensitivity to different factors. For example, it is often the case that the optimal choice in decisions with continuous options (e.g., drink X ounces of alcohol, wait Y minutes before driving) is relatively unaffected by moderate variations in assessed probabilities and values (von Winterfeldt & Edwards, 1982).[1] Although such situations are, in a sense, easy for decision makers, they can be difficult for investigators. Where many combinations of options, beliefs, and values could lead to the same choice, observers cannot confidently infer which perceptions actually motivated the decision maker's actions (Dawes, 1979). Thus, if different sets of perceptions could lead adolescents to drive with drinkers, then one must be cautious in trying to interpret (or alter) their behavior.

This realization had a powerful influence on the study of decision making. Many earlier studies had modeled decision-making strategies with multiple regression, attempting to discern the weight that people

---

[1]This analysis assumes that decision makers act optimally on the basis of their perceptions.

give to different concerns (or *cues*) in making choices (Goldberg, 1968; Hammond, Hursch, & Todd, 1964; Hoffman, 1960). However, formal analyses showed that linear models were such powerful predictors that many weighting schemes would produce similar predictions, as long as they contained the same variables (or highly correlated surrogates; Dawes & Corrigan, 1974; Wilks, 1938). The good news in this result is that any linear combination of relevant variables will have some predictive success. The bad news is that it can be very difficult to distinguish alternative strategies. Thus, linear models can have considerable practical value, at the same time as they have limited ability to illuminate decision-making processes (Camerer, 1981; Dawes, Faust, & Meehl, 1989). As a result, the use of linear models, like expectancy-value models, has come to be treated as a sort of cognitive task analysis, for identifying critical variables, rather than as a way to describe decision-making processes. Experimental methods are seen as necessary for discerning the finer structure of how decisions are made (Fischhoff, Goitein, & Shapira, 1982).

Formal analysis can also estimate the sheer difficulty of the decisions that people face. Just how many options, consequences, and uncertainties must they consider? Is there a dominating alternative to be found, one that is at least as good as all others in all respects? Are there awkward trade-offs to be made (e.g., money vs. health)? Are there irreducible uncertainties? As the difficulty of decision making increases, so might the chances of suboptimal performance and the decision makers' degree of frustration. Adolescents might be particularly disturbed by the realization that decision making is not always facilitated by concentrated thought. Accepting the fact that life is a gamble is a part of maturation and may be a buffer against the emotional stress generated by insoluble problems.

Selecting Information for Health Communications

An explicit analysis of the decisions facing individuals can also provide a reasoned basis for selecting information to present to them, in health communications. All too often, public health messages seem to tell people things that they already know or else do not need to know, wasting their valuable attention and demonstrating insensitivity to their informational needs. For example, in its report, *Confronting AIDS*, the Institute of Medicine (1986) lamented a survey showing that only 41% of the public knew that AIDS is caused by a virus. Yet one would be hard pressed to identify any decision that would be affected by knowledge of this fact. (One also might wonder whether 41% of the population really knew what a virus was.) The absence of standards for determining which information is relevant for making a particular decision can complicate life for information providers as well as for information recipients.

Some studies have found that adolescents' decisions to drink are unrelated to how much they know about the effects of alcohol (Berberian, Gross, Lovejoy, & Paparella, 1976; Botvin, 1986). That could mean that information makes no difference, or that one needs to look at adolescents' understanding of the information that they receive. For example, in a study in progress (Quadrel, Fischhoff, & Palmgren, 1994), we asked teenagers to interpret information about risk, including several posters designed to deter them from drinking and driving. Five of 19 subjects (26%) reported that these ads told them not to get drunk and drive.[2] When asked to describe someone who was drunk, respondents typically used descriptions such as "had 10 glasses of beer," "would go into a blackout," or "can't stand up." These teens understood that accidents may result from drinking, and that heavy drinking results in observable effects on judgment and coordination. However, there was little indication that they realized the detrimental effect on a person's judgment of just one or two drinks. (Two subjects did say that some people could be legally drunk from a "couple" or "three" beers, and one noted that the "legal alcohol level is lower than most people recognize as being drunk.")

In principle, communications should attempt to provide the pieces of information that have the largest possible impact on pending decisions. Value-of-information analysis is the general term for techniques that determine the sensitivity of decisions to different information (Raiffa, 1968). Merz (1991) applied value-of-information analysis to a well-specified medical decision, whether to undergo carotid endarterectomy. Both this procedure, which involves scraping out an artery that leads to the head, and its alternatives have a variety of possible positive and negative effects. These effects have been the subject of extensive research, which has provided quantitative risk estimates of varying precision. Merz created a simulated population of patients who varied in their physical conditions and relative preferences for different health states. He found that knowing about a few, but only a few, of the possible side effects would change the preferred decision for a significant portion of patients. He argued that communications fo-

---

[2]This result was also observed in Quadrel (1990), where teenagers were asked to estimate the probability of becoming involved in a car crash while driving after drinking. Our goal was to uncover what information respondents assumed or requested in order to make their judgments. Although no information was provided on how much the person had to drink, more than 50% assumed that the driver in question was drunk.

cused on these few side effects would make better use of patients' attention than would laundry lists of undifferentiated possibilities. He also argued that his procedure could provide an objective criterion for identifying the information that must be transmitted to insure medical informed consent.

Performing such analyses requires an explicit decision-making model. It envisions individuals as waiting for quantitative estimates, in order to compute the expected utility of different courses of action. At times, however, people are in a predecisional state, just trying to understand the processes involved in creating and controlling risks. In such cases, information selection could be guided by a modeling of those processes, in order to identify the most critical risk factors. Communications could then be directed at those issues that are most important to science and least understood by individuals (as determined by descriptive studies of their beliefs), in order to convey a comprehensive picture of the processes creating (and controlling) a risk. Bridging the gap between lay mental models and expert models could require adding missing concepts, correcting erroneous beliefs, strengthening correct beliefs, and deemphasizing peripheral ones (Morgan, Fischhoff, Bostrom, Lave, & Atman, 1992). Particular attention would be paid to correct the critical "bugs" in recipients' beliefs: cases where people confidently hold incorrect beliefs that could lead to inappropriate actions (or lack enough confidence in correct beliefs).

The choice among these approaches would depend on, among other things, how much time is available for communication, how well the decisions are formulated, and what scientific risk information exists. For example, calibration analysis might be particularly useful for identifying the focal facts for PSAs. Such facts might both grab recipients' attention and change their behavior. Contrasting lay and expert perceptions of the full set of processes governing risks might be more suited for the preparation of explanatory brochures or curricula. Value-of-information analysis might suit common decisions with well-characterized options and consequences (e.g., in medicine). In all cases, it is important to remember the imperfections in expert knowledge. Typically, it is surrounded by some uncertainty; occasionally, it may be more poorly informed than the beliefs of laypeople who have experienced the risks more directly.

DESCRIPTIVE ANALYSIS

As opposed to normative analysis, descriptive analysis attempts to show how people actually make decisions. Like other kinds of behavioral research, approaches to identifying deviations from a normative model can be divided into those that are structured and those that are open-ended. The former approaches assume that decision makers share the model's qualitative description, then focus on how its quantitative components (i.e., the probabilities and tradeoffs) are judged. The latter approaches accept the possibility that critical pieces (i.e., options, consequences, uncertainties) may be missing entirely from people's thought processes or, if present, may be defined differently than the way they appear in the normative analysis.

What follows is a discussion of these approaches. Their respective merits turn on the difficulties, in different circumstances, of measuring decision theory's central concepts (e.g., the perceived probabilities of adverse consequences). These difficulties are often quite daunting. However, to the decision theorist, that difficulty is an inherent feature of decision-making situations, which are brought into relief by decision theory's explicit perspective. For example, surveys often ask people general questions about the "importance" of different decision criteria (e.g., pay vs. benefits vs. fulfillment—in choosing a job, style vs. performance vs. safety—in buying a car). From a decision-theoretic perspective, however, importance depends on context; pay matters only if job offers vary on that dimension. Or, people are often described in terms of their degree of *risk aversion*. However, the term is ill-defined in situations where all options entail some degree of some kind of risk. Then, people might perhaps show a relative aversion to one kind of risk (e.g., the chance of physical harm) over another kind (e.g., the chance of social censure)—to the extent that those consequences vary across the available options. Recognizing these possibilities, decision theory views importance and risk aversion as context dependent. If this entails more complex measurement procedures, with more obvious limitations, then that is a fact of life, rather than a failing of the perspective (e.g., Keeney & Raiffa, 1976; von Winterfeldt & Edwards, 1986). A sampling of these issues are described in the following sections.

STRUCTURED APPROACHES

Absolute Judgments of Risk

Of decision theory's two quantitative components, people's probability judgments are typically much easier to evaluate than their value trade-offs. Often, there are relatively hard statistics against which those judgments can be compared, unlike trade-offs, which are matters of personal opinion. Comparisons between risk judgments and statistics are the basis of such claims as, "people overestimate the likelihood of overreported events" (Combs & Slovic, 1979; Tversky & Kahneman, 1974). Eliciting such judgments requires attention to many methodological details, in order to cope with people's inexperience in making explicit numerical estimates (Fischhoff et al., 1987; Linville, Fischer, & Fischhoff, 1993; Poulton, 1988). One cannot just look up a risk estimate in a table and then ask people to guess at it, in whatever unit happens to be used there. For example, Fischhoff and MacGregor (1983) found that changes in the response mode for eliciting judgments could produce hundredfold differences in estimates of the risk of dying from a disease (e.g., tuberculosis) among those afflicted by it.[3]

Although, to the best of our knowledge, people have not been asked for quantitative estimates about the specific health risks in Fig. 4.1, studies have elicited estimates of the population risk of motor vehicles crashes (e.g., Lichtenstein, Slovic, Fischhoff, Layman, & Combs, 1978). These risks are judged fairly accurately, suggesting that they are observed roughly in proportion to their actual frequency. Perceptions of personal risks from these sources, however, seem less trustworthy. For example, most people judge themselves to be safer and more skilled than the average driver (e.g., Svenson, 1981), a claim that could be true for at most 50% of the population. This exaggerated sense of personal control over accident situations would be encouraged by the difficulty of observing other drivers' intoxication and one's own unintentional lapses (even when one has not been drinking). The tendency to view oneself as less at risk than others has been observed in many other settings (Weinstein, 1987).

Judgments of Relative Risk

Ironically, this evidence of perceived personal invulnerability comes almost exclusively from studies with adults—even though one common claim about adolescents is that they harbor an "illusion of invulnerability." Because invulnerability is such a widely accepted

---

[3]Specifically, the (conditional) risks were much larger when people were asked, for example, "for each person who dies of mumps, how many have it and survive?" than when they were asked, "of each 100,000 people who had mumps, how many died?" As in other studies, the relative risk from different sources was largely independent of response mode.

explanation of teenagers' risk-taking behavior, we recently conducted a study comparing the illusion of invulnerability among 86 matched pairs of adolescents and adults (parents of the teenagers) from middle-class neighborhoods. Among other risks, we asked about the probability of becoming an alcoholic. The adolescents showed no more illusion of invulnerability for this question than did the adults. Some 62% of both teenagers and adults estimated their risk to be smaller than that of an acquaintance; 19% of teenagers (compared to 23% of adults) reported that they were as likely as an acquaintance to become alcoholic, whereas 20% of the teenagers (compared to 15% of the adults) saw themselves as facing greater risk. A group of high-risk teenagers, drawn from group homes for teens with legal and chemical abuse problems, provided similar judgments (Quadrel, Fischhoff, & Davis, 1993).

Subjects judged the probabilities of eight such events, occurring to themselves or various others. Four of these events were *active*, in the sense of offering relatively large possibilities for personal control (e.g., auto accidents, unwanted pregnancy), whereas the other four were *passive* (e.g., radiation poisoning). The most common response pattern was to see no difference between one's own risk level and that faced by the target others. Where subjects did distinguish the two risk levels, they were twice as likely to see the target individual as facing the greater risk. Subjects assigned a risk probability of zero (or "no chance") to themselves about 10% of the time, to others about one half as often.

The prevalence of these various expressions of invulnerability was very sensitive to the event in question. Specifically, it was much higher with the four active events, especially among those subjects who saw themselves as having greater control than the target. This sensitivity to perceived controllability was greater among adults. However, there was little overall difference in perceived invulnerability. Teenagers were more likely to distinguish their risk from that of the target. That might reflect a heightened tendency to overdifferentiate their personal situation, akin to Elkind's (1967) notion of "personal fable." However, it might also reflect more intense observation of friends and acquaintances than is possible for adults (whose lives are often more private). In any case, having made these additional distinctions, teenagers often judged themselves to have the greater risk. Indeed, by most of the measures used in the study, the low-risk teens showed less perceived invulnerability than did their parents. Much of that difference came from the fact that both groups saw the teenagers as facing more risk from auto accidents and unwanted pregnancy—arguably, appropriate judgments.

Psychological Processes in Comparative Risk Judgments

The most straightforward account of these results is that adults and teenagers rely on similar, moderately biased psychological processes in estimating these risks. Those processes lead them to see themselves as facing less risk than the target others—who, presumably, see themselves as being safer. As suggested by Weinstein (1980) and others, both cognitive and motivational processes could contribute to exaggerating one's own safety. On the cognitive side, for example, the precautions that one takes (or at least plans to take) should be much more visible than those taken by others, especially for active events (where control is more possible). It would take unusual perceptiveness to undo the biases in such readily available evidence (Tversky & Kahneman, 1973). On the motivational side, wishful thinking might deflate perceptions of personal risk, possibly through indirect processes (e.g., which friends and acquaintances one chooses for comparisons).

From this perspective, the behavior of parents and teenagers would differ to the extent that their different life circumstances affect the operation of these common psychological processes. Thus, speculatively, low-risk teens might have a strong need to see their parents as safe, whereas the parents' aura of personal invulnerability may not extend to their children (whom they are, after all, entrusted with protecting). Adults might be more sensitive to the active–passive difference because they have acquired a larger repertoire of control mechanisms (which they imagine themselves as using) and greater individual autonomy that enables them (in principle) to exercise those options.

Adults' cumulative experience may not have affected their overall perception of personal invulnerability because that experience carried no systematic message. For example, seeing others suffer a misfortune may give rise to very different interpretations. It could lead one to blame the victims in hindsight, exaggerating how much they could have done to avoid the risk, thereby creating the illusion that one has learned the lesson vicariously (Fischhoff, 1975; Hoch & Loewenstein, 1989). Or it could lead one to sympathize with the victim and conclude that "it could have happened to anyone." Or, it could signal an ambient threat in the shared environment, creating concern over when one's own turn will come.

Confidence in Judgments of Risk

People cannot know every fact about every risk in their lives. As a result, it is critical that they understand the limits of their own knowledge, so that they know when to hedge their bets or when to collect more information. Many studies have found that people are only moderately successful in assessing how much they know, with the most common overall result being overconfidence (Lichtenstein, Fischhoff, & Phillips, 1982; Nelson, 1992; Yates, 1990).

Quadrel, Fischoff, and Halpern (1994) found a similar pattern in responses to a quiz with 100 two-alternative questions about risk behaviors, including drinking and driving. For each question, respondents chose the alternative they believed to be true, and then assessed the probability that their answer was correct. Respondents were divided into three groups: middle-class teenagers, their parents, and high-risk teenagers (drawn from group homes). Results for the first two groups were similar and indicated moderate overconfidence (e.g., they had chosen the correct answer to the questions only about 85% of the time when they were 100% certain of having done so). The high-risk youths were much more overconfident (and had many fewer correct answers), despite their greater direct experience with the effects of alcohol. For example, only 45% of the high-risk teenagers knew that having a beer would affect their driving as much as drinking a shot of vodka. However, the mean of their estimates of the probability of having answered this question correctly was .84 (meaning that one would have expected them to be correct 84% of the time). For this particular question, the adults were just as overconfident as the high-risk youth, whereas the low-risk teenagers judged their chances of a correct response more realistically. Such local misconceptions might qualify as the sort of bug in thinking that deserves focused attention in communications.

Imprecise Response Modes

The studies reported here require subjects to report their risk estimates using numerical scales. However, most surveys of risk perceptions, including ones studying teenagers' perceptions of alcohol-related risks (American School Health Association, 1988; Bauman, 1985; Bauman & Bryan, 1983; Institute for Social Research, 1988), rely on nonquantitative scales. For example, the National Adolescent Student Health Survey (American School Health Association, 1988) asked: "How much do you think people risk harming themselves (physically or in other ways) if they drink alcoholic beverages occasionally?" The response options were: *no risk, slight risk, moderate risk,* and *great risk* (with a *can't say—drug unfamiliar* category). Similarly, Bauman (1985) asked respondents to estimate the likelihood of each of 57 possible consequences of drinking one beer or glass of liquor each week. Response options were:

sure it would happen, it probably would happen, it probably would not happen, and *sure it would not happen.*

Unfortunately, responses to such verbal scales are difficult to interpret because they may connote very different numerical values to different people in a given context or to the same person in different contexts. A great risk of feeling drunk after four beers may indicate a 70% or 80% likelihood, whereas even 1% may constitute a great risk of having a fatal accident (Beyth-Marom, 1982; Wallsten, Budescu, Rapoport, Zwick, & Forsyth, 1986). The same ambiguity can arise in risk communications. Being told that rain is "likely" may suffice when deciding whether to have a picnic or carry an umbrella. Being told that AIDS in the blood supply is "rare" or that there is a "great risk" of car crashes from drinking may not convey enough information for effective decision making (Merz, Small, & Fischbeck, 1992).

Imprecise Stimuli

Similar ambiguity frequently characterizes the wording of the questions that respondents evaluate as well as the scales that they use to convey their beliefs. For example, a National Center for Health Statistics survey (Dawson, Cynamon, & Fitti, 1987) posed the following question: "How likely do you think it is that a person will get the AIDS virus from sharing plates, forks, or glasses with someone who had AIDS?" We presented this question to a relatively homogeneous group, psychology students at an Ivy League college (Fischhoff, 1989). After answering, they were asked what they had understood to be the frequency and intensity of the sharing.[4] There was considerable disagreement among respondents about the presumed frequency of sharing: single occasion (endorsed by 39% of respondents), several occasions (20%), routinely (28%), and uncertain (12%). There was considerable agreement about intensity: sharing utensils during a meal (82%), using the same washed utensils (11%), and uncertain (6%). Even if there was complete agreement among the subjects, their responses would only be interpreted appropriately if readers could guess what that consensual definition was. Interestingly, all of the subjects who reported uncertainty about the frequency and intensity of sharing still made likelihood judgments (whereas those uncertain about the likelihood reported no uncertainty about the event). If people are willing to respond to survey questions that they do not understand, any relationship between beliefs and behaviors would tend to be blurred. That

---

[4]Readers might want to guess at their answers before reading the results in the text.

would, in turn, lead observers to think that "information does not work with teens; their actions are unrelated to their knowledge." If so, that would be a special case of the general tendency for poor measurement to reduce the power of research designs.

Assessing Values

Measuring the other quantitative component of decisions, people's values, presents its own methodological challenges (von Winterfeldt & Edwards, 1986). Evaluating the quality of what has been measured is, however, a rather different enterprise. It is not as easy, as it is with risk estimates, to claim that experts know what the right answer is. Claiming that people have the wrong values means denying them sovereignty over their own choices.[5] Rather than assume this role, investigators interested in the quality of value judgments have focused on identifying inconsistencies (which people would, presumably, wish to avoid). An extensive literature now documents the changes in expressed values that can accompany seemingly trivial variations in how questions are posed (Dawes, 1988; Fischhoff, 1991; Hogarth, 1982; Tversky & Kahneman, 1981). These problems arise not because the wording of the elicitation questions is unclear, but because respondents' feelings are. As a result, different perspectives, and responses, can be evoked by different ways of presenting the same problem.

For example, we recently found 88% of a sample of college students willing to allow a condom to be labeled as "effective" if it had a 95% success rate in stopping transmission of the AIDS virus; however, the endorsement rate dropped to 42% when the condom was described as having a 5% failure rate (Linville et al., 1993). Slovic, Fischhoff, and Lichtenstein (1978) found that seatbelt usage was judged more positively when the risks of driving were described in terms of the lifetime chance of a fatal accident rather than in terms of the (formally equivalent) one-trip risk. In such situations, people's choices are sensitive to how decisions happen to be posed or viewed at the moment they are made. An additional complication with this particular "framing" problem is that, even when people do evoke the long-term consequences of repeatedly engaging in an act such as drinking and driving, they may

---

[5]Some of the most controversial research on adolescents has, in fact, centered on the possibility that they reject values that adult society would have them adopt (e.g., Brown, 1990; Gardner, Scherer, & Tester, 1989; Luker, 1975).

greatly underestimate the cumulative risks (Shaklee & Fischhoff, 1990).[6]

OPEN-ENDED APPROACHES

One methodological implication of these results is that it may not always be possible to measure people's values with conventional survey questions. A common strategy in the social sciences is to work hard to formulate the precise question whose answer is needed to test a theory. Investigators then assume that respondents will quickly be able to assemble and express their thoughts in the form required by the survey. No provision is made for helping respondents to think through the question or to offer alternative formulations (of the sort that respondents themselves might generate, if they just had time to think). Little provision is made for respondents to express alternative views or indicate confusion. One good reason for such formulaic techniques is that they reduce the opportunities for overtly reactive measurement, by constraining the direct communication between respondent and investigators. A second is that they allow larger samples. Less worthy reasons for their use are that they greatly simplify data analysis and allow investigators to operate at a safe distance from their subjects.

The previous sections provided several examples in which more open-ended approaches could have clarified the strengths and limits of results obtained with structured approaches, by revealing mismatches between lay and expert perspectives. Open-ended approaches can also provide some insight into how laypeople think. This section describes several other studies that have attempted to exploit the descriptive possibilities that are only possible with open-ended approaches.

The inconsistencies between decision makers' responses to single and multiple exposures to a given risk raise the question of how people naturally think about such risks. An open-ended approach would seek to answer this question by asking how people actually structure their decision making, rather than assuming the appropriateness of a particular perspective. Adapting one possible strategy, Quadrel, Fischhoff, and Palmgren (1994) asked adolescents to think aloud as they tried to assess the probabilities of several deliberately ambiguous events, such as "getting into an accident when driving after drinking." Other ques-

---

[6]For example, on average, the subjects in Linville et al. (1993) estimated the probability of the AIDS virus being transmitted from a male to a female as 5% in 1 case of protected sex (a great overestimate, according to public health estimates) and as 20% in 100 cases (a more reasonable estimate, but much too small given their one-case estimates).

tions pertained to the risks of sexual behavior and the use of cigarettes, marijuana, and cocaine. With respect to drinking and driving, 48 out of 61 subjects spontaneously made assumptions or asked for information about how much drinking was involved; far fewer (6) asked about how much driving. With varying frequency, subjects also wanted to know about a number of other factors, differing in their objective relevance (e.g., driving skill, age, the social atmosphere, the type of alcohol, physical tolerance).

Respondents routinely raised the issue of dose (e.g., how much drinking) for seven of nine ambiguous events (e.g., the probability of getting cancer from smoking cigarettes or of becoming alcoholic from drinking). However, for the two events concerning sex, they did not spontaneously consider dose (i.e., the amount of sex) as a determinant of risk: only 2 of 61 subjects mentioned dose in relation to AIDS, whereas only 6 of 61 did so for pregnancy. Theoretically, these results suggest that adolescents have a more accurate intuitive understanding of the cumulative effects of drinking and other drug use than they do of the risks of sexual behavior. Methodologically, they suggest that survey questions asking adolescents to evaluate alcohol-related risks without specifying dose are too vague to produce meaningful answers.

This study brought potential consequences of risk behaviors directly to respondents' attention. A study conducted by Beyth-Marom, Austin, Fischhoff, Palmgren, and Quadrel (1993) weakened this kind of structure. They asked subjects to list consequences of a teenager choosing either to engage in or to reject a possible risk behavior, including the accept-ride and reject-ride options in Fig. 4.1. Responses from 69 matched pairs of middle-class adults and teenagers were quite similar with respect to the number and type of consequences mentioned. One modest difference was that teenagers were more likely than adults to mention the physical (e.g., being hurt in an accident) and legal (e.g., being caught by police) consequences of accepting the ride. Adults were more likely to mention continuing behaviors (e.g., one drink leads to another).

Fischhoff and Furby (1991) further weakened the degree of structure by letting teenagers choose three recent difficult decisions in their lives, to be described in their own terms. None of the decisions that the 105 teenagers chose dealt with drinking and driving, although quite a few dealt with drinking. For those decisions that were mentioned, few had an option structure as complicated as that in Fig. 4.1. Rather, most were described in terms of a single option (e.g., whether to go to a party where alcohol would be served). In a two-option decision, as in Fig. 4.1, the consequences of the alternative option are logically implied. However, that need not mean that they are intuitively obvious to the decision maker. Indeed, Beyth-Marom et al. (1993) found that the consequences produced for engaging in a risky behavior were not the mirror image of the consequences of rejecting that opportunity. These are but suggestive results. Structured and unstructured studies are needed to piece together a full account of adolescents' judgments and decisions about alcohol. Normative decision theory provides a conceptual framework for determining what topics to study. Descriptive decision theory provides some of the methodological and theoretical tools for pursuing that study. All are imperfect. However, in combination, they can begin to provide the sort of complex descriptions that people's decisions about complex topics deserve. Attention to methodological detail is critical when studying drinking decisions (or any other ones). Decision variables will explain little if they are measured poorly.

CONCLUSION

From decision theory's perspective, any account of teenagers' drinking behavior needs to consider the different components of decisions: options, beliefs, values. If teenagers are drinking in ways that are ill advised, it maybe due to failings in any (or all) of these domains, each of which may be subject to somewhat different interventions. For example, teenagers might be ignoring options that would make it more attractive not to drink; if so, then life-skills training programs may be able to create such options by teaching "refusal skills," socially adroit ways to avoid taking risks (e.g., Botvin, 1986; Schinke & Gilchrist, 1984). Or drinking decisions by youths might be hampered by faulty beliefs about the consequences of the options that they consider; if so, then they might be affected most directly by communications directed at the "bugs" in their mental models—misconceptions that have somehow escaped correction despite the great volume of communications directed at them. Or, adolescents might reject the values that would lead to adult-approved behaviors; if so, then interventions could focus on changing their motivation. Those efforts might have a global or local focus, trying to change either teenagers' overall values or the specific incentives surrounding particular decisions. For example, agreeing to drive teenagers home from parties, with no questions asked, changes the trade-offs in those specific decisions; over some period of time, it might change broader trade-offs (e.g., parent–teenager relationships).

Or, adolescents may just have difficulty making sense of complex decisions and keeping track of all the relevant considerations. As a result, they may resort to quick solutions, reflecting an incomplete mix of their personal beliefs and values. At the margin, such last-minute decision making may be disproportionately influenced by transient, visceral incentives (e.g., sexual drives). If that were the case, then poor decision-making processes might encourage more impulsive decisions, in addition to whatever tendency there is for impulsivity to short-circuit decision-making processes. Suitable interventions might attempt either to teach decision making as a general cognitive skill (Baron & Brown, 1991) or to preprogram choices, so that teens would not have to make decisions under real-time pressures.

The theoretical and policy implications of these studies depend on the generality of the phenomena that they document. Ultimately, that is a matter for future research. In the meantime, one might look at those features of these studies with the greatest potential for inducing unrepresentative behavior. For example, they tend to be administered in circumstances that might encourage subjects to impress the investigators, that direct subjects to consider issues that they might otherwise ignore, that insulate subjects from the social pressures accompanying actual decision making, and that isolate them from normal social support. The time pressures that these studies create may be qualitatively different from those of real life (sometimes greater, sometimes less). The mix of these threats to generalizability obviously varies across tasks.

It is a matter of considerable debate in behavioral decision theory whether these are conditions that tend to enhance or impair performance (Arkes & Hammond, 1986; Kahneman et al., 1982). One critical developmental question is whether these situational factors affect adults and adolescents differently. If so, then similar performance in experiments might still mask differences in everyday life. Many speculations are possible (Fischhoff, 1992b). They need to be disciplined with fact, in the sense of collecting the requisite data.

A second critical developmental question is whether similar performance deficits have similar consequences for adults and adolescents. Generally speaking, judgmental errors can cause more damage when decisions have irreversible consequences, when stakes are large, when decision makers lack the resources needed to recover from failures, when the domain is unfamiliar (requiring heavier reliance on judgment), and when decision makers lack structural protections (shielding them from the opportunity to make decisions that place them at great risk). Thus, for example, the same degree of exaggerated perceived invulnerability should create more actual vulnerability for those who rely more on judgments of personal risk. There is no simple summary of adults' and adolescents' relative degrees of such exposure. For example, many adults run much of their lives by routine, choosing among modest variations on habitual responses, acquired through trial and error, where they cannot go too far wrong. Yet they, too, sometimes work without a net, as when they ponder their first equity investment, extramarital liaison, power tool, independent presidential candidate, or hazardous waste facility (as a potential neighbor). The same rate of poor decisions will create more problems for those who make more decisions.

Recognizing these possibilities, various experts have advocated protecting adults from the consequences of their fallible judgments, with such paternalistic strategies as banning "unhealthy" products and publications or excluding laypeople from decisions about complex technologies. Such proposals, in which parents are treated like children, often generate strong negative responses (Fischhoff, 1990). They might be borne in mind when considering adolescents' responses to policies that would "protect" them by restricting their freedom.

A recurrent theme in this chapter is that poor measurement and incomplete conceptualization of cognitive processes can blur the role played by those processes in teenagers' decision making. As a result, youths' behavior seems less orderly, less related to their beliefs, and less responsive to health communications. Inadequate attention to these issues does more than just impede the progress of science. Poorly documented claims about the incompetence of adolescents encourage frustration with teenagers behavior and paternalistic solutions for dealing with it. As a result, such claims threaten to stigmatize and disenfranchise adolescents. If teenagers seem impervious to information, it may be easier to deny them the right to govern their own actions, to view them as a societal problem (rather than as a resource), and to interfere with the experimentation that is part of the business of adolescence. Such claims make teenagers, rather than society, responsible for adolescents' problems. They place adults in the flattering position of knowing what is right (Baumrind, 1968; Fischhoff, 1992b; Gardner et al., 1989).

As with other conceptual frameworks, decision theory has limitations. One is a temptation to assume, without adequate evidence, that people follow the model of optimal decision making (i.e., they always make the choice that is in their own self-defined best interests). Although that assumption is not made in the account presented here, it can be found in those theories falling closer to the economic roots of decision theory.[7] With its cognitive focus, the decision theoretic ap-

---

[7]A slavish commitment to rationality is often imputed to the field of decision making by people who have but a passing familiarity with it. Such a caricature provides an easy basis for dismissing the approach as implausible.

proach may pay less attention to the roles of emotion (Fiske & Taylor, 1990; Janis & Mann, 1979), self-control (Thaler & Shefrin, 1981) and social forces in shaping cognitive processes (Bronfenbrenner, 1986; Majoribanks, 1979). Often, though, those factors can be given cognitive representations. For example, parental pressure can be treated as one a consequence of a decision, namely, the censure or approval that would follow from it (Beyth-Marom et al., 1993). The best defenses against these potential pitfalls are awareness and a willingness to entertain more complex accounts than are possible when working entirely within one paradigm (Fischhoff, 1992b).

This discussion has also highlighted a number of methodological challenges in applying a decision-theoretic perspective to the question of adolescent drinking behavior. These include specifying the risks to be evaluated, measuring values and beliefs, and identifying the information needed to make decisions. These could be viewed as limits to the perspective, in the sense of representing daunting challenges facing those who would apply it. Alternatively, they could be viewed as properties of the complex reality with which teenagers must deal. One large potential complication that plays relatively little role in this approach is that of individual differences. One reason is that persistent efforts have seldom found individual difference measures with cross-situational validity (Bromiley & Curley, 1992). A second reason is cognitive psychologists' tendencies to assume similarity in how people think, while acknowledging differences in what people believe. A third reason is a predisposition to look for differences in the circumstances of people's decisions, within which similar cognitive processes are applied. Collaboration with investigators experienced with these issues might be a productive direction for future research.

One cannot study everything at once. Decision theory examines some dimensions of difference, while ignoring others. Clearly, multimethod approaches are necessary, including open-ended questions that allow the discovery of decision variables not anticipated by investigators.

REFERENCES

American School Health Association, Association for the Advancement of Health Education, and the Society for Public Health Education. (1988). *National adolescent student health survey: A report on the health of America's youth.* Oakland, CA: Third Party Publishing.

Arkes, H. R., & Hammond, K. R. (Eds.). (1986). *Judgment and decision making: An interdisciplinary reader.* New York: Cambridge University Press.

Baron, J., & Brown, R. (Eds.). (1991). *Teaching decision making to adolescents.* Hillsdale, NJ:

Lawrence Erlbaum Associates.

Bauman, K. E. (1985). The consequences expected from alcohol and drinking behavior: A factor analysis of data from a panel study of adolescents. *International Journal of the Addictions, 20*, 1635–1647.

Bauman, K. E., & Bryan, E. S. (1983). Adolescent beer drinking: Subjective expected utility and gender differences. *Youth & Society, 15*, 157–170.

Baumrind, D. (1968). Authoritarian vs. authoritative control. *Adolescence, 3*, 255–272.

Beach, L. R., Townes, B. D., Campbell, F. L., & Keating, G. W. (1976). Developing and testing a decision aid for birth planning decisions. *Organizational Behavior and Human Performance, 15*, 99–116.

Berberian, R. M., Gross, C., Lovejoy, J., & Paparella, S. (1976). The effectiveness of drug education programs: A critical review. *Health Education Monographs, 4*, 377–398.

Beyth-Marom, R. (1982). How probable is probable? Numerical translation of verbal probability expressions. *Journal of Forecasting, 1*, 257–269.

Beyth-Marom, R., Austin, L., Fischhoff, B., Palmgren, C., & Quadrel, M. J. (1993). Perceived consequences of risky behaviors. *Developmental Psychology, 29*, 549–563.

Botvin, G. J. (1986). Substance abuse prevention research: Recent developments and future directions. *Journal of School Health, 56*, 369–374.

Bromiley, P., & Curley, S. P. (1992). Individual differences in risk taking. In J. F. Yates (Ed.), *Risk-taking behavior* (pp. 88–132). Chichester: Wiley.

Bronfenbrenner, U. (1986). Ecology of the family as a context for human development: Research perspectives. *Developmental Psychology, 22*, 723–742.

Brown, B. B. (1990). Peer groups and peer cultures. In S. S. Feldman & G. R. Elliot (Eds.), *At the threshold: The developing adolescent* (pp. 171–196). Cambridge, MA: Harvard University Press.

Camerer, C. (1981). General conditions for the success of bootstrapping models. *Organizational Behavior and Human Performance, 27*, 411–422.

Combs, B., & Slovic, P. (1979). Causes of death: Biased newspaper coverage and biased judgments. *Journalism Quarterly, 56*, 837–843.

Coombs, C., Dawes, R. M., & Tversky, A. (1970). *Introduction to mathematical psychology.* Englewood Cliffs, NJ: Prentice-Hall.

Dawes, R. M. (1979). The robust beauty of improper linear models in decision making. *American Psychologist, 34*, 571–582.

Dawes, R. M. (1988). *Rational choice in an uncertain world.* San Diego, CA: Harcourt Brace Jovanovich.

Dawes, R. M., & Corrigan, B. (1974). Linear models in decision making. *Psychological Bulletin, 81*, 95–106.

Dawes, R. M., Faust, D., & Meehl, P. E. (1989). Clinical versus actuarial judgment. *Science, 243*, 1668–1674.

Dawson, D. A., Cynamon, M., & Fitti, J. E. (1987, August). *AIDS knowledge and attitudes.* (Provisional data from the National Health Interview Survey: United States. Advance Data from Vital and Health Statistics. No. 146. DHHS Pub. No. [PHS]88-1250). Hyattsville, MD: Public Health Service.

Dryfoos, J. G. (1990). *Adolescents at risk: Prevalence and prevention.* New York: Oxford University Press.

Eddy, D. M. (1982). Probabilistic reasoning in clinical medicine: Problems and opportunities. In D. Kahneman, P. Slovic, & A. Tversky (Eds.), *Judgment under uncertainty: Heuristics and biases* (pp. 249–267). New York: Cambridge University Press.

Elkind, D. (1967). Egocentrism in adolescence. *Child Development, 38*, 1025–1034.

Feldman, S. S., & Elliott, G. R. (Eds.). (1990). *At the threshold: The developing adolescent.*

Cambridge, MA: Harvard University Press.

Fischhoff, B. (1975). Hindsight ≠ foresight: The effect of outcome knowledge on judgment under uncertainty. *Journal of Experimental Psychology: Human Perception and Performance, 104,* 288–299.

Fischhoff, B. (1988). Judgment and decision making. In R. J. Sternberg & E. E. Smith (Eds.), *The psychology of human thought* (pp. 153–187). New York: Cambridge University Press.

Fischhoff, B. (1989). Making decisions about AIDS. In V. Mays, G. Albee, & S. Schneider (Eds.), *Primary prevention of AIDS* (pp. 168–205). Newbury Park, CA: Sage.

Fischhoff, B. (1990). Psychology and public policy: Tool or tool maker? *American Psychologist, 45,* 57–63.

Fischhoff, B. (1991). Value elicitation: Is there anything in there? *American Psychologist, 46,* 835–847.

Fischhoff, B. (1992a). Giving advice: Decision theory perspectives on sexual assault. *American Psychologist, 47,* 577–588.

Fischhoff, B. (1992b). Risk taking: A developmental perspective. In J. F. Yates (Ed.), *Risk taking behavior* (pp. 133–162). Chichester: Wiley.

Fischhoff, B., & Furby, L. (1991). Making risky decisions. In. L. Lipsitt & L. Mitnick (Eds.), *Self-regulation & risk-taking behavior: Causes and consequences* (pp. 231–239). Norwood, NJ: Ablex.

Fischhoff, B., Furby, L., & Morgan, M. (1987). Rape prevention: A typology and list of strategies. *Journal of Interpersonal Violence, 2*(3), 292–308.

Fischhoff, B., Goitein, B., & Shapira, Z. (1982). The experienced utility of expected utility approaches. In N. Feather (Ed.), *Expectancy, incentive and action* (pp. 315–339). Hillsdale, NJ: Lawrence Erlbaum Associates.

Fischhoff, B., & MacGregor, D. (1983). Judged lethality: How much people seem to know depends upon how they are asked. *Risk Analysis, 3,* 229–236.

Fiske, S. T., & Taylor, S. (1990). *Social cognition* (2nd ed.). Reading, MA: Addison-Wesley

Gardner, W., Scherer, D., & Tester, M. (1989). Asserting scientific authority: Cognitive development and adolescent legal rights. *American Psychologist, 44,* 895–902.

Goldberg, L. R. (1968). Simple models or simple processes? *American Psychologist, 23,* 483–496.

Hammond, K. R., Hursch, C. J., & Todd, F. J. (1964). Analyzing the components of clinical inference. *Psychological Review, 71,* 438–456.

Hoch, S., & Loewenstein, G. (1989). Outcome feedback: Hindsight and information. *Journal of Experimental Psychology: Learning, Memory and Cognition, 15,* 605–619.

Hogarth, R. (1982). *New directions for methodology of social and behavioral science: Question framing and response consistency.* San Francisco: Jossey-Bass.

Hoffman, P. J. (1960). The paramorphic representation of clinical judgment. *Psychological Bulletin, 57,* 116–131.

Institute for Social Research. (1988). *Monitoring the future: A continuing study of the life styles and values of youth.* Ann Arbor: University of Michigan.

Institute of Medicine. (1986). *Confronting AIDS: Directions for public health, health care, and research.* Washington, DC: National Academy Press.

Janis, I. L., & Mann, L. (1979). *Decision making: A psychological analysis of conflict, choice, and commitment.* New York: The Free Press.

Jervis, R. (1976). *Perception and misperception in international politics.* Princeton, NJ: Princeton University Press.

Kahneman, D., Slovic, P., & Tversky, A. (Eds.). (1982). *Judgments under uncertainty: Heuristics and biases.* New York: Cambridge University Press.

Keeney, R., & Raiffa, H. (1976). *Decisions with multiple objectives: Preferences and value trade-offs.* New York: Wiley.

Lebow, R. N., & Stein, J. (1987). Beyond deterrence. *Journal of Social Issues, 43,* 5–71.

Lichtenstein, S., Slovic, P., Fischhoff, B., Layman, M., & Combs, B. (1978). Judged frequency of lethal events. *Journal of Experimental Psychology: Human Learning and Memory, 4,* 551–578.

Lichtenstein, S., Fischhoff, B., & Phillips, L. D. (1982). Calibration of probabilities: State of the art to 1980. In D. Kahneman, P. Slovic, & A. Tversky (Eds.), *Judgment under uncertainty: Heuristics and biases* (pp. 306–334). New York: Cambridge University Press.

Linville, P. W., Fischer, G. W., & Fischhoff, B. (1993). AIDS risk perceptions and decision biases. In J. B. Pryor & G. D. Reeder (Eds.), *The social psychology of HIV infection* (pp. 5–38). Hillsdale, NJ: Lawrence Erlbaum Associates.

Luker, K. (1975). *Taking chances: Abortion and the decision not to contracept.* Berkeley: University of California Press.

Majoribanks, L. (1979). *Families and their learning environments: An empirical analysis.* London: Routledge & Kegan.

Merz, J. F. (1991). *Toward a standard of disclosure for medical informed consent: Development and demonstration of a decision-analytic methodology.* Unpublished doctoral dissertation, Carnegie Mellon University, Pittsburgh, PA.

Merz, J. F., Small, M., & Fischbeck, P. (1992). Measuring decision sensitivity: A combined Monte Carlo-logistic regression approach. *Medical Decision Making, 12,* 189.

Millstein, S., Peterson, A., & Nightingale, E. (Eds.). (1993). *Promoting the health of adolescents.* New York: Oxford University Press.

Morgan, M. G., Fischhoff, B., Bostrom, A., Lave, L., & Atman, C. J. (1992). Communicating risk to the public. *Environmental Science and Technology, 26,* 2048–2056.

Nelson, T. O. (Ed.). (1992). *Metacognition: Core readings.* Boston: Allyn & Baron.

Poulton, E. C. (1988). *Bias in quantifying judgment.* Hove and London: Lawrence Erlbaum Associates.

Quadrel, M. J. (1990). *Elicitation of adolescents' risk perceptions: Qualitative and quantitative dimensions.* Unpublished doctoral dissertation, Carnegie Mellon University, Pittsburgh, PA.

Quadrel, M. J., Fischhoff, B., & Davis, W. (1993). Adolescent (in)vulnerability. *American Psychologist, 48,* 102–116.

Quadrel, M. J., Fischhoff, B., Fischhoff, M., & Halpern S. (1994). *Calibration of adolescents' and adults' confidence judgments.* Unpublished manuscript.

Quadrel, M. J., Fischhoff, B., & Palmgren, C. (1994). *Adolescents' definitions of risk behaviors.* Manuscript submitted for review.

Raiffa, H. (1968). *Decision analysis.* Reading, MA: Addison-Wesley.

Schinke, S. P., & Gilchrist, L. D. (1984). *Life skills counseling with adolescents.* Austin, TX: Pro-ed Publishers.

Shaklee, H., & Fischhoff, B. (1990). The psychology of contraceptive surprises: Judging the cumulative risk of contraceptive failure. *Journal of Applied Psychology, 20,* 385–403.

Slovic, P., Fischhoff, B., & Lichtenstein, S. (1978). Accident probabilities and seat-belt usage: A psychological perspective. *Accident Analysis and Prevention, 10,* 281–285.

Svenson, O. (1981). Are we all less risky and more skillful than our fellow drivers? *Acta Psychologica, 47,* 143–148.

Thaler, R., & Shefrin, H. M. (1981). An economic theory of self-control. *Journal of Political Economy, 89,* 391–406.

Tversky, A., & Kahneman, D. (1973). Availability: A heuristic for judging frequency and probability. *Cognitive Psychology, 4,* 207–232.

Tversky, A., & Kahneman, D. (1974). Judgment under uncertainty: Heuristics and biases. *Science, 185*, 1129–1131.

Tversky, A., & Kahneman, D. (1981). The framing of decisions and the psychology of choice. *Science, 21*, 453–458.

von Winterfeldt, D., & Edwards, W. (1982). Cost and payoffs in perceptual research. *Psychological Bulletin, 91*, 609–622.

von Winterfeldt, D., & Edwards, W. (1986). *Decision analysis and behavioral research.* New York: Cambridge University Press.

Wallsten, T., Budescu, D. V., Rapoport, A., Zwick, R., & Forsyth, B. (1986). Measuring the vague meanings of probability terms. *Journal of Experimental Psychology: General, 115*, 348–365.

Watson, S., & Buede, D. (1988). *Decision synthesis: The principles and practice of decision analysis.* New York: Cambridge University Press.

Weinstein, N. D. (1980). Unrealistic optimism about future life events. *Journal of Personality and Social Psychology, 39*, 800–820.

Weinstein, N. D. (Ed.). (1987). *Taking care: Understanding and encouraging self-protective behavior.* New York: Cambridge University Press.

Wilks, S. S. (1938). Weighting systems for linear functions of correlated variables where there is no dependent variable. *Psychometrika, 8*, 23–40.

Yates, J. F. (1990). *Judgment and decision making.* New York: Wiley.

Yates, J. F. (Ed.). (1992). *Risk-taking behavior.* New York: Wiley.

5

Alcohol Expectancy Theory and the Identification of High-Risk Adolescents

Gregory T. Smith
University of Kentucky

Mark S. Goldman
University of South Florida

Attempts to prevent teenage problem drinking have been hindered by the relative lack of available theory on the causes of alcohol problems—theory that could then guide prevention efforts. One common result of this limitation is that prevention efforts have often led to attitude changes without reductions in drinking behavior (see reviews by Moscowitz, 1989; Nathan, 1983). Recent adaptations of expectancy theory to the study of alcohol may help fill this gap by offering a theoretical model for understanding teens' acquisition of problem-drinking behaviors. In this article, we provide an overview of alcohol expectancy theory and a selective review of supporting research; we then present new findings that support application of this model to the task of identifying high-risk adolescents.

BASIC EXPECTANCY THEORY: LEARNING AND MEMORY

The expectancy-learning model can be traced to James (1890), was explicitly formulated by Tolman (1932), and was further developed by MacCorquodale and Meehl (1954), Rotter (1954), Bolles (1972), and others. It represents one specific version of a number of related theories, each of which is concerned with the cognitive mechanisms by which early learning experiences come to influence later behavioral choices (see, e.g., Bagozzi, 1992). Early mechanistic, behavioral learning models have given way to an appreciation of the importance of memory and cognitive encoding of both interoceptive and exteroceptive experience when modeling the causal sequences that control later behavior. This family of models can be contrasted both with purely behavioral learning theories and biological or personality theories; it also can be integrated with processes and mechanisms from each of these domains.

Expectancy theory, then, is a memory-based cognitive-learning theory—that is, a theory of how any new behavior is acquired. Briefly, the repeated perception of an association between a given behavior and certain outcomes leads to the storage of these associations in memory in the form of expectancies of if–then relations between the behavior and its consequences. These stored associations then influence decisions made at future choice points; expectations of valued reinforcers from a given behavior increase the likelihood of that behavior. In this manner, early learning experiences (as well as biological characteristics) can serve as early or distal influences on later behavior. Their influence is transmitted forward in time by stored information concerning the behavior, (i.e., *expectancies*), which function as the proximal influence that mediates the influence of distal factors on current behavior (Goldman, in press; Goldman, Brown, Christiansen, & Smith, 1991; Goldman & Rather, 1993; Henderson, Goldman, Coovert, & Carnevalla, in press; Sher, Walitzer, Wood, & Brent, 1991; Smith, 1989; Stacy, Newcomb, & Bentler, 1991). In recent years, expectancy formulations have been usefully applied to a wide range of topics in psychology, including classical and operant conditioning (Anderson, 1983; Bolles, 1972; Rescorla, 1988), psychopathology (Alloy & Tabachnik, 1984), hypnosis (Kirsch, 1985), interpersonal processes (Jones, 1986; D. T. Miller & Turnbull, 1986), and even affect (Carver & Scheier, 1990).

APPLICATION OF EXPECTANCY THEORY TO ALCOHOL USE

A number of risk factors for alcohol-related problems among teens have been identified. These include: (a) parental modeling (McKenna & Pickens, 1983); (b) personality characteristics, including such genetically influenced factors as temperament (Cloninger, 1987; P. M. Miller & Smith, 1990); (c) biological vulnerability (Schuckit, 1987); (d) peer influences (cf. Akers, Krohn, Lanza-Kaduce, & Radosevich, 1979); (e) sociocultural factors, such as gender, race, socioeconomic status, and ethnic and religious variables (cf. Cahalan & Cisin, 1968); and (f) mass media or cultural influences (cf. Finn & Strickland, 1982). None of these variables, however, necessarily includes a mechanism that directly and automatically compels an adolescent to drink. Rather, they are risk factors because they increase the probability that a child will have learning experiences that dispose him or her toward future, excessive alcohol use. For example, genetic factors may lead to an enhanced subjective response (i.e., provide greater reinforcement) to alcohol (Newlin & Thomson, 1990) and, thus, indirectly may lead to greater drinking. Children whose parents (a) excessively rely on alcohol to relax or to facilitate social interactions and (b) provide few examples of alternative coping strategies vicariously experience the association between alcohol use and these needs. Media influences (e.g., advertising) may also demonstrate particular positive outcomes from alcohol use. These learning events—made more likely by the broad risk factors just cited—can be thought of as early or distal influences on adolescent alcohol misuse.

As just noted, expectancy theory proposes a mechanism by which these early learning experiences come to exert an influence on drinking choices later in time (Goldman et al., 1991; Goldman & Rather, 1993; Smith, 1989). Information from these experiences relating alcohol consumption to anticipated reinforcement is stored in memory; such information then influences the decision to drink at later drinking-choice points. *Expectancy* is a summary label for this stored information. (Peer influence may be among the few circumstances that require little or no cognitive mediation in that pressure to use from peer group members may operate in the absence of information about alcohol.)

The acquisition of alcohol expectancies need not involve direct experience with alcohol. Modern social learning formulations (cf. Abrams & Niaura, 1987; Bandura, 1985) emphasize the role of vicarious learning or modeling, and numerous studies indicate that young children without appreciable drinking experience form clear views of both the propriety (Casswell, Gilmore, Silva, & Brasch, 1988; Spiegler, 1983) and the effects (Bauman & Bryan, 1980; Dunn & Goldman, 1993; Kraus, Smith, & Ratner, in press; P. M. Miller, Smith, & Goldman, 1990) of drinking alcohol. This is an important feature of the model because it suggests that children may form expectancies before they begin to drink. Alcohol expectancy theory holds that predrinking expectancies for positive outcomes from drinking lead to more positive initial drinking experiences, which in turn lead to still more positive expectancies, and so forth (Goldman, Brown, & Christiansen, 1987; Smith, Goldman, & Christiansen, 1992). For a more extensive review of alcohol expectancy theory cast as a modern network theory of memory (based on the work of Collins & Loftus, 1975, and others) see Goldman and Rather (1993) and Rather, Goldman, Roehrich, and Brannick (1992).

It follows from this theory that measuring alcohol expectancies formed on the basis of early learning experiences should provide a more direct assessment of risk than the measurement of many sociocultural and genetic factors, family influences, temperament, and so forth. In principle, measured expectancies reflect an important proximal influence on drinking—one that incorporates the combined influences of many possible distal factors. In what follows, we present initial longitudinal evidence of the usefulness of expectancies for risk assessment.

It also follows that intervening at the expectancy level—attempting to modify expectancies to reduce teenage drinking—may prove fruitful because, by targeting expectancies, one is (a) focusing directly on the learning process itself, rather than on factors indirectly related to that process, (b) targeting the current, causally active cognitive mechanisms by which learning is thought to influence the behavior of concern, and (c) attempting to interrupt the vicious cycle of increased consumption. In this way, the expectancy model provides a theoretical framework that can guide prevention efforts.

EMPIRICAL EVIDENCE FOR ALCOHOL EXPECTANCY THEORY

We describe four steps in a progression of studies undertaken in our laboratories to investigate the hypothesized role of expectancy in teenage problem drinking. Although a great deal of research in this burgeoning field has recently come from other laboratories as well, the scope and space limitations of this article constrain extensive review of this material. Interested readers are advised to consult any of a number of recent reviews (cf. Connors & Maisto, 1988; Connors, Maisto, & Dermen, 1992; Goldman et al., 1991; Goldman & Rather, 1993).

Step 1: Expectancies Correlate With Drinking Behavior

The initial phase of this research identified the domain of adult and adolescent alcohol expectancies and assessed whether they, in fact, covary with drinking behavior. Hence, Brown, Goldman, Inn, and Anderson (1980) interviewed men and women from widely divergent drinking backgrounds to elicit their expectancies, they statistically refined a questionnaire constructed from subjects' statements on a second sample, and they factor analyzed the responses to the measure by a third sample to derive a set of six expectancy dimensions. Expectancies were found to correlate significantly with drinking behavior; expectancies for social and physical pleasure and for social assertiveness proved important for all drinkers, and increased expectancy for sexual and aggressive behavior was found in heavier drinkers. Notably, subsequent investigations in different laboratories produced generally similar findings (cf. Leigh, 1987; Mooney, Fromme, Kivlahan, & Marlatt, 1987; Southwick, Steele, Marlatt, & Lindell, 1981).

Following these demonstrations with adults, Christiansen, Goldman, and Inn (1982) identified adolescent expectancies that closely paralleled adult-held expectancies. They found that adolescents believe alcohol: (a) is a powerful agent that makes global, positive transformations of experience; (b) can enhance or impede social behavior; (c) improves cognitive and motor functioning; (d) enhances sexuality; (e) leads to deteriorated cognitive and behavioral functioning; (f) increases arousal; and (g) promotes relaxation. To date, numerous studies have documented the relationship between expectancies and the drinking behavior both of adults—from low-level social drinkers to alcoholics (cf. Brown, 1985a, 1985b; Brown, Goldman, & Christiansen, 1985; Connors, O'Farrell, Cutter, & Thompson, 1986; Cooper, Russell, Skinner, Fromme, & Mudar, 1992; Mann, Chassin, & Sher, 1987)—and of adolescents (Brown, Creamer, & Stetson, 1987; Christiansen & Goldman, 1983; Christiansen, Smith, Roehling, & Goldman, 1989; Sher et al., 1991; Smith & Goldman, 1990; Stacy et al., 1991), leaving little doubt that alcohol expectancy correlates highly with drinking behavior across a wide range of age and drinking groups.

Step 2: Expectancies Predict Future
Onset of Teen Drinking

Documentation of the expectancy–drinking behavior relationship represents a necessary but far-from-sufficient condition for demonstration of a possible causal relation between the two variables (J. Cohen & P. Cohen, 1983). As Bollen (1989) and others have noted, two other conditions that support a causal inference are demonstration that the putative cause temporally precedes the putative effect (which can be addressed by prospective studies) and isolation of the putative cause from other potential causes (which can be addressed by experimental designs). In Step 2, the question of directionality was investigated using longitudinal designs in which the putative cause (i.e., expectancy) naturally preceded the effect (i.e., problem-drinking behavior); this approach makes it possible to assess the influence of expectancy, measured prior to onset of problem drinking, on teens' subsequent engagement in problem drinking. In the first such study, Christiansen et al. (1989) studied young adolescents, many of whom were engaging in their first drinking experiences. Expectancies held by seventh and eighth graders—most of whom had consumed four or fewer drinks in their lives and so were considered nondrinkers—were found to predict drinking levels 12 months later, accounting for 25.6% of the variance in Year 2 drinking behavior. Moreover, five of seven expectancy scales at Time 1 successfully discriminated between nonproblem drinkers and those teens who subsequently became problem drinkers over the ensuing 1-year period.

A different approach from this "natural experiment" design is to control statistically for early-use levels when evaluating expectancy's prediction of later use. Using this method, Stacy et al. (1991) found that adolescent expectancies predict adult drug use 9 years later, controlling for adolescent drug use. Therefore, over short- and long-term longitudinal periods, whether using a natural experiment, by studying teens making the transition to problem-drinking behavior, or using statistical means to control for prior use, and whether measuring alcohol consumption alone or other drugs as well, expectancy appears to predate and predict subsequent use. Indirect support also comes from P. M. Miller et al. (1990), who reported initial evidence that alcohol expectancies may form as early as the third grade, with some indication that expectancies may be present in first graders (Dunn & Goldman, 1993; P. M. Miller et al., 1990), and even earlier (Noll, Zucker, & Greenberg, 1990).

Step 3: Expectancies Mediate Learning Influences on Teen Drinking

Before moving to isolate expectancy as an inferred cause of drinking through experimental manipulation, two other aspects of alcohol expectancy theory should be addressed: first, whether expectancies, in fact, mediate the influence of early learning influences on adolescent drinking; and second, whether expectancies operate in a vicious cycle of positive expectancy influencing heavier drinking, which, in turn, influences more positive expectancy, and so forth.

To address the first of these issues, Smith and Goldman (1990) compiled a composite index of family drinking variables to represent the likely influence of such variables on adolescent consumption, using a sample of high-school juniors and seniors. The index included (a) the history of alcoholism in first-, second-, and third-degree relatives; (b) the history of problems associated with drinking in the same relatives; (c) parents' experience of a set of life problems associated with drinking, including hangovers, blackouts, family problems, work problems, legal difficulties, fighting, early morning drinking, and drinking alone; (d) frequency of both father's and mother's drinking; and (e) each parent's attitude toward adult drinking. The mediation hypothesis was tested following Baron and Kenny (1986), who described the conditions necessary for demonstration of mediation: (a) the bivariate correlations among the predictor (i.e., family drinking), the putative mediator (i.e., expectancy), and the criterion (i.e., adolescent drinking) are found to be significant; and, also, (b) the indirect path from the predictor (i.e., family drinking) to the criterion (i.e., teen drinking) through the mediator (i.e., expectancy) is significant. This set of relationships results in a significant drop in the predictor–criterion correlation when the mediator is controlled (Hoyle & Smith, in press).

Smith and Goldman (1990), in fact, found just such a set of relationships: All three variables were significantly related, and the drop in the relationship between family variables and teen drinking when expectancy was controlled was statistically significant. Interestingly, expectancy accounted for more than 10 times the variance in teen drinking than did the family influence composite by itself (nearly 40% vs. 3.6%). Perhaps expectancies mediate other, as yet unspecified, early causes as well. It is also possible, however, that individuals' formation of expectancies may involve an active, dynamic process that goes beyond the simple linear combination of inputs (i.e., observable learning events). In other words, one's expectancy may be more than the sum of the individually contributing learning experiences.

Expectancy's mediational influence was only partial; with expectancies included, the family variables' independent influence on teen drinking, though smaller (accounting for 1% of the variance), remained statistically significant. Two other recent studies (Henderson, Goldman, Brannick, & Carnevalla, in press; Sher et al., 1991) also support the partial mediating influence of expectancies.

An important related notion is that individuals who drink while holding positive expectancies are therefore more likely to experience the event positively, thus reinforcing the expectancies and making further drinking all the more likely. This concept was tested (Smith et al., 1992) using a three-wave longitudinal design with teens who were nondrinkers at the study's outset (i.e., they had consumed fewer than four drinks in their lifetimes). The findings showed that (a) high-expectancy nondrinkers were more likely to begin drinking by the following year, (b) their early drinking experiences predicted the subsequent endorsement of still more positive expectancies for alcohol's effects, and (c) these higher expectancies predicted still higher drinking levels by the following year. It appeared that expectancy, although already in place before drinking began, also mediated the influence of early drinking experiences on later drinking. In contrast to this cyclical process, the original low-expectancy nondrinkers maintained low levels of expectancy and drinking behavior over the 3 years.

Step 4: Experimental Manipulation of
Expectancy Reduces Alcohol Consumption

All correlational designs are, at best, quasi-experimental in nature, and experimental manipulations that isolate the proposed cause provide more compelling evidence for causal inference. Three recent studies used a true experimental design (including random subject assignment, manipulation of an independent variable, and appropriate control groups) to test whether expectancies could be manipulated with a consequent change in drinking levels. The first two studies (Henderson & Goldman, 1987; Massey & Goldman, 1988) were designed to develop the expectancy "challenge" procedures using samples of females who drank low to moderate amounts of alcohol. In Henderson and Goldman's (1987) study, subjects were given a placebo alcoholic beverage in a context that encouraged the display of intoxicated behavior and only told of the placebo nature of the beverage after they had behaved in an intoxicated fashion. Massey and Goldman (1988) told subjects in advance they might or might not receive alcohol in a masked beverage, and they challenged them to identify those peers who had actually received alcohol. In addition, these subjects were asked to monitor environmental cues for expectancies (e.g., advertising, media influences, and other drinkers). In both studies, the results suggested that these manipulations could effectively disrupt the linkages between expectancies and alcohol use or, to be more precise, might produce competing (i.e., incongruent) expectancies that interfered with alcohol use.

The third study (Darkes & Goldman, 1993) put the techniques refined in the previously mentioned studies to their most stringent test. A sample of college men that included subjects who drank up to problematic levels were subjected to Massey and Goldman's (1988) format: Subjects knew they might be receiving alcohol, and they were called on to identify those who had been given alcohol. The challenge was repeated on two occasions, and subjects were again called on to monitor external expectancy stimuli. Two control groups were used: a "traditional" college program for teaching responsible drinking condition and a no-treatment condition. In addition, expectancies were assessed using an instrument (Levine & Goldman, 1989) sensitive to situational and short-term changes in expectancies. These results showed that only the expectancy manipulation reduced drinking over the 2 weeks following the experimental manipulation; it also showed that drinking decreases paralleled decreases in measured expectancies. It was noteworthy that the expectancy challenge showed the most striking impact on the heaviest drinkers, suggesting that these procedures might be influencing a central drinking mechanism. These findings, of course, have implications for the development of future prevention and intervention programs, but further studies using more extensive challenges, and follow-ups of a considerably longer period, are certainly necessary to establish the utility of these practical applications.

Ongoing Controversies

Although a growing body of converging evidence supports the general hypotheses of alcohol expectancy theory, some controversies as to the structure and domain of expectancies continue. Some investigators (Leigh, 1989) have argued that the classical factor analytic criterion of perfect simple structure should be applied to test whether expectancy factors or scales are relatively "pure," and they have suggested that such outcomes might best be achieved by applying a priori domains to expectancy measurement (e.g., behavioral, cognitive, and affective domains). We have advanced the alternative position that models of concept formation and similarity (cf. Collins & Loftus, 1975; Goldman & Rather, 1993; Nosofsky, 1992; Rosch, 1975; Simon & Kaplan, 1990; Smith & Medin, 1981) that note the probablistic nature of concept elements and that result in "fuzzy" categories more accurately reflect the likely cognitive structure of expectancies (see Goldman et al., 1991). Such structure may be more faithfully modeled using similarity scaling techniques coupled with Euclidian distance-based proximity algorithms, such as multidimensional scaling and hierarchical clustering (Medin, Goldstone, & Gentner, 1993; Nosofsky, 1992; Rather & Goldman, 1992). Limitations are always present in the mathematical representation of complex human processes, and choices must necessarily be made about appropriate formal models. It would be convenient if phenomena in the real world happened to precisely fit such mathematical formalisms as perfect simple structure but, most often, these formalisms prove to be aspirational. Findings from similarity scaling and factor analytic methods may converge as hierarchical factorial structures become testable with the advent of new hierarchical confirmatory factor analytic (CFA) models that include common and specific factors. The ultimate criteria for utility of differing models should be sought in the form of validity as measured by percentage of variance

accounted for both in the measurement model and in drinking outcomes as well as in the model's capacity to generate further experimental tests of expectancy operation (see Goldman, in press and Goldman
& Rather, 1993, for further discussion of these complex issues).

Differing conceptualizations of expectancy structure (sometimes explicit and sometimes implicit) have also led to other discussions about
the necessary aspects of expectancy measurement. Although no investigator has suggested that expectancies of negative drinking outcomes
are not present in human drinkers, different levels of theoretical importance have been associated with negative expectancies. Some researchers have emphasized their importance (e.g., Leigh, 1989)
whereas others have noted that they appear to have less impact on
ongoing drinking decisions (Goldman et al., 1991; Goldman & Rather,
1993). The impact of negative expectancies may also relate to the question of whether most drinking is controlled by automatic processes or
effortful (i.e., conscious) decision making (Goldman et al., 1991). In a
similar vein, some authors (Fromme, Stroot, & Kaplan, 1993) have
suggested that expectancy measurement can be improved by independent measurement of expectancies and their valuation. Future research
should help clarify all these issues although the fundamental issue of
expectancy as a valid predictor and mediator appears reasonably well-
established by now.

THIS STUDY: APPLYING EXPECTANCY
THEORY TO HELP IDENTIFY HIGH-RISK
ADOLESCENTS

As promising as alcohol expectancy theory and other models of risk
are, a great deal of work remains to apply these correlational findings
to the far greater challenge of identifying individual teens at risk of
becoming problem drinkers. Although limits undoubtedly exist as to
how many teens can be accurately identified—particularly because
adolescence involves so much rapid change—any means of improving
prediction will enhance the targeting of preventive efforts. If, as the
evidence suggests, alcohol expectancies represent the currently active
distillation of one's prior alcohol-related learning history, assessment
of teens' expectancies may well contribute to this task.

There are, however, significant costs to the misclassification of teens.
We strongly believe, therefore, that risk-assessment decisions must rely
on multiple sources of information to reduce such errors. Hence, we do
not advocate the use of expectancy or any other single measure as a
sole determinant of risk. The following preliminary data, then, should

be viewed as an exploration of expectancy's power to discriminate high-risk from low-risk teens and not as a basis for premature clinical use of this method.

METHOD

Subjects

Subjects were 203 seventh graders participating in a multiyear study of the development of drinking behavior in adolescence. These subjects represent all seventh graders (the youngest cohort in the study, chosen here to focus on early onset drinking) who had not yet begun to drink at the study's inception and for whom data were available from each of three annual data collections. (There were 245 seventh graders for whom complete data were available; this sample of original nondrinkers accounts for 82.8% of the larger group.) Subjects (48% male) came from two suburban Detroit public-school districts, one comprising primarily middle- to upper-middle-class professionals and the other including predominately low-middle class blue-collar workers. Diverse ethnic and national backgrounds and a variety of religious backgrounds and levels of religious involvement were represented. Parental drinking behavior (as described by their children) ranged widely and approximated previously reported figures for the U.S. population. Thirty-five percent of subjects reported some member of their family (nuclear or extended) to be alcoholic. For a detailed description of the sample, consent procedures, and subject retention, see Christiansen et al. (1989) and Smith et al. (1992).

Measures

Alcohol Expectancy Questionnaire–Adolescent Form (AEQ–A). Of the seven scales of the AEQ–A, Scale 2—Alcohol Can Enhance or Impede Social Behavior—has consistently proved to be the strongest predictor of adolescent drinking behavior (Christiansen & Goldman, 1983; Christiansen et al., 1982; Christiansen et al., 1989). In multiple regression analyses, the incremental validity of the other scales over and above Scale 2, though significant, has been of small magnitude in comparison to the magnitude of variance explained by this scale (Christiansen et al., 1982). For this reason, Scale 2 was used to identify high-risk adolescents. As noted previously (Christiansen et al., 1989), prior reports of good internal consistency were replicated in the present sample (coefficient alpha for Scale 2 averaged .83 over the 3 years).

Drinking Styles Questionnaire. This adolescent self-report instrument assessed drinking quantity/frequency, problem drinking and drunkenness, and typical drinking context. Its quantity/frequency and problem-drinking scales have been shown to be highly reliable, stable, and valid (Smith, Goldman, & Christiansen, 1989). To provide the most sensitive measure of teen drinking possible, the two scales were summed in this study to form a composite; the internal consistency of this index of quantity, frequency, frequency of drunkenness, and alcohol-related problems was $\alpha = .92$ in each of Years 2 and 3.

Procedure

As described previously (Christiansen et al., 1989), subjects were tested over a two-day period in October in their regular classrooms. Teachers were not present during the testing. Strict procedures to ensure confidentiality were followed to protect students, and these procedures were explained thoroughly to students to maximize response accuracy.

RESULTS

As Table 5.1 shows, the 24-month period from Year 1 (Grades 7 and 8) to Year 3 (Grades 10 and 11) was one of transition into drinking behavior for many adolescents. By Year 3, over one half of this originally nondrinking sample had become drinkers and over one fourth reported getting drunk two to four times per year or more.

Criterion of Significant Drinking Behavior

Adolescent problem drinking can take a variety of forms not limited to traditional conceptualizations of adult alcoholism (Smith & Miller,

TABLE 5.1
Self-Reported Drinking Behavior Change[a]

Drinking Behavior	Year 2	Year 3
Drinker status	24.4	52.2
Drink 3–4 times per year or more	22.4	48.6
Typically drink 2–3 drinks or more	14.3	41.0
Get drunk 2–4 times per year or more	10.0	28.2
Get drunk more than half of all drinking episodes	4.8	15.4

Note. Figures reported are percentages. Subjects were nondrinkers at Year 1, so all table values for that year would be zero.
[a]$N = 203$.

1992); frequent or heavy drinking, drunkenness, and engaging in high-risk behaviors while drinking can all be considered forms of teen problem drinking. Hence, an inclusive criterion of significant drinking behavior, defined as being above the median of all same-grade peers—including those who are drinking at Year 1—on our composite drinking index, was employed. The median was computed separately for Years 2 and 3 of the study. Alcohol expectancies of seventh graders who had not yet begun to drink were used to predict which of these teens fell above the median for alcohol consumption in their age cohort 1 year and then 2 years later.

Determination of Cutting Score on Expectancy Scale 2

For both the 1- and 2-year predictions, the sample was split in half. A cutting score was chosen that maximized successful prediction in one sample; the discriminative power of using this score to demarcate high- and low-risk status was then replicated on the second sample. Final results are presented for the combined sample. Because avoiding false negatives (i.e., failure to identify high-risk subjects) is a priority, a cutting score was chosen to emphasize both high overall hit rate and low false negative errors as goals. In each case, a cutting score of 0 on Scale 2 was obtained; high-risk teens were defined as those with scores greater than or equal to 0. (In this study, the scale was scored in a bipolar fashion, with seven items keyed in the direction of expectancies for social impediment and 10 keyed for social enhancement. A score of 0, therefore, reflected a roughly even balance between positive and negative social expectancy. An alternative scoring approach is to eliminate negative scores by assigning 1 point for either the endorsement of a positive expectancy or the failure to endorse a negative expectancy.)

An expedient means often used to identify high-risk status is simply to ascertain history of alcoholism in the family. For comparison purposes, we present classification results using this method along with results based on expectancy assessment. This comparison does not represent the most sophisticated risk assessment based on in-depth knowledge of familial factors; it is offered only as a common approach that may find real-world use due to its expediency.

Tables 5.2 and 5.3 present the classification results for the 12-month and 24-month predictions, respectively. For both the short- and long-prospective intervals, the social expectancy scale produced overall hit rates of approximately 64%, and sensitivity between 65% and 69% (i.e., using the expectancy cutoff, 69% of those teens who were found to be drinking significantly 1 year later were identified, and 65% of those drinking

TABLE 5.2
Prediction of Significant Eighth-Grade Drinking Among Nondrinking Seventh Graders:
12-Month Time Lag

Risk Assessment	Significant Eighth-Grade Drinking		%
	No	Yes	
Expectancy risk factor			
Low	70	27	
High	43	59	
Total	113	86	
Base rate for drinking			43.22
Sensitivity of measure			68.60
Overall hit rate			64.82
Family history risk factor			
No	91	63	
Yes	24	25	
Total	115	88	
Base rate for drinking			43.35
Sensitivity of marker			28.41
Overall hit rate			57.14

Note. Expectancy risk factor is: social expectancy > 0. Totals vary slightly because of missing data.

TABLE 5.3
Prediction of Significant Ninth-Grade Drinking Among Nondrinking Seventh Graders:
24-Month Time Lag

Risk Assessment	Significant Ninth-Grade Drinking		%
	No	Yes	
Expectancy risk factor			
Low	65	32	
High	40	60	
Total	105	92	
Base rate for drinking			46.70
Sensitivity of measure			65.22
Overall hit rate			63.45
Family history risk factor			
No	84	69	
Yes	22	26	
Total	106	95	
Base rate for drinking			47.26
Sensitivity of marker			27.37
Overall hit rate			54.73

Note. Expectancy risk factor is: social expectancy > 0. Totals vary slightly because of missing data.

significantly 2 years later were identified).[1] By contrast, prediction based on simple identification of a positive family history proved much less successful. Although hit rates were over 50%, the low base rate of positive family history led to very little sensitivity for this marker: Only 28% of teens drinking significantly were identified by this means.

These analyses were then performed separately for boys and girls. The expectancy risk marker was slightly more successful for boys: The 12-month hit rate and sensitivity were 68% and 80%, respectively, for boys, as compared to 61% and 57%, respectively, for girls. Over 24 months, the figures were 63% and 77%, and 64% and 58%, respectively. Sample-size constraints did not permit cross-sample replication of the male–female difference.

DISCUSSION

In the first part of this article, we described a causal-mediational model of alcohol expectancy and reviewed the growing body of evidence supporting its validity. In particular, data from a number of cross-sectional, longitudinal, and experimental investigations point to the role expectancy plays in the acquisition of problem-drinking behaviors by adolescents. In addition to contributing to our understanding of the causes of problem drinking, these data illustrate the potential advantages of modifying expectancies both for intervention with heavy drinkers (Darkes & Goldman, 1993) and for prevention with children (Kraus et al., in press).

This model was then applied to the thorny problem of identifying individual high-risk adolescents prior to drinking onset. Four conclusions can be drawn from these results. First, the results were encouraging: Hit rates of roughly 64% and sensitivity as high as 69% were obtained across considerable time lags during the tumultuous years of adolescence. Split-half, cross-validation analyses indicated these results were generally stable, particularly so over the 12-month prospective period. Second, the expectancy marker proved much more successful than the simple marker of positive family history. Third, despite the promise of this approach, numerous errors of individual prediction were made. For example, 38% of those below the median for Year 2 drinking were identified as high risk by this method, and 31% of those above the median were classified as low risk (i.e., false negatives). Therefore, although these results augur well for the inclu-

---

[1]For 12-month prediction, the derivation sample hit rate was 63.20% and its sensitivity was 70.83%. On cross-validation, the hit rate and sensitivity were 66.67% and 65.79%, respectively. For 24-month prediction, the derivation sample produced a hit rate of 66.98% and sensitivity of 71.15%. The cross-validated hit rate was 59.34% and sensitivity was 57.50%.

sion of expectancy (as measured by the AEQ–A) in a more comprehensive risk-assessment protocol, the potential stigma from false positive identifications as well as the failure to identify others because of false negatives argue against use of this approach by itself. Future improvements in measurement and understanding of expectancy operation may decrease these prediction "misses." Fourth, the findings of differential predictive success by gender should be cross-validated. Whether this reflects superior prediction for boys, is an artifact of earlier onset drinking by males, or is due to some other, unstable cause should be investigated.

In sum, prediction of future alcohol problems among early adolescents is both difficult and sensitive. The potential harm to the sizable number of teens who, at present, are likely to be misclassified argues for a cautious approach. These results do, however, establish new possibilities for such prediction. Further, ambitious efforts to achieve this aim, which is so crucial to successful prevention, are clearly needed. We encourage multifactor approaches that evaluate the unique, incremental contribution of each putative risk factor.

ACKNOWLEDGMENTS

Portions of this research were supported by National Institute on Alcohol Abuse and Alcoholism Grants 2R01AA06123, to Gregory T. Smith, and R37AA08333 (MERIT), to Mark S. Goldman.

REFERENCES

Abrams, D. G., & Niaura, R. S. (1987). Social learning theory. In H. T. Blane & K. E. Leonard (Eds.), *Psychological theories of drinking and alcoholism* (pp. 131–178). New York: Guilford.

Akers, R. L., Krohn, M. D., Lanza-Kaduce, L., & Radosevich, M. (1979). Social learning and deviant behavior: A specific test of a general theory. *American Sociological Review, 44,* 636–655.

Alloy, L. B., & Tabachnik, N. (1984). Assessment of covariation by humans and animals: The joint influence of prior expectations and current situational information. *Psychological Review, 91,* 112–149.

Anderson, J. R. (1983). A spreading activation theory of memory. *Journal of Verbal Learning and Verbal Behavior, 22,* 261–295.

Bagozzi, R. P. (1992). The self-regulation of attitudes, intentions, and behavior. *Social Psychology Quarterly, 55,* 178–204.

Bandura, A. (1985). *Social foundations of thought and action.* Englewood Cliffs, NJ: Prentice-Hall.

Baron, R. M., & Kenny, D. A. (1986). The moderator–mediator variable distinction in social psychological research: Conceptual, strategic, and statistical considerations. *Journal of Personality and Social Psychology, 51,* 1173–1182.

Bauman, K. E., & Bryan, E. S. (1980). Subjective expected utility and children's drinking.

Journal of Studies on Alcohol, 41, 952–958.

Bollen, K. A. (1989). *Structural equations with latent variables.* New York: Wiley.

Bolles, R. C. (1972). Reinforcement, expectancy, and learning. *Psychological Review, 79,* 394–409.

Brown, S. A. (1985a). Expectancies versus background in the prediction of college drinking patterns. *Journal of Consulting and Clinical Psychology, 53,* 123–130.

Brown, S. A. (1985b). Reinforcement expectancies and alcoholism treatment outcome after a one-year follow-up. *Journal of Studies on Alcohol, 46,* 304–308.

Brown, S. A., Creamer, V. A., & Stetson, B. A. (1987). Adolescent alcohol expectancies in relation to personal and parental drinking practices. *Journal of Abnormal Psychology, 96,* 117–121.

Brown, S. A., Goldman, M. S., & Christiansen, B. A. (1985). Do alcohol expectancies mediate drinking patterns of adults? *Journal of Consulting and Clinical Psychology, 53,* 512–519.

Brown, S. A., Goldman, M. S., Inn, A. M., & Anderson, L. (1980). Expectations of reinforcement from alcohol: Their domain and relation to drinking patterns. *Journal of Consulting and Clinical Psychology, 48,* 419–426.

Cahalan, D., & Cisin, I. H. (1968). American drinking practice: A summary of findings from a national probability sample: Vol. 1. Extent of drinking by population subgroups. *Quarterly Journal of Studies on Alcohol, 29,* 130–151.

Carver, C. S., & Scheier, M. F. (1990). Origins and functions of positive and negative affect: A control process view. *Psychological Review, 97,* 19–35.

Caswell, S., Gilmore, L. L., Silva, P., & Brasch, P. (1988). What children know about alcohol and how they know it. *British Journal of Addictions, 83,* 223–227.

Christiansen, B. A., & Goldman, M. S. (1983). Alcohol-related expectancies versus demographic/background variables in the prediction of adolescent drinking. *Journal of Consulting and Clinical Psychology, 51,* 249–258.

Christiansen, B. A., Goldman, M. S., & Inn, A. (1982). Development of alcohol-related expectancies in adolescents: Separating pharmacological from social learning influences. *Journal of Consulting and Clinical Psychology, 50,* 336–344.

Christiansen, B. A., Smith, G. T., Roehling, P. V., & Goldman, M. S. (1989). Using alcohol expectancies to predict adolescent drinking behavior after one year. *Journal of Consulting and Clinical Psychology, 57,* 93–99.

Cloninger, C. R. (1987). Neurogenetic adaptive mechanisms in alcoholism. *Science, 236,* 410–416.

Cohen, J., & Cohen, P. (1983). *Applied multiple regression/correlation analysis for the behavioral sciences* (2nd. ed.). Hillsdale, NJ: Lawrence Erlbaum Associates.

Collins, A. M., & Loftus, E. F. (1975). A spreading activation theory of semantic processing. *Psychological Review, 82,* 407–428.

Connors, G. J., & Maisto, S. A. (1988). The alcohol expectancy construct: Overview and clinical applications. *Cognitive Therapy and Research, 12,* 487–504.

Connors, G. J., Maisto, S. A., & Dermen, K. H. (1992). Alcohol-related expectancies and their applications to treatment. In R. R. Watson (Ed.), *Drug and alcohol abuse reviews: Vol. 3. Alcohol abuse treatment* (pp. 203–231). Totowa, NJ: Humana.

Connors, G. J., O'Farrell, T. J., Cutter, H. S. G., & Thompson, D. L. (1986). Alcohol expectancies among male alcoholics, problem drinkers, and nonproblem drinkers. *Alcoholism: Clinical and Experimental Research, 10(6),* 667–671.

Cooper, M. L., Russell, M., Skinner, J. B., Fromme, M. R., & Mudar, P. (1992). Stress and alcohol use: Moderating effects of gender, coping, and alcohol expectancies. *Journal of Abnormal Psychology, 101,* 139–152.

Darkes, J., & Goldman, M. S. (1993). Expectancy challenge and drinking reduction: Experimental evidence for a mediational process. *Journal of Consulting and Clinical Psychology, 61,* 344–353.

Dunn, M. E., & Goldman, M. S. (1993, June). *Children's alcohol expectancies: Development and relationship to adult drinking patterns.* Paper presented at the annual meeting of the Research Society on Alcoholism, San Antonio, TX.

Finn, T. A., & Strickland, D. E. (1982). A content analysis of beverage alcohol advertising: Vol. 2. Television advertising. *Journal of Studies on Alcohol, 43,* 964–989.

Fromme, K., Stroot, E., Kaplan, D. (1993). Comprehensive effects of alcohol: Development and psychometric assessment of a new expectancy questionnaire. *Psychological Assessment, 5,* 19–26.

Goldman, M. S. (in press). Issues in the assessment, prevention, and treatment of alcohol problems using alcohol expectancies. *Applied and Preventive Psychology.*

Goldman, M. S., Brown, S. A., & Christiansen, B. A. (1987). Expectancy theory: Thinking about drinking. In H. T. Blane & K. E. Leonard (Eds.), *Psychological theories of drinking and alcoholism* (pp. 181–226). New York: Guilford.

Goldman, M. S., Brown, S. A., Christiansen, B. A., & Smith, G. T. (1991). Alcoholism etiology and memory: Broadening the scope of alcohol expectancy research. *Psychological Bulletin, 110,* 137–146.

Goldman, M. S., & Rather, B. C. (1993). Substance use disorders: Cognitive models and architecture. In P. Kendall & K. S. Dobson (Eds.), *Psychopathology and Cognition.* Orlando, FL: Academic.

Henderson, M. J., & Goldman, M. S. (1987, November). *Effect of a social manipulation on alcohol expectancies and subsequent drinking.* Paper presented at the 21st meeting of the Association for the Advancement of Behavior Therapy, Boston.

Henderson, M. J., Goldman, M. S., Coovert, M. D., & Carnevalla, N. (in press). Covariance structure models of expectancy. *Journal of Studies on Alcohol.*

Hoyle, R. H., & Smith, G. T. (in press). Formulating clinical research hypotheses as structural equation models: A conceptual overview. *Journal of Consulting and Clinical Psychology.*

James, W. (1890). *The principles of psychology* (Vol. 1). New York: Holt.

Jones, E. E. (1986). Interpreting interpersonal behavior: The effects of expectancies. *Science, 234,* 41–46.

Kirsch, I. (1985). Response expectancy as a determinant of experience and behavior. *American Psychologist, 40,* 1189–1202.

Kraus, D., Smith, G. T., & Ratner, H. H. (in press). Modifying alcohol-related expectancies in grade-school children. *Journal of Studies on Alcohol.*

Leigh, B. C. (1987). Beliefs about the effects of alcohol on self and others. *Journal of Studies on Alcohol, 48,* 467–475.

Leigh, B. C. (1989). In search of the seven dwarves: Issues of measurement and meaning in alcohol expectancy research. *Psychological Bulletin, 105,* 361–373.

Levine, B., & Goldman, M. S. (1989, August). *Situational variations in expectancies.* Paper presented at the 97th annual convention of the American Psychological Association, New Orleans, LA.

MacCorquodale, K. M., & Meehl, P. E. (1954). Preliminary suggestions as to a formalization of expectancy theory. *Psychological Review, 60,* 53–60, 125–129.

Mann, L. M., Chassin, L., & Sher, K. J. (1987). Alcohol expectancies and the risk for alcoholism. *Journal of Consulting and Clinical Psychology, 55,* 411–417.

Massey, R. F., & Goldman, M. S. (1988, August). *Manipulating expectancies as a means of altering alcohol consumption.* Paper presented at the 96th annual convention of the American Psychological Association, Atlanta, GA.

McKenna, T., & Pickens, R. (1983). Personality characteristics of alcoholic children of alcoholics. *Journal of Studies on Alcohol, 44*, 688–700.

Medin, D. L., Goldstone, R. L., & Gentner, D. (1993). Respects for similarity. *Psychological Review, 100*, 254–278.

Miller, D. T., & Turnbull, W. (1986). Expectancies and interpersonal processes. *Annual Review of Psychology, 37*, 233–256.

Miller, P. M., & Smith, G. T. (1990, August). *Dispositional and specific learning history risk factors for alcohol abuse.* Paper presented at the annual meeting of the American Psychological Association, Boston.

Miller, P. M., Smith, G. T., & Goldman, M. S. (1990). Emergence of alcohol expectancies in childhood: A possible critical period. *Journal of Studies on Alcohol, 51*, 343–349.

Mooney, D. K., Fromme, K., Kivlahan, D. R., & Marlatt, G. A. (1987). Correlates of alcohol consumption: Sex, age, and expectancies relate differentially to quantity and frequency. *Addictive Behaviors, 12*, 235–240.

Moscowitz, J. M. (1989). The primary prevention of alcohol problems: A critical review of the research literature. *Journal of Studies on Alcohol, 50*, 54–88.

Nathan, P. (1983). Failures in prevention: Why we can't prevent the devastating effect of alcoholism and drug abuse. *American Psychologist, 38*, 459–467.

Newlin, D. B., & Thomson, J. B. (1990). Alcohol challenge with sons of alcoholics: A critical review and analysis. *Psychological Bulletin, 108*, 383–402.

Noll, R. B., Zucker, R. A., & Greenberg, G. S. (1990). Identification of alcohol by smell among preschoolers: Evidence for early socialization about drugs occurring in the home. *Child Development, 61*, 1520–1527.

Nosofsky, R. M. (1992). Similarity scaling and cognitive process models. *Annual Review of Psychology, 43*, 25–53.

Rather, B. C., Goldman, M. S., Roehrich, L., & Brannick, M. (1992). Empirical modeling of an alcohol expectancy memory network using multidimensional scaling. *Journal of Abnormal Psychology, 101*, 174–183.

Rescorla, R. A. (1988). Pavlovian conditioning. *American Psychologist, 43*, 151–160.

Rosch, E. H. (1975). Cognitive representations of semantic categories. *Journal of Experimental Psychology: General, 104*, 192–233.

Rotter, J. B. (1954). *Social learning and clinical psychology.* Englewood Cliffs, NJ: Prentice-Hall.

Schuckit, M. A. (1987). Biological vulnerability to alcoholism. *Journal of Consulting and Clinical Psychology, 55*, 301–309.

Sher, K. J., Walitzer, K. S., Wood, P. K., & Brent, E. E. (1991). Characteristics of children of alcoholics: Putative risk factors, substance use and abuse, and psychopathology. *Journal of Abnormal Psychology, 100*, 427–448.

Simon, N. A., & Kaplan, C. A. (1990). Foundations of cognitive science. In M. I. Posner (Ed.), *Foundations of cognitive science* (pp. 1–47). Cambridge, MA: MIT Press.

Smith, E. E., & Medin, D. L. (1981). *Categories and concepts.* Cambridge, MA: Harvard University Press.

Smith, G. T. (1989). Expectancy theory and alcohol: The situation insensitivity hypothesis. *Psychology of Addictive Behavior, 2*(3), 108–115.

Smith, G. T., & Goldman, M. S. (1990, August). *Toward a mediational model of alcohol expectancy.* Paper presented at the annual meeting of the American Psychological Association, Boston.

Smith, G. T., Goldman, M. S., & Christiansen, B. A. (1989, August). *The Drinking Styles Questionnaire: Adolescent drinking self-report.* Paper presented at the annual meeting of the American Psychological Association, New Orleans.

Smith, G. T., Goldman, M. S., & Christiansen, B. A. (1992). *The divergent paths of high-expectancy and low-expectancy adolescents.* Manuscript submitted for publication.

Smith, G. T., & Miller, T. L. (1992). Toward a developmental framework for the treatment of adolescent alcohol abuse: Current findings and future directions. In R. R. Watson (Ed.), *Drug and alcohol abuse reviews: Vol. 3. Alcohol abuse treatment* (pp. 87–113). Totowa, NJ: Humana.

Southwick, L., Steele, C., Marlatt, A., & Lindell, M. (1981). Alcohol-related expectancies: Defined by phase of intoxication and drinking experience. *Journal of Consulting and Clinical Psychology, 49,* 713–721.

Spiegler, D. L. (1983). Children's attitudes toward alcohol. *Journal of Studies on Alcohol, 44,* 545–552.

Stacy, A. W., Newcomb, M. D., & Bentler, P. M. (1991). Cognitive motivation and drug use: A 9-year longitudinal study. *Journal of Abnormal Psychology, 100,* 502–515.

Tolman, E. G. (1932). *Purposive behavior in animals and man.* New York: Appleton-Century-Crofts.

6

The Path to Alcohol Problems Through Conduct Problems: A Family-Based Approach to Very Early Intervention With Risk

Eugene Maguin
University of Pittsburgh

Robert A. Zucker
Hiram E. Fitzgerald
Michigan State University

According to national epidemiologic data, substance abuse can be expected to affect approximately 17% of the adult population sometime during their lives (Regier et al., 1990); if one narrows the problem solely to alcohol abuse/dependence among males, the lifetime prevalence figure runs to approximately one fourth of the U.S. population (Helzer, Burnam, & McEvoy, 1991). How might one intervene very early on in a preventive way with what ultimately grows into such a large clinical problem? The program of work reported here began with the epidemiologic fact just noted, added several pieces of evidence pertaining to the development of risk, considered what interventions might likely alleviate such risk, and then crafted a population-based intervention regimen to address these issues quite early in the life course. The risk marker selected for access to the population was also derived from the previously mentioned data; it involved selecting male children from households in which the father was already alcoholic.

Such children are a compelling target group for preventive activity for a variety of reasons. Not only does substantial trouble already exist in the parental generation, but the children are at significantly greater risk to become alcohol or drug abusers themselves. (Current estimates put this figure at four to six times the likelihood in the general population; Russell, 1990.) In addition, elevated risk is present for a wide variety of other difficulties that begin even earlier in the life cycle than substance abuse. Such difficulties include hyperactivity, oppositional behavior and conduct problems, and their developmentally more advanced manifestations—including delinquency and the development of antisocial patterns of adaptation in adulthood (Sher, 1991; Zucker, 1989). Moreover, much recent work links the causal paths into adolescent alcohol and other drug abuse to those very same factors that are identified as more prevalent in early childhood among male children of alcoholics (COAs; cf. Kellam, Ensminger, & Simon, 1980; Pihl & Peterson, 1991; Zucker, 1989). Finally, as commonly noted in reviews of this area (Patterson, DeBaryshe, & Ramsey, 1989; Zucker & Fitzgerald, 1991), this risk envelope is very similar to the one known to be related to the emergence and continued development of antisociality even into adulthood (Olweus, 1979). In addition, continuity of process appears most likely to take place when the earlier nonalcohol specific risks are of greater severity (Loeber & LeBlanc, 1990; Tartar & Vanukov, in press).

Thus, the promise is offered that by addressing risk for conduct-related difficulty in early childhood and using preventive intervention techniques originally designed to alleviate it, one may be able to intervene, and arrest risk development, in the highest risk environments out of which alcohol and other forms of substance abuse are known to emerge. The program described here, the Michigan State University Multiple Risk Child Outreach Program (Zucker, Maguin, Noll, Fitzgerald, & Klinger, 1990),[1] was formulated with these goals in mind. Its first goal, therefore, was the arrest of conduct problems in young children. The long-term hypothesis is that such work would serve dual functions: (a) It would be useful in its own right and (b) it would intervene on processes that are believed to be causal to later alcohol abuse and alcoholism (Zucker & Gomberg, 1986; Zucker & Noll, 1987). The specific program we put in place represents an effort that focuses on a considerably earlier developmental period than the vast majority of preventive intervention programming currently being done (Hawkins, Catalano, & J. Y. Miller, 1992). It incorporates a broadly based, systemic model that includes a focus on family factors as well as individual child factors (G. E. Miller & Prinz, 1990), and its recruitment methodology is based on a primary preven-

---

[1]The original name for this program was the Michigan State University Prevention of Conduct Disorders Project (Zucker & Noll, 1987).

tion/outreach model that used a population net to access children at risk.

More concretely, in the present study, a group of families with pre-school-age sons were accessed using a population screening procedure. Once identified, families were randomly assigned to either of two service delivery formats of an intervention program that has been found to be effective in producing significant and long-lasting decreases in aggression and noncompliance in both clinic- and self-referred families (Patterson, Chamberlain, & Reid, 1982; Webster-Stratton, 1981, 1982). Two delivery formats were used. In the first, only mothers were involved; in the second, both parents were involved.

On the basis of the success of parent-training programs with both clinic- and self-referred populations, it was expected that irrespective of delivery format, compared to families not participating in the program, intervention group families would report (a) significantly lower levels of such negative child behaviors as aggression and noncompliance, (b) significantly higher levels of such prosocial child behavior as minding and cooperative play, and (c) significantly higher levels of affectionate behavior toward the parents at the midtreatment, program termination, and follow-up assessments.

The both-parents format was added on the basis of both the family therapy (Minuchin, 1974) and the marital discord literatures (Gottman & Katz, 1989), which suggest that addressing family issues with both parents present should lead to more effective long-term outcomes; the empirical literature is currently equivocal on this point (Budd & O'Brien, 1982; Horton, 1984; Webster-Stratton, 1985). Nonetheless, from Webster-Stratton (1985), it was anticipated that the both-parents format, compared to the mother-only format, would show significantly lower levels of negative behavior and higher levels of prosocial and affectionate behavior at the midtreatment, termination, and follow-up assessments.

METHOD

Subjects

Program participants were the first 104 families recruited from district courts in four mid-Michigan counties who, as part of the program protocol, were initially asked to take part in "a study of child health and family development." At that point, only casual mention was made of the possibility of later child-focused work. The initial assessment of child and family functioning involved a substantial (10-session) protocol. Families had to meet the following inclusion criteria: conviction of the father for driving while impaired (DWI) or driving under the influence of liquor (DUIL), with a blood alcohol concentration (BAC) of at least 15 mg per 100 ml (0.15%) when arrested and no prior DWI or DUIL arrests or a BAC of at least 0.12% and multiple arrests; subsequently, the father had to pass a protocol screen ensuring that he also met Feighner diagnostic criteria (Feighner et al., 1972) for probable or definite alcoholism (approximately 90% met the *definite* level); and, in addition, a biological son, ages 3.0 to 6.0 years, as well as the child's biological mother had to be living with the father at the time of first contact.

Although all fathers met the criteria for alcoholism, almost none of them identified themselves as alcoholic. In addition, the fact that these men were convicted drunk drivers indicates that their alcoholism was more heavily combined with antisociality than is true of other types of alcoholics (Babor & Dolinsky, 1988). Other analyses we conducted show that 60% are classified as Type 2 alcoholics according to Cloninger's (1987) typology, 25% are classified as Type 1 (nonantisocial, later onset), and 14% are classified as indeterminate (Zucker, Ellis, & Fitzgerald, in press). Thus, the present group is most representative of the subset of alcoholics known as the most damaged, as having the most antisocial comorbidity and earliest onset, and as the group most likely to have substance abuse manifested among their offspring (Zucker & Fitzgerald, 1991).

Demographic characteristics of the sample are as follows: mean age of the parents at first assessment contact was 29.3 years for the mothers and 31.4 years for the fathers. Although 16% of the mothers and 21% of the fathers had not finished high school, 42% of mothers and 38% of fathers had some post-high-school education. The biological parents in 99 of the families were married to each other and had been for a mean of 7.3 years.

At the time of the initial evaluation, families were randomly assigned to either of the two intervention formats or to a control group. At the conclusion of the evaluation, those families that were still intact and lived within 30 miles of the university were invited to participate in a sustained follow-up program on the basis of their earlier protocol designation. The treatment assignments involved two different intervention alternatives, both of which were described as "a program to improve parent–child communication patterns." Families whose random assignment was to the control condition were asked to take part in three follow-up assessments spaced at approximately 6-month intervals.

Of the 104 families initially recruited, 81 families met intervention protocol eligibility criteria and 23 families did not (12 had separated, 5 had moved from the intervention area, and 6 had failed to complete the initial evaluation). Comparisons between eligible and ineligible families revealed no significant demographic differences. On the Child Behavior Checklist (CBCL; Achenbach & Edelbrock, 1983), more, though not significantly, ineligible than eligible boys (36.8% vs. 23.5%, respectively) scored in the clinical range ($T > 63$) of the externalizing behavior scale. Although the families that were not eligible for the intervention protocol are not relevant to the issue of treatment success, they are relevant to the issue of outreach generalizability and the likely implementation success of population-based programs. The reader is referred to Maguin (1991) and Zucker et al. (1990) for detailed information about recruitment and retention of subjects as well as about procedural details.

Intervention Regimen

The intervention regimen (Zucker, 1991; Zucker, Noll, Kriegler, & Cruise, 1986) employed was a modification and extension of social learning therapy, a behavior modification strategy developed for the treatment of older aggressive/antisocial children at the Oregon Social Learning Center (OSLC; Patterson, Reid, Jones, & Conger, 1975). Although the OSLC parent-training protocol formed the core of the child intervention, the Michigan State University protocol had some significant differences in both clientele and implementation. First, the average age of the target child was about 4.4 years at the first contact, compared to the average of about 12 years reported by Patterson (1974). Second, the protocol involved outreach to an already designated high-risk population, but the offering of help was not made within the context of offering treatment. Thus, families were neither self-selected nor court referred, and some needed to be convinced of the usefulness of the program. Third, the program was offered as an educational package rather than as treatment; it was described as one that would enhance parent–child communication and improve parent–child relationships. Thus, the families were volunteers rather than clients. Fourth, fathers typically were initially much less convinced of the need for the program. Because of this not-uncommon reluctance, much of the early work involved finding some common ground around which the intervention could legitimately proceed. Last, family conflict and marital dissatisfaction were frequently encountered. A common source of dissatisfaction among wives was spouse's drinking and related difficulties. Thus, any effort to work with the children—even in the early sessions—had to also confront this problem, which included the wife's anger at her husband's drinking and the husband's dissatisfaction with his spouse's nagging. As a result, although not a part of the framework for recruitment, special attention was routinely paid to the parents' alcohol and drug problems and marital functioning as part of the intervention program. Where indicated, referrals to Alcoholics Anonymous, as well as community treatment agencies, were made for focused work on these difficulties, and the extent of compliance with these referrals was then monitored as part of the intervention work.

The study design is diagrammed in Fig. 6.1. The overall length of the intervention was 28 sessions, spanning approximately 1 year, and it was divided into two phases. During Phase 1, intervention staff taught child management skills (i.e., tracking, contracting, and time-out) through weekly sessions with families and twice-weekly telephone contacts. Phase 1 ended when the family had either (a) satisfactorily acquired the child management skills or (b) had completed between 12 and 16 sessions. In this latter instance, the exact Phase 2 transition was determined by staff decision. During Phase 2, interveners conducted 12 biweekly face-to-face sessions, along with at least weekly telephone contacts, to support and reinforce child management skills and address significant marital issues and individual substance abuse issues.

Although the nominal physical setting for the intervention was the Clinical Center at Michigan State University, about 45% of the families received some or all of the intervention program in their homes. The treatment staff were primarily post-masters-level doctoral students in clinical psychology who additionally received approximately 20 hours of training in the treatment paradigm and 4 hours of group supervision each week from one of two licensed clinical psychologists.

Procedure

Both parents in all families, irrespective of the family's eligibility or intervention status, were asked to take part in all three posttest assessments, for which they received compensation. Posttest 1 (PT 1) was conducted between the first and second sessions of Phase 2 for the intervention families and at a nominal 26-week interval after initial assessment completion for all other families. Posttest 2 (PT 2) was conducted at the conclusion of the intervention program for intervention families and at a nominal 26 weeks after Posttest 1 completion for all other families. Posttest 3 was conducted at a nominal 26 weeks after completion of Posttest 2 for all families (see also Figure 1). Although the nominal 26-week interval was dictated by the study design, the actual interval between posttests was monitored regularly and adjustments were made in posttest scheduling for control and ineligible intervention group families so as to maintain an approximately equal interval between posttests for both intervention and other families.

INTERVENTION DESIGN

BOTH PARENTS AND MOTHER ONLY CONDITIONS

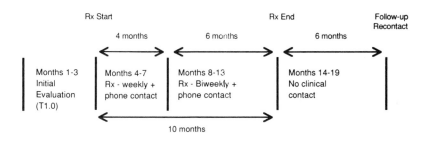

EVALUATION DESIGN

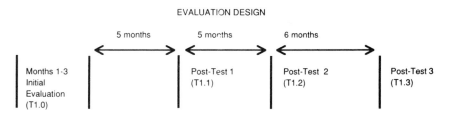

FIG. 6.1. Schedule of initial assessment, intervention program, and posttest assessments for the intervention and control groups.

Evaluation Instruments

Each of the following four evaluation instruments was completed by both of the child's parents.

Child Behavior Checklist–Revised (CBCL–R). The CBCL–R (Achenbach & Edelbrock, 1983) is perhaps the most commonly used parent rating scale in clinical use. It was used here to provide a standardized index of the level of symptomatic functioning of the study children.

Conners Parent Questionnaire–Modified (CPQ–M). CPQ–M is a 51-item shortened and slightly modified version of the original Conners Parent Questionnaire and the Revised Conners Parent Questionnaire (Conners, 1973; Goyette, Conners, & Ulrich, 1978); it uses the same 4-point response format.

Child Behavior Rating Scale–Preschool Version (CBRS–P). The CBRS–P (Noll & Zucker, 1985a) is an 84-item child behavior questionnaire consisting of 49 desirable child behavior items (e.g., minds, shows affection, appropriately expresses anger) and 35 undesirable child behavior items (e.g., pushes or hits, inappropriately expresses anger), which are rated on a 7-point scale ranging from *never* (1) to *always* (7).

Parent Daily Report–Modified (PDR–M). The PDR–M (Noll & Zucker, 1985b) uses 22 items taken verbatim from the CBRS–P to which parents respond by reporting whether each of the behaviors had occurred in the previous 24 hours. At each assessment, each parent was interviewed by telephone on alternate days for 3 days each.

Outcome Measures

Outcome measures were built in a three-step process, originally involving a content analysis of the four outcome instruments administered, followed by confirmatory factor analysis on data pooled over parents and assessments to evaluate the provisionally identified clusters (see Hunter & Gerbing, 1982), and concluding with a second-order confirmatory factor analysis to evaluate the possible existence of higher order constructs. From this work three outcome measures were developed that (a) met necessary construct development criteria of internal consistency, along with parallelism with other variables, and (b) were judged suitable in content to evaluate intervention effects. These measures were *negative behavior composite, prosocial behavior composite,* and *affectionate behavior.*

The negative behavior composite comprised four more specific negative behavior constructs (anger arousal, aggression, hyper, and defiant). The behaviors included in these scales describe children who, in the negative extreme, are seen as being aggressive, rude, defiant, oppositional, restless and overactive, and given to sharp and dramatic explosions of anger. The prosocial behavior composite consisted of three more specific prosocial behavior constructs (compliant, polite, and plays well). The behaviors included in these scales describe children who, in the positive extreme, are seen as being compliant to parent requests, respectful of the rights of other children and adults, and able to play easily with other children. The affectionate behavior measure consisted of a single construct that is a measure of the parent's perception of the target child's expressed affection toward the parent.

Under a model that treated parents as equal raters or observers of their child's behavior, the construct score was the mean of each parent's score on the construct, and the reliability of that score was the between-parent correlation corrected by the Spearman-Brown formula for two measurements. The resulting reliability estimate was .70 for the negative behavior composite, .55 for the prosocial behavior composite, and .58 for affectionate behavior.

Analysis of Change

The impact of the intervention was computed by the change score (i.e., the difference in the averaged within-parent construct scores) for each pair of time points. The resulting change scores were then correlated with intervention group membership (Yes–No) to yield a point biserial correlation as an index of whether significant change took place.

RESULTS

Initial Symptomatic Status

Although none of the study children had clinical contact, the CBCL–R was used to provide an index of the extent to which clinically significant problems were present. On the basis of a T score of more than 63 on the externalizing scale, 23.5% of the eligible boys were in the clinical range, which was not significantly different than the ineligible boys' scores.

Final Intervention Status

At the conclusion of the intervention program, a review showed that 17 of the 23 families (74%) offered the mother-only protocol and 12 of the 28 families offered the both-parents protocol (43%) had completed the entire intervention sequence. Over the course of the intervention, an additional 4 families (3 in the mother-only group and 1 in the both-parents group) had separated and thus became ineligible. Of the families that did not complete the intervention protocol, 4 mother-only families and 3 both-parents families received partial treatment because they completed at least five sessions before withdrawing, and 12 both-parents families and 3 mother-only families either refused the intervention or failed to complete five sessions. Significantly more families in the both-parents condition than in the mother-only condition either refused the intervention offer or withdrew before completing five sessions, $\chi^2(1, N = 15) = 4.27, p < .05$. Overall, the attrition rate for the intervention group was 43%, which is certainly comparable to intervention outreach studies (e.g., 25% to 50%, from Andrews et al., 1982; or 28%, from Garber, 1988) but is somewhat high compared to self- or clinic-referred parent-training programs ($M = 28\%$, range: 0% to 50%; Forehand, Middlebrook, Rogers, & Stiffle, 1983).

We also compared families that refused treatment with those completing treatment on a variety of demographic, parent-functioning, and child-behavior variables, but we found no differences (Maguin, 1991). Because of the small sample size, however, the power of the tests was quite low. Of the 26 eligible families assigned to the control group, 3 families refused to complete all three scheduled posttests and were counted as dropouts from the control group.

Intervention effects were examined using the subset of 52 families that either completed the intervention or—in the case of the controls—continued to remain eligible for it (i.e., the families were still intact and living in the immediate geographic area of the program).

Overall Intervention Effects

It was expected that the group receiving the intervention would show a significant decrease in negative behavior and a significant increase in prosocial behavior relative to the control group. Table 6.1 presents the means and standard deviations of the composite construct measures for the intervention and control groups at the four measurement points. A higher score indicates that a child has "more" of the construct. Table 6.2 presents the measures of change of the intervention group relative to the control group, as assessed by point biserial correlations. Correlations were computed to assess change (a) at midtreatment, (b) over the whole of the intervention period, and (c) over the whole of the intervention as well as the follow-up period. A significant positive correlation here indicates that the intervention group increased more than the control group between the two time points, and a significant negative correlation means that the intervention group decreased more than the control group.

As predicted, the correlations for negative behavior composite (Table 6.2) show negative behavior decreased more in the intervention group compared to the control group at both the midtreatment probe ($r = -.23$) and at treatment termination ($r = -.30$) relative to the initial assessment. Change in the level of negative behavior over the period from initial assessment to follow-up, however, did not favor the intervention group over the control group. Table 6.1 shows that the means for the intervention group decreased steadily from pretest to termination, with no change thereafter. In addition, as one would anticipate, the means for the control group vary over this interval. This variation included a substantial decrease in negative behavior from termination to follow-up. Unfortunately, on these grounds, a clear interpretation of the follow-up effects is not possible.

As predicted, correlations for the prosocial behavior composite indicate that the level of prosocial behavior increased significantly more in

TABLE 6.1
Across-Time Means and Standard Deviations for Intervention and Control Groups
on the Composite Intervention Measures

Scale	Pretest	Midtreatment	Termination	Follow-Up
Negative composite				
Intervention				
M	3.08	2.98	2.90	2.92
SD	0.56	0.58	0.60	0.65
n	29	29	28	29
Control				
M	2.94	3.01	2.96	2.82
SD	0.56	0.61	0.61	0.58
n	23	23	23	22
Prosocial composite				
Intervention				
M	2.70	3.12	3.17	3.11
SD	0.57	0.53	0.60	0.60
n	29	29	28	29
Control				
M	2.86	2.77	2.98	2.98
SD	0.49	0.64	0.69	0.56
n	23	23	23	22
Affectionate				
Intervention				
M	3.11	3.06	3.03	2.89
SD	0.75	0.94	0.88	0.76
n	29	29	28	29
Control				
M	3.21	3.11	2.80	2.82
SD	0.60	0.86	0.69	1.05
n	23	23	23	22

TABLE 6.2

Relationship of Group Membership (Intervention Vs. Control) to Across-Time Change
on the Composite Intervention Measures (Point Biserial Correlations)

	Time Period		
Scale	Pretest to Midtreatment[a]	Pretest to Termination[b]	Pretest to Follow-Up[c]
Negative composite			
r	−.23*	−.30*	−.04
Prosocial composite			
r	.42**	.26*	.26*
Affectionate			
r	.04	.24*	.13

Note. A positive correlation indicates that the intervention group increased more than
did the control group.

[a]$n = 52$. [b]$n = 51$. [c]$n = 51$.

*$p < .05$. **$p < .01$. (Both are one-tailed.)

the intervention group compared to the control group over the period from initial assessment to midtreatment probe ($r = .42$), from initial assessment to treatment termination ($r = .26$), and from initial assessment to follow-up ($r = .26$). Thus, increases in prosocial behavior remained after the intervention had ceased.

Correlations for affectionate behavior toward parents show an advantage for the intervention group only at the conclusion of the intervention (i.e., the initial assessment to posttest correlation, $r = .24$, is positive and significant). The data do not show an advantage for the intervention group at either the midtreatment probe or at the posttreatment, 6-month follow-up. Thus, the benefits of increased affection from child to parents were not lasting.

Comparison of Intervention Formats

The second hypothesis predicted that the both-parents intervention would be more effective than the mother-only format. Table 6.3 presents the means and standard deviations of the three outcome measures for the two intervention protocols, and Table 6.4 compares their relative success by means of point biserial correlations between format and change score. A positive coefficient indicates the both-parents format showed an advantage relative to the mother-only format, and a negative coefficient indicates the converse.

The effect correlations for the negative behavior composite show an overall pattern of small effects at each time period with no advantage to either intervention format. In contrast, the results for the prosocial behavior composite show a consistent pattern of advantage for the both-parents format. Although the effect correlation is not significant at the midtreatment probe, it is in the same direction as the significant effects at posttest ($r = .36$) and also at follow-up ($r = .27$). The results for affectionate behavior show no clear evidence favoring one format over the other.

DISCUSSION

The predicted increases in prosocial child behavior for intervention families were found at midtreatment, termination, and follow-up. Predicted decreases in negative child behavior for intervention group families were found at midtreatment and termination but not at follow-up. A significant increase in affectionate behavior among intervention families was found only at termination. Thus, the intervention program was successful in not only increasing prosocial

TABLE 6.3
Across-Time Means and Standard Deviations for Mother-Only and Both-Parents
Formats on the Composite Intervention Measures

Scale	Pretest	Midtreatment	Termination	Follow-Up
Negative composite				
Mother only				
M	3.09	2.96	2.94	2.95
SD	0.54	0.63	0.56	0.63
n	17	17	16	17
Both parents				
M	3.05	3.01	2.84	2.86
SD	0.61	0.54	0.67	0.69
n	12	12	12	12
Prosocial composite				
Mother only				
M	2.81	3.13	3.08	3.10
SD	0.39	0.39	0.45	0.53
n	17	17	16	17
Both parents				
M	2.54	3.10	3.28	3.13
SD	0.75	0.71	0.77	0.72
n	12	12	12	12
Affectionate				
Mother only				
M	3.27	3.27	3.08	3.02
SD	0.56	0.67	0.67	0.66
n	17	17	16	17
Both parents				
M	2.87	2.76	2.96	2.71
SD	0.93	1.19	1.12	0.88
n	12	12	12	12

TABLE 6.4
Intervention Format Contrasts (Both Parents Vs. Mother Only)
as Related to Across-Time Change on the Composite Intervention Measures
(Point Biserial Correlations)

	Time Period		
	Pretest to Midtreatment[a]	Pretest to Termination[b]	Pretest to Follow-Up[c]
Negative composite			
r	.14	$-.03$	$-.06$
Prosocial composite			
r	.22	.36*	.27[†]
Affectionate			
r	$-.10$	.21	.07

Note. A positive correlation indicates that the both-parents protocol was more effective
in producing change in the expected direction than was the mother-only protocol.
[a]$n = 29$. [b]$n = 28$. [c]$n = 29$.
*$p < .05$. [†]$p < .10$. (Both are one-tailed.)

behavior at the conclusion of the program but the increase also persisted after the program had ended. Although the program succeeded in decreasing negative behavior during treatment and at termination, differences between the intervention children and controls did not persist at follow-up. Similarly, although a positive impact on affectionate behavior was observed at termination, this effect did not persist. Finally, comparison of the two intervention formats showed the anticipated advantage for the both-parents format over the mother-only format only for prosocial behavior; both delivery formats were equally effective in reducing negative behavior.

The effect for negative behavior noted at midtreatment (i.e., the conclusion of the child management skills teaching) is most comparable to termination data for those programs that ended with time-out and contracting or included an assessment near the end of the child-focused program (e.g., Forehand & King, 1977; Patterson & Reid, 1973; Webster-Stratton, Kolpacoff, & Hollinsworth, 1988). Although reports of prosocial behavior change have been less frequently examined, two studies (Fleischman & Szykula, 1981; Webster-Stratton, Kolpacoff, & Hollinsworth, 1988) included a measure that combined prosocial and affectionate behaviors. The Webster-Stratton, Kolpacoff, & Hollinsworth study, which is the most directly comparable because it was a pre–post design, also found a significant improvement in prosocial behavior.

The significant decrease in negative behavior found at termination is quite comparable to that reported in the literature. A comparison of the effect correlation at midtreatment ($r = -.23$) with that at termination ($r = -.30$) suggests that a further reduction in negative behavior did not occur during the latter, parent-focused portion of the intervention. An analysis of the Patterson (1974) data by Maguin (1991) showed the same result. The increase in prosocial behavior at termination found here is similar to that found by Fleischman and Szykula (1981). Comparison of the correlations at midtreatment and termination, however, indicates that some attenuation of the prosocial effect occurred.

Almost all parent-training studies (e.g., Fleischman, 1981; Fleischman & Sykula, 1981; Forehand, Griest, & Wells, 1979; Forehand & King, 1977; Patterson & Reid, 1973) have found a significant decrease in negative behavior from pretest to follow-up. Although, in this study, we did not find such a decrease, an inspection of the across-time means for both intervention and control groups shows that this is more attributable to the variability of the control group than to an increase in negative behavior by the intervention group. By contrast, the finding of a significant increase in prosocial behavior at the follow-up is also reported by Fleischman and Szykula (1981).

Finally, the weak intervention format difference effects are generally consistent with the small literature on father involvement in parent training. Horton's (1984) review of father involvement consisted of just three studies and found no evidence of a convincing advantage for the both-parents format relative to the mother-only format for negative behavior. The differences in prosocial behavior that we observed here cannot be contrasted against this earlier work because none of those studies included measures of prosocial behavior.

Nonetheless, the question of the benefits of one- versus two-parent involvement may, to some extent, be miscast. In very recent analyses of our study data, Nye, Zucker, and Fitzgerald (1993) examined the dimension of a family's involvement in the work of the program. They found that families did not uniformly benefit from the intervention and that the level of involvement rather than whether one or two parents participated mediated the response to the program.

More generally, an examination of how the participating families in this program differed from families in other programs and how the present intervention program met the unique circumstances of the participating families is useful in understanding the mixed, and partially discrepant, results observed here. All families in this program were characterized by the presence of severe alcohol problems and in many cases by significant drug and marital problems as well. Because previous parent-training studies have selected samples solely on the basis of child behavior, they have, to some degree, also sampled other family characteristics that are associated with conduct problems. The degree to which these other factors may have played a role in enhancing or detracting from outcome is, however, indeterminate, because parent characteristics have typically not been well-specified. In contrast, the use of a clearly identifiable familial risk factor, paternal alcoholism, the use of an outreach model, and the absence of an avowedly clinical focus all set this study apart in significant ways.

To elaborate on these points, the father's drunk-driving conviction and the severity of the alcohol-impairment selection criteria meant that his alcoholism frequently was a prominent factor in the life of the family. For example, some of these men were not able to drive legally because their licenses had been suspended and, when some of them did, that created even more of a problem. Concomitantly, successful implementation of the program required sustained attention to the child management regimen to ensure its effective implementation.

Last, and perhaps most important, despite the father's frequently visible alcoholism (and sometimes also the mother's), the intervention only gradually was able to move in on these issues given that families were recruited on the basis of child difficulty. Although this orientation may provide initial entre to a population that seeks assistance only reluctantly and tentatively, it also means that the motivational impetus to seek help is different from that of self-referred or court-referred parents. In addition, although virtually all mothers in the program acknowledged that their child was a problem at times, this was not as common among the fathers.

Thus, intervention staff were required to address both child and parent problems from a disadvantaged status, and they needed to walk a line that balanced issues of holding the families in the protocol against the need to confront and take risks about addressing ongoing alcohol and other family-related difficulty. In retrospect, the outreach, population-based, rather than problem-focused, nature of the original contract was seen as hobbling the intervention team's efforts, and it also likely contributed to the weak treatment effects.

This study illustrates the significant accomplishments, as well as difficulties, related to the implementation of a community-based, substance abuse risk prevention activity (see also Lorion & Ross, 1992). When family problems are severe, such work tests the envelope of applicability of coping/behavioral enhancement intervention efforts. Within this framework, the long-term question of how early to intervene, and for how long, to produce lasting change, cannot yet be answered. Our work indicates that efforts lasting as long as even a year have demonstrable, but only modest, impact. Nonetheless, a chronic-disease framework for such work, which would specify the need for periodic "inoculations" to maintain control of the disorder (as in diabetes), would suggest that over fairly long spans of developmental time, the problematic behavior can be brought under full control. A similar perspective has been advocated, beginning during early childhood, for the reduction and prevention of juvenile delinquency (Zigler, Taussig, & Black, 1992), and it is consistent with some of the evidence amassed during our study. Within this context, the work of O'Farrell (1989), relating to the issue of relapses in family work with alcoholics, is particularly relevant. O'Farrell made the point that relapses are a common occurrence during the initial stages of drinking cessation and that booster sessions at later intervals are needed to address relapses. In a parallel vein, families might benefit from booster sessions—such as were used by Patterson (1974)—after completing the intervention program (see also Lochman, 1992).

Finally, it may be that additional external pressure needs to be brought to bear on those families that are most deeply troubled and also of highest risk. Such pressure could be applied if a public-health model were used by the courts in working with this subset of alcoholic families. Within this framework, a more clearly pressured approach (e.g., by way of court order) would be required to bring the family into the treatment net in a manner that would allow immediate and direct attention to the substance abuse issues that are so central to the maintenance and embellishment of child risk. Our group is currently engaging in pilot work that will evaluate the workability of such an alternative approach (Zucker & Bermann, 1992), with the hope that such work will allow us to more carefully specify a menu of alternative preventive interventions, that can be differentially applied to families with different risk profiles and that may thereafter be evaluated in a long-term way.

ACKNOWLEDGMENTS

This work was primarily supported by grants to Robert A. Zucker, Robert B. Noll, and Hiram E. Fitzgerald from the Michigan Department of Mental Health, Prevention Services Unit, and from the Governor's Initiative Against Alcohol and Drug Abuse Grant Program of the Office of Substance Abuse Services, Michigan Department of Public Health.

We are indebted to Robert B. Noll for his substantial involvement in earlier phases of this project, including supervision of a part of the intervention protocol. We also especially thank Susan K. Refior, Patricia Wehner, and Susan Lotus, who served as field coordinators and initial recruiters of the study families. Susan K. Refior, in particular, deserves a special note of thanks for the substantial work that permitted effective follow-up.

Robert A. Zucker is now at the Departments of Psychiatry and University of Michigan Alcohol Research Center, University of Michigan.

REFERENCES

Achenbach, T. M., & Edelbrock, C. (1983). *Manual for the Child Behavior Checklist.* Burlington: University of Vermont.
Andrews, S. R., Blumenthal, J. B., Johnson, D. L., Kahn, A. J., Ferguson, C. J., Lasater, T.

M., Malone, P. E., & Wallace, D. B. (1982). *The skills of mothering: A study of parent–child development centers*. Monographs of the Society for Research in Child Development, 47(6, Serial No. 198).

Babor, T. F., & Dolinsky, Z. S. (1988). Alcoholic typologies: Historical evolution and empirical evaluation of some common classification schemes. In R. M. Rose & J. Barret (Eds.), *Alcoholism: Origins and outcome* (pp. 245–266). New York: Raven.

Budd, K. G., & O'Brien, T. P. (1982). Father involvement in parent training: An area in need of research. *Behavior Therapist, 5(3)*, 85–89.

Cloninger, R. (1987). Neurogenetic adaptive mechanisms in alcoholism. *Science, 236*, 410–416.

Conners, C. K (1973). Rating scales for use in drug studies with children [Special issue: Pharmacotherapy of children]. *Psychopharmacology Bulletin*, 24–29.

Feighner, J. P., Robins, E., Guze, S., Woodruff, R. A., Winokur, G., & Munoz, R. (1972). Diagnostic criterion for use in psychiatric research. *Archives of General Psychiatry, 26*, 57–63.

Fleischman, M. J. (1981). A replication of Patterson's *Intervention for boys with conduct problems*. *Journal of Consulting and Clinical Psychology, 2*, 342–351.

Fleischman, M. J., & Szykula, S. A. (1981). A community setting replication of a social learning treatment for aggressive children. *Behavior Therapy, 12*, 115–122.

Forehand, R., Griest, D. L., & Wells, K. C. (1979). Parent behavioral training: An analysis of the relationship between multiple outcome measures. *Journal of Abnormal Child Psychology, 7*, 229–242.

Forehand, R., & King, H. E. (1977). Noncompliant children: Effects of parent training on behavior and attitude change. *Behavior Modification, 1*, 93–108.

Forehand, R., Middlebrook, J., Rogers, T., & Stiffle, M. (1983). Dropping out of parent training. *Behavior Research and Therapy, 21*, 663–668.

Garber, H. L. (1988). *The Milwaukee Project: Preventing mental retardation in children at risk*. Washington, DC: American Association of Mental Retardation.

Gottman, J. M., & Katz, L. F. (1989). Effects of marital discord on young children's peer interaction and health. *Developmental Psychology, 25*, 373–381.

Goyette, C. H., Conners, C. K., & Ulrich, R. F. (1978). Normative data on Revised Conners Parent and Teacher Rating Scales. *Journal of Abnormal Child Psychology, 6*, 221–236.

Hawkins, J. D., Catalano, R. F., & Miller, J. Y. (1992). Risk and protective factors for alcohol and other drug problems in adolescence and early adulthood: Implications for substance abuse prevention. *American Journal of Orthopsychiatry, 54*, 415–425.

Helzer, J. E., Burnam, A., & McEvoy, L. T. (1991). Alcohol abuse and dependence. In L. N. Robins & D. A. Regier (Eds.), *Psychiatric disorders in America: The epidemiologic catchment area study* (pp. 81–115). New York: Free Press.

Horton, L. (1984). The father's role in behavioral parent training: A review. *Journal of Clinical Child Psychology, 13*, 274–279.

Hunter, J. E., & Gerbing, D. W. (1982). Unidimensional measurement, second order factor analysis, and causal models. In B. Staw (Ed.), *Research in organizational behavior* (Vol. 4, pp. 267–320). Greenwich, CT: JAI.

Kellam, S. G., Ensminger, M. E., & Simon, M. B. (1980). Mental health in first grade and teenage drug, alcohol, and cigarette use. *Drug and Alcohol Dependency, 5*, 273–304.

Lochman, J. E. (1992). Cognitive-behavioral intervention with aggressive boys: Three-year follow-up and preventive effects. *Journal of Consulting and Clinical Psychology, 60*, 426–432.

Loeber, R., & LeBlanc, M. (1990). Toward a developmental criminology. In M. Tonry & N. Morris (Eds.), *Crime and justice: A review of the research* (Vol. 12, pp. 375–473). Chicago: University of Chicago Press.

Lorion, R., & Ross, J. G. (1992). Programs for change: a realistic look at the nation's potential for preventing substance abuse among high risk youth [Special issue: Programs for change: Office for Substance Abuse Prevention models]. *Journal of Community Psychology*, 3–9.

Maguin, E. (1991). *Evaluation of a community program for the prevention of conduct problems among preschool sons of alcoholic fathers*. Unpublished doctoral dissertation, Michigan State University, East Lansing.

Miller, G. E., & Prinz, R. J. (1990). Enhancement of social learning family interventions for childhood conduct disorder. *Psychological Bulletin, 108*, 291–307.

Minuchin, S. (1974). *Family and family therapy*. Cambridge, MA: Harvard University Press.

Noll, R. B., & Zucker, R. A. (1985a). *Child Behavior Rating Scale*. Unpublished manuscript, Michigan State University, East Lansing.

Noll, R. B., & Zucker, R. A. (1985b). *Parent Daily Report–Modified*. Unpublished manuscript, Michigan State University, East Lansing.

Nye, C. L., Zucker, R. A., & Fitzgerald, H. E. (1993, August). *Treatment predictors of child outcome in a early intervention program*. Paper presented at the meeting of the American Psychological Association, Toronto, Canada.

O'Farrell, T. J. (1989). Marital and family therapy in alcoholism treatment. *Journal of Substance Abuse Treatment, 6*, 23–29.

Olweus, D. (1979). Stability of aggressive reaction patterns in males: A review. *Psychological Bulletin, 86*, 852–857.

Patterson, G. R. (1974). Retraining of aggressive boys by their parents: Review of recent literature and a followup evaluation. *Canadian Psychiatric Association Journal, 19*, 142–161.

Patterson, G. R., Chamberlain, P., & Reid, J. B. (1982). A comparative evaluation of a parent training program. *Behavior Therapy, 13*, 638–650.

Patterson, G. R., DeBaryshe, B. D., & Ramsey, E. (1989). A developmental perspective on antisocial behavior. *American Psychologist, 44*, 329–335.

Patterson, G. R., & Reid, J. B. (1973). Intervention for families of aggressive boys: A replication study. *Behavior Research and Therapy, 11*, 383–394.

Patterson, G. R., Reid, J. B., Jones, R. R., & Conger, R. E. (1975). *A social learning approach to family intervention: Vol. 1. Families with aggressive boys*. Eugene, OR: Castalia.

Pihl, R. O., & Peterson, J. B. (1991). Attention-deficit hyperactivity disorder, childhood conduct disorder, and alcoholism: Is there an association? *Alcohol Health and Research World, 15*, 25–31.

Regier, D. A., Farmer, M. E., Rae, D. S., Locke, B. Z., Keith, S. J., Judd, L. L., & Goodwin, F. K (1990). Comorbidity of mental disorders with alcohol and other drug abuse. *Journal of the American Medical Association, 264*, 2511–2518.

Russell, M. (1990). Prevalence of alcoholism among children of alcoholics. In M. Windle & J. S. Searles (Eds.), *Children of alcoholics: Critical perspectives* (pp. 9–38). New York: Guilford.

Sher, K. J. (1991). *Children of alcoholics*. Chicago: University of Chicago Press.

Tartar, R. E., & Vanukov, M. M. (in press). Stepwise developmental models of alcoholism etiology. In R. A. Zucker, J. Howard, & G. M. Boyd (Eds.), *The development of alcohol problems: Exploring the biopsychosocial matrix of risk* . Rockville, MD: National Institute of Alcohol Abuse and Alcoholism.

Webster-Stratton, C. (1981). Modification of mothers' attitudes and behaviors through a videotape modeling group discussion program. *Behavior Therapy, 12*, 634–642.

Webster-Stratton, C. (1982). The long-term effects of a videotape modeling parent-training program: Comparison of immediate and 1-year follow-up results. *Behavior Therapy, 13,* 702–714.

Webster-Stratton, C. (1985). The effects of father involvement in parent training for conduct problem children. *Journal of Child Psychology and Psychiatry and Allied Disciplines, 26,* 801–810.

Webster-Stratton, C., Kolpacoff, M., & Hollinsworth, T. (1988). Self-administered videotape therapy for families with conduct problem children: Comparison with two cost-effective treatments and a control group. *Journal of Consulting and Clinical Psychology, 56,* 558–566.

Zigler, E., Taussig, C., & Black, K (1992). Early childhood intervention: A promising preventative for juvenile delinquency. *American Psychologist, 47,* 997–1006.

Zucker, R. A. (1989). Is risk for alcoholism predictable? A probabilistic approach to a developmental problem. *Drugs & Society, 4,* 69–93.

Zucker, R. A. (1991). *Protocol details of the Michigan State University Multiple Risk Child Outreach Program.* (Available from R. A. Zucker, Departments of Psychiatry and University of Michigan Alcohol Research Center, University of Michigan, Ann Arbor, MI, 48109.)

Zucker, R. A., & Bermann, E. (1992). *Michigan State University–University of Michigan pilot project on family intervention with substance abusive families.* Unpublished manuscript, Michigan State University, Department of Psychology and Longitudinal Studies Program, East Lansing.

Zucker, R. A., Ellis, D. A., & Fitzgerald, H. E. (in press). Developmental evidence for at least two alcoholisms: Vol. 1. Biopsychosocial variation among pathways into symptomatic difficulty. *Annals of the New York Academy of Science.*

Zucker, R. A., & Fitzgerald, H. E. (1991). Early developmental factors and risk for alcohol problems. *Alcohol Health and Research World, 15,* 1–24.

Zucker, R. A., & Gomberg, E. S. L. (1986). Etiology of alcoholism reconsidered: The case for a biopsychosocial process. *American Psychologist, 41,* 783–793.

Zucker, R. A., Maguin, E. T., Noll, R. B., Fitzgerald, H. E., & Klinger, M. T. (1990, August). *A prevention program for preschool C.O.A.s: Design and early effects.* Paper presented at the meeting of the American Psychological Association, Boston.

Zucker, R. A., & Noll, R. B. (1987). The interaction of child and environment in the early development of drug involvement: A far ranging review and a planned very early intervention. *Drugs & Society, 2,* 57–97.

Zucker, R. A., Noll, R. B., Kriegler, J., & Cruise, K A. (1986). *A program for the prevention of conduct disorders: Intervention manual.* Unpublished manual, Michigan State University, Department of Psychology, East Lansing.

7

School-Based Research on the Prevention of Adolescent Alcohol Use and Misuse: Methodological Issues and Advances

T. E. Dielman
University of Michigan

The purposes of this chapter are to provide an evaluative summary of school-based research on the prevention of adolescent alcohol use and misuse (AAUM) in the context of some of the problems associated with prevention research and to review methodological and theoretical advances in that area. Early efforts in drug-use prevention in general, of which the research in the school-based prevention of AAUM is a subset, were marked by a lack of theoretical and methodological sophistication. This was also characteristic of the journals that published prevention articles prior to the period of methodological, quantitative, and theoretical advances from the late 1970s to the present. The early work provided the basis for many methodological advances; this review provides a summary of the lessons learned, rather than a critique of the early research. The National Institute on Alcohol Abuse and Alcoholism began stressing prevention studies during the late 1970s and especially the early 1980s; the associated rigor demanding for successful peer review and funding has resulted in a considerable increase in methodological, quantitative, and theoretical sophistication during the past 15 years. The focus of this chapter is on school-based, individual-level (i.e., micro-level) research. For discussions of macro-level research, such as the effects of policy changes concerning minimum purchase age, outlet density, pricing, drinking and driving laws and their enforcement, the reader is referred to recent reviews in that area (e.g., Bukoski, 1991; Saffer & Grossman, 1987; Treno, Parker, & Holder, 1993).

Social psychology had become an established discipline by the 1950s, with the development of mini-theories of attitude formation and change as well as clever confirmatory experiments. It was natural, in this context, that early attempts at prevention were based on the assumption that if one could succeed in establishing negative attitudes concerning a given behavior (e.g., the use or misuse of alcohol) or, similarly, pair such behavior with fear arousal, one should observe a concomitant reduction in the adoption of the behavior in question. The early fear arousal and/or information dissemination programs were based on the related assumption that if the audience received factual information concerning the negative effects of alcohol use, behavioral adoption would be less likely to occur. Reviews of these studies indicate that none were successful in reducing adoption of alcohol use or misuse. As pointed out by Young (1968); Berberian, Gross, Lovejoy, and Paparella (1976); Staulcup, Kenward, and Frigo (1979); and Kinder, Pape, and Walfish (1980), the underlying premise was incorrect; changes in attitudes or knowledge were not correlated with subsequent behavioral changes.

In addition, the earliest of these studies were conducted without the benefit of Campbell's (1957) thoughtful analysis of sources of confounding as threats to the internal and external validity, and many did not employ an experimental design. This problem was not immediately remedied with the appearance of Campbell's article, as indicated by Kinder, Pape, and Walfish (1980) in their review of more than 100 studies; only 18 were found to have at least some systematic, data-based evaluation. To test the effectiveness of an alcohol use or misuse prevention program, an evaluation should compare differences between preintervention and postintervention measures with changes that occur during the same time period in a control group. A no-treatment comparison group is essential to control for a variety of possible sources of confounding, such as attrition and extraneous (i.e., historical) events. To optimize the internal and external validity of the experiment, among other steps, one ideally would randomly assign subjects from the target population to the experimental and control groups. In practice, however, especially in school-based prevention research, school buildings or classrooms, rather than individuals, are assigned (again, random assignment is the goal) to experimental and control groups. This procedure underscores the necessity of correcting for the *design effect*, which is becoming increasingly recognized in prevention research (see Campanelli, Dielman, Shope, Butchart, & Renner, 1989; Dielman, in press; Dielman, Shope, & Butchart, 1989a; Kish, 1965;

Murray & Hannan, 1990). The design effect refers to the tendency for behaviors or attitudes to be somewhat correlated within groups, such as neighborhoods, schools, and churches. The random assignment of units such as these, rather than individuals to experimental conditions, reduces the error variance on the dependent variable to the extent that there is a within-group correlation. The correction for the design effect, based on the intraclass correlation, adjusts for this tendency.

The early studies were also characterized by inadequate theoretical formulation of the correlates and causes of the adoption of AAUM as well as a concomitant inadequate formulation of intervention goals. In many programs, stated goals were not congruent with the dependent variable measurement. For example, it was not uncommon for interventions to be developed with the stated goal of reducing alcohol use and/or misuse but to be evaluated using knowledge gain or attitude change as the dependent variable. During this time, values clarification and self-esteem enhancement approaches to the reduction of adolescent problem behavior, including AAUM, became popular and these approaches drew increased criticism regarding the validity of the dependent variable measures. Increased criticism was also quite likely due to the appearance in 1959 of another thoughtful article, by Campbell and Fiske, concerning the desiderata for evidence of the convergent and discriminant validity of measures of unobserved constructs (now often referred to as latent variables) such as values and self-esteem.

In one review, Goodstadt (1986) criticized early studies for not attending to the existing evidence concerning relative program effects on the components of knowledge, attitudes, and behavioral skills. Goodstadt concluded that knowledge and attitudes are seldom strongly correlated with behavior, and behavior is the component most difficult to influence. Mauss, Hopkins, Weisheit, and Kearney (1988) also published a critical review of the early work and suggested methodological improvements in prevention programs and study designs to address the weaknesses previously discussed. Although changes in knowledge and attitudes have not been shown to produce changes in behavior, many studies have continued to focus exclusively on the analysis of change in knowledge and attitudes as well as other intervening variables, such as self-esteem, locus of control, and values. Differences between treatment and control groups on these intervening variables are not necessarily followed by group differences on the behavioral outcome measures that are of primary concern. As recent studies have shown, however, consideration of the changes in the intervening variables is important for understanding the mechanisms through which the intervention has its effect (i.e., the indirect influence on behavior through the direct influence of the intervention on hypothesized intervening variables). Such indirect, as well as direct, effects can now be estimated through the use of structural equation analysis techniques (e.g., Bollen, 1987; Dielman, Butchart, & Shope, 1993; Dielman, Butchart, Shope, Campanelli, & Caspar, 1989; Dielman, Kloska, Leech, Schulenberg, & Shope, 1992; Dielman, Schulenberg, Leech, & Shope, 1991; Hayduk, 1987; Long, 1988; Newcomb & Bentler, 1988; Schaie & Hertzog, 1985).

The early studies were especially prone to adopting unrealistic program goals. If the stated objective is the prevention of any alcohol use, adolescents who have a sip of wine at religious or other special occasions with their parents constitute program failures. Exclusive reliance on any use of alcohol as the outcome of interest can obscure important program effects on patterns of alcohol use. This suggests the inclusion of a greater variety of outcome measures, such as the frequency and quantity of use, problems with others as a result of use, or the involvement in a variety of situations placing one at increased risk as a consequence of drinking.

A related problem in assessing behavioral outcomes was exclusive reliance on short-term (i.e., 1 year at most) differences between groups. As Goodstadt (1986) pointed out, reliance on the evaluation of short-term results is almost guaranteed to result in apparent failure of the prevention program; behavioral changes are difficult to produce in the short term, but they may be attainable over a longer term. Bangert-Drowns (1988) conducted a meta-analysis of substance abuse prevention studies and provided evidence suggesting that successful programs may produce "delayed effects" on behavior. His results indicated that, on the average, successful substance abuse prevention programs have typically produced short-term and long-term effects on information and attitudes but no short-term and only slight long-term effects on behavior. The components of information, attitudes, and behavioral skills may therefore show differential effects over different time periods. A purely quantitative methodological point related to Goodstadt's observation is that prevention programs, by definition, should focus on groups in which the behavior to be prevented is not of high prevalence. In evaluating the effectiveness of a prevention program, it is necessary to wait a sufficient length of time to allow the treatment and control group prevalence rates to diverge enough for a statistically significant difference to be detected. The degree of divergence required depends on the sample and effect sizes as well as other factors.

Many early studies also suffered from lack of standardization in program implementation. Once a substance abuse prevention program has been conceptualized, the program objectives specified, and the procedures developed and refined, it is necessary to train the program implementation staff thoroughly and to systematically monitor program implementation. The early studies were hindered in their effectiveness by the differential quality of program material presentation. In the Cambridge and Sommerville Program for Alcoholism Rehabilitation (CASPAR) program, for example, 31% of the students were classified as having received an improperly implemented curriculum. These students showed no change in attitudes from pretest to posttest, whereas the students who were classified as having received a properly implemented curriculum showed a sizable positive change in the targeted attitudes (DiCicco, 1978).

Goodstadt (1986) has identified an additional dimension in the formulation of evaluation plans for substance abuse prevention programs: the possible moderating effects of prior use. As demonstrated in recent studies by Dielman et al. (Dielman, Kloska, Leech, Schulenberg, & Shope, 1992; Dielman, Kloska, Leech, & Shope, 1993; Dielman et al., 1989a), interventions can result in differential effects on youths who have already begun to use alcohol and those who have not. Combining prior users and nonusers in the analysis of outcome data can attenuate or completely mask program effects that would be detected if the sample were stratified by prior use.

In summary, the early efforts in the area of school-based substance abuse prevention have not been shown to be effective. These pioneer studies suffered from shortcomings in theory, conceptualization, implementation, and evaluation. However, these studies did provide a foundation and impetus for improvements in program design and research methodology, and more recent research in this area has been characterized by increased rigor. The new generation of research has sought to strengthen the theoretical bases of the prevention programs. The recently developed social skills and social norms approaches provide promising theoretical approaches to the prevention of alcohol misuse among adolescents. These approaches have their theoretical bases in the social learning theory of Bandura (1977), Festinger's (1957) cognitive dissonance model, McGuire's (1969) communication persuasion model, and Hansen's (Hansen & Graham, 1991; Hansen, Johnson, Flay, Graham, & Sobel, 1988) social norms model. The social skills approach postulates that to prevent the adoption of an undesirable behavior, the subject must first be "inoculated" by exposure to the negative argument or model, followed by a strong counterargument and extensive opportunity to practice the desired coping behaviors (cf. Forman & Linney, 1991). In the social norms model, the behavior of adolescents is hypothesized to be based in large measure on their (often incorrect) perceptions of peer norms and related behavior. Recent research using these theoretical frameworks and more sophisticated analytic methods have shown positive results (e.g., G. J. Botvin, Baker, Dusenbury, Tortu, & E. M. Botvin, 1990; Dielman, Kloska, Leech, Schulenberg, & Shope, 1992; Dielman et al., 1993; Dielman et al., 1985; Dielman et al., 1989a; Dielman et al., 1991; Hansen & Graham, 1991; Hansen et al., 1988; Johnson et al., 1990; Pentz et al., 1989).

The refusal skills/social skills approach to prevention was initially used successfully by Evans (1976) and his colleagues (e.g., Evans, Henderson, Hill, & Raines, 1979; Evans et al., 1978) to deter adolescent smoking behavior. McAlister, Perry, Killen, Slinkard, and Maccoby (1980) used a similar approach to increase the resistance of junior-high-school students to the use of alcohol and other drugs. Duryea (1983) and colleagues (Duryea, Mohr, Newman, Martin, & Egwaoje, 1984), in a prevention program based on inoculation theory, reported significant gains in students knowledge and attitudes, although there was no difference between experimental and control groups on a frequency of drinking variable at an early posttest, and AAUM was not reported at the 6-month posttest. G. Botvin (1983b, 1986) and colleagues (e.g., G. Botvin, Baker, E. Botvin, Filazzola, & Millman, 1984; G. Botvin, Baker, Renick, Filazzola, & E. Botvin, 1984) expanded on the earlier social skills approach and developed the life skills training curriculum (e.g., G. Botvin, 1983a), which has been used with some success in Grades 7 through 10 in New York schools. Using this approach, which is directed at increasing social skills and reducing interpersonal pressures to drink, G. J. Botvin et al. (1990) found less frequent drinking and less excessive drinking in their experimental groups of junior-high-school students. Other important recent prevention studies include those of Hansen and his colleagues, who have found that changing adolescents' perceptions of the prevalence of peers substance use behavior and peer approval of such behavior (i.e., peer norms) is an important and effective focus for school-based prevention programs (Hansen & Graham, 1991; Hansen et al., 1988). In addition, large-scale, comprehensive community prevention programs, including school-based components, have been successful in reducing the rate of increase in adolescent substance use (e.g., Johnson et al., 1990; Pentz et al., 1989). Additional reviews providing current researchers with excellent critical analyses of problems encountered in prevention research, and solutions to those problems posed to date, include those by Tobler (1987), Bangert-Drowns (1988), Moskowitz (1989), and Hansen (1992).

THE ALCOHOL MISUSE PREVENTION STUDY

With the benefit of hindsight provided by some of the critical reviews mentioned previously, in 1983, my colleagues and I began the Alcohol

Misuse Prevention Study (AMPS). This prevention effort is based on solutions proposed to earlier problems encountered in the field, and some interesting findings have resulted from the study to date. Some space will therefore be devoted to a description of AMPS and those results considered by the investigators to be most important. The AMPS curriculum was based on a social influences (including peer use and norms) approach, and it seeks to provide students with the social skills necessary to prevent inappropriate use of alcohol and the serious problems that are frequently associated with it. The *misuse* of alcohol was targeted, in addition to the prevention of alcohol *use*, because of the emphasis in the literature on setting realistic goals for prevention programs (Bartlett, 1981; Rachel et al., 1980).

The development and evaluation of the AMPS program was guided by a conceptual model that hypothesized direct and indirect program effects on the intervening and outcome variables as well as interrelationships among those variables. Schools were first matched on ethnic composition, student achievement, and socioeconomic status (SES); they were then randomly assigned to a combination of pretest–no pretest and treatment–control groups. The intervention was delivered by study staff, who were trained and monitored by the investigators. Evaluation included longitudinal follow-up of individual subjects, and corrections were made for intraclass correlations on the dependent variables to adjust for the design effects. Learning gains by the treatment group were regarded as a necessary first result of the intervention. Behavioral differences between the treatment and control groups were hypothesized to follow at later posttest occasions. A "booster treatment" condition was included in the design.

This initial study, which involved a theory-based, large-scale, longitudinal elementary school AMPS program design, implementation, and evaluation, provides an unique opportunity for the continued, iterative development and improvement of a conceptual model of antecedents of AAUM and for the refinement of a prevention program based on that model. There is now an existing longitudinal, multivariate data base on the students involved in the first (AMPS 1) study—in Grades 5 and 6 and followed through Grade 12—and on those involved in the second (AMPS 2) study in Grades 6, 7, and 8, followed through Grade 10. The tests of the initial conceptual model, involving intrapersonal and peer influence constructs, and evaluation of the AMPS program based on that model have been conducted. Structural equation tests have also been conducted on the revised and expanded model, adding parent and sibling constructs to the initial model, that was developed and employed during the second grant period. The testing of the effectiveness of the revised and expanded intervention based on the new model tests with the AMPS 2 data are beginning as of this writing.

AMPS has resulted in a number of published findings. There are several primary findings that I regard as especially relevant to the this discussion:

1. The refusal skills/social skills approach was effective in reducing the rate of increase in the prevalence of AAUM.
2. The effects of a prevention program implemented in Grade 6 have endured through Grade 12—the last posttest occasion analyzed as of this writing.
3. The effectiveness of the program was especially apparent among adolescents who had already started to experiment with the use of alcohol by Grade 6 in settings where no adults were present.
4. The effectiveness of the program was grade dependent, suggesting, perhaps, an optimal age for intervention implementation.
5. The importance of peer influences was confirmed.
6. The degree of the adolescents susceptibility to peer pressure as an important mediating variable, sensitive to the intervention program, was established.
7. The importance of parental influences, independent of the effects of peer influences, was confirmed.

Each of these findings is discussed in more detail.

Program Efficacy and Enduring Effects

The success of the intervention approach was established during the first 4 years of the study (1984–1988) with students who were pretested and experienced the intervention in Grade 6. These students were posttested at the end of their sixth, seventh, and eighth grade years during this period. An overall comparison of the comparative rates of increase of alcohol misuse, defined by 10 variables involving problem consequences, such as becoming sick, hangovers, problems with others, and increased risky behavior, in the experimental and control groups, showed a significant Treatment × Occasion interaction, with the rate of increase for the control group being significantly greater than that of the experimental group. There was a similar but smaller interaction in the analysis of the students alcohol use. The results were still somewhat disappointing in that the overall experimental versus control group differences, unstratified by prior use, although significant, were not extremely large (about .1 SD for misuse, and somewhat less for use). In addition, there was no significant effect noted for students who entered the study in Grade 5 (Dielman et al., 1989a). This led us to investigate the differential effectiveness hypothesis, the duration of intervention effects, and the influence of age at intervention on program effectiveness.

Differential Effectiveness

The differential effectiveness hypothesis was based on Goodstadt's (1986) argument that because students entered prevention studies with differential experience with respect to the substance in question, they should be treated differently, at least in the data analysis. Goodstadt proposed that standard approaches to prevention may be more effective for students who had not yet begun to experiment with the substance in question than for those who had. In fact, we found just the opposite to be the case. With the benefit, again, of hindsight, the reason for this finding is quite clear. We were able to separate the students in the study into three groups on the basis of settings in which they had used alcohol prior to the intervention: abstainers (constituting about one half of the students at the early occasion (Grade 5/6), those who had used alcohol only at home under adult (usually parental) supervision (another one third of the sample), and those who had used alcohol with peers, unsupervised by adults (the remaining one sixth of the sample). Data from students who received the intervention in Grade 6 were analyzed using this categorization as a stratification variable in a three-way repeated measures analysis of variance (ANOVA; Treatment Condition $\times$ Prior Drinking Experience $\times$ Occasion) of the third posttest data (end of Grade 8). A significant three-way interaction was found, which persisted through the early Grade 12 posttest, the last follow-up analyzed as of this writing. The interaction remained significant after correction for the design effect (Campanelli et al., 1989; Dielman, in press; Dielman et al., 1993; Dielman et al., 1989a; Donner, Birkett, & Buck, 1981; Kish, 1965; Murray & Hannan, 1990). Figure 7.1 shows the mean levels of alcohol misuse over time for each of the six treatments by prior experience conditions; the control group students, who had prior unsupervised experience with alcohol, increased their rate of alcohol misuse over twice as much as their treatment group counterparts. The results were similar with respect to alcohol use. The intervention was therefore quite effective for high-risk students (i.e., those who had already started to experiment with alcohol in unsupervised settings). Sixth-grade students who at pretest had no experience, or only supervised experience, with alcohol, increased very little in their alcohol use and misuse through Grade 12, regardless of treatment condition. The fact that these latter two groups constituted about five sixths of the sample resulted in a marked attenuation of the treatment

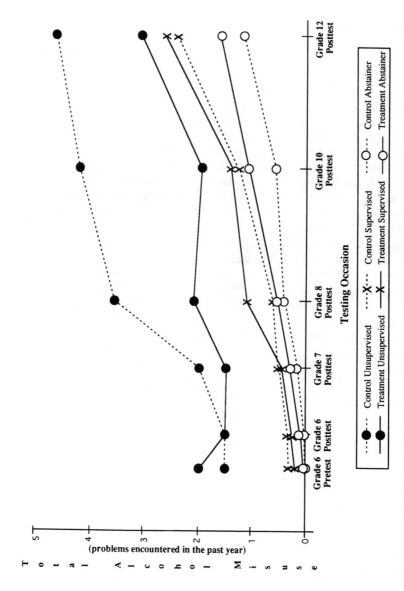

FIG. 7.1. Total alcohol misuse: Treatment condition by type of prior drinking experience by occasion interaction. Early Grade 12 pretest through Grade 12 posttest, initial Grade 6 posttest, initial Grade 6 students. Spacing between points on abscissa is proportional to the different intervals between measurement occasions.

by occasion effect when the total sample was analyzed without stratification on the basis of prior drinking experience. The often-heard complaint that "school substance abuse prevention programs do not work" may therefore be a premature conclusion, and the failure to find significant program effects in some of the earlier studies may have been due to the failure to stratify by prior experience with the substance. These results through Grade 8 and the mediating effects of susceptibility to peer pressure have been published (Dielman, Kloska, Leech, Schulenberg, & Shope, 1992; Dielman et al., 1989a; see Dielman, in press, for results through Grade 12).

In AMPS, we also considered differential attrition from the comparison groups. A three-way ANOVA of attrition rates (by treatment condition, prior drinking experience, and occasion) did not result in a significant three-way interaction, indicating none of the comparison subgroups of interest differed in rates of attrition over time (Dielman et al., 1993). The problem of attrition, or experimental mortality as Campbell (1957) referred to it, must be considered in any longitudinal experiment. The issue is whether the attrition was nonrandom. There are at least two subissues: (a) was attrition different between or among the comparison groups, and (b) were those more likely to develop alcohol misuse problems also more likely to drop out of the study (or school) than those who were not likely to develop such problems? If the answer regarding the first question is *yes,* the internal validity of the study is compromised *if* the dropouts differentially changed the prevalence estimates across time for the various groups. If the answer to the first question is *no* but the answer to the second is *yes,* the internal validity of the study is not compromised but the external validity is, and the prevalence rates are underestimated for all experimental conditions. The attrition rates were somewhat higher among previous drinkers across all subgroups, however. These findings indicate that, although the internal validity of the AMPS experiment was valid, attempts to generalize from the observed rates of alcohol use/misuse prevalence in the later grades would be underestimates, across all groups, of AAUM prevalence rates in the population. The degree of underestimation of AAUM prevalence was approximately 5%.

These findings highlight the methodological issue of determining appropriate comparisons for testing program efficacy. If my observation of differential program effectiveness is characteristic of many prevention programs, gross comparisons of the rate of increase for all experimental and control students generally results in attenuated effect sizes. Unfortunately, the decisions underlying choice of comparisons and program goals are often guided more by personal value judgments than by scientific considerations. From a theoretical view-point, although it may be appropriate to set the program goal in cigarette smoking prevention as total abstinence, it may be more reasonable in our society to set alcohol misuse (i.e., overindulgence and the associated consequences) prevention as the goal in alcohol prevention programs. It may well be that different program goals can be set for different societal subgroups. When abstinence is the subgroup norm, because of religion or family values, it is probably a reasonable goal. When abstinence is not the subgroup family norm, however, the prevention of alcohol misuse is probably a more achievable goal.

Optimal Age and Timing of Intervention and Posttests

One issue that must be considered from both theoretical and practical viewpoints is the optimal age of the target population for the delivery of a prevention program. From a purely logical viewpoint, a prevention program, by definition, needs to be targeted at a population in which the prevalence of the behavior to be prevented is nearly zero. From epidemiologic studies we know that, in general, the prevention of AAUM needs to be targeted at populations no later than late elementary or very early junior high school, although there is regional variation in age-specific prevalence rates (Johnston, O'Malley, & Bachman, 1991; National Institute on Drug Abuse, 1991; Oetting & Beauvais, 1990; O'Malley, Bachman, & Johnston, 1988). Although some investigators have adhered to the initiation of AAUM prevention programs in Grade 7 (e.g., G. J. Botvin et al., 1990), this is based more on tradition, following the early work of Evans (1976; Evans et al., 1979; Evans et al., 1978) and McAlister et al. (1980), than on research concerning the relative effectiveness of intervention at different ages. Dielman and colleagues (Dielman, Kloska, Leech, Schulenberg, & Shope, 1992; Dielman et al., 1993; Dielman et al., 1985; Dielman et al., 1989a) and others (e.g., Johnson et al., 1990) have found significant intervention effects when the program was implemented in Grade 6. Further, recent data have documented alcohol use and misuse as early as Grade 4 or 5, with considerable increases beginning in Grade 6 (Oetting & Beauvais, 1990). It is my perspective that as an *ecological transition*, the transition from elementary to junior high school is a very important factor, and interventions must be implemented prior to this transition (Dielman, Butchart, Shope, & Miller, 1990–1991; Dielman, Kloska, Leech, Schulenberg, & Shope, 1992; Dielman et al., 1985; Dielman et al., 1989a; Dielman et al., 1993; Dielman, Shope, Butchart, & Campanelli, 1986; Dielman, Shope, Campanelli, & Butchart, 1987). School districts do vary, however, in the grade level at which this transition occurs. The solution to this problem is to conduct prevalence surveys of the population in which the prevention program is to be implemented and design the program appropriately.

It must be noted that the hypothesized three-way interaction was not found for the AMPS students who began the study in Grade 5 and were in Grade 7 at the time of the last AMPS 1 posttest analysis. We reasoned that this result could have occurred because either (a) the control group prevalence had not yet reached a high enough level at the Grade 7 posttest for a difference to be detected or (b) Grade 5 was too early for the students to benefit from the intervention. We were able to partially test these competing hypotheses. As shown in Figure 1, when we conducted the treatment by prior drinking experience by occasion repeated measures analysis at Grades 10 and 12, we found that the significant interaction effect noted at Grade 8 for the original Grade 6 students was still present, although in somewhat attenuated form. Among the students who received the intervention in Grade 5 only, there was no suggestion of an overall intervention effect or an interaction between prior use and treatment condition at the Grade 10 posttest. There did appear to be such an interaction, however, when students who received a booster intervention in Grade 6, in addition to receiving the Grade 5 intervention, were compared with controls. The interaction did not reach significance, because of, in part, the small subgroup sample size. The absence of any indication of an intervention effect for those students who experienced the intervention only in Grade 5, and the appearance of an effect among those who received the intervention in Grade 5 in addition to the booster in Grade 6, suggests that Grade 5 may have been too early for the intervention to be useful. These results have been submitted for publication (Dielman et al., 1993).

As an aside, the importance of the ecological transition from elementary to junior high school in the initiation of AAUM behavior, coupled with the studies indicating that earlier initiation is associated with a greater likelihood of subsequent problem use and other adjustment problems (e.g., Blyth, Simmons, & Carlton-Ford, 1983; Crockett, Petersen, Graber, Schulenberg, & Ebata, 1989; Simmons & Blyth, 1987), would recommend to educators that this transition occur as late as possible within the context of educational theory. In practice, however, the timing of this transition is usually determined by convenience, classroom availability, and the number of students at each grade level rather than recommendations from educational and behavioral research. It is essential that decision making by educators become more informed by research.

A related evaluation issue is the appropriate timing (i.e., frequency and intervals) of posttests, which should be determined on the basis of the theoretical model and the usual considerations for power analysis. Some preliminary prevalence data by grade level for the area in which the program is to be implemented are needed to estimate the expected rate of growth of the prevalence in the control group. An estimate of the reduction in this rate of increase that will result from the prevention program, or a goal for a minimum program effect, is also needed. One can then plot the expected, or hypothesized, prevalence rates for the control and experimental groups from the point just prior to the programs implementation until the control group prevalence reaches asymptote. The point at which the control and treatment group prevalence curves diverge significantly, given the number of participants per group and the acceptable probabilities of Type 1 and Type 2 errors, indicates the necessary minimum duration of follow-up. As a practical consideration, attrition rate influences the maximum length of follow-up. The initiation of follow-up is seldom necessary in the same year during which the pretest and intervention were conducted, but it may be useful to test students annually to facilitate tracking. This suggests a minimum follow-up interval of 1 year. If theory or previous data suggests significant divergence or convergence of subgroup curves in shorter intervals, the follow-up interval should be adjusted appropriately. This suggests that follow-up intervals need not be equally spaced. I have seen very few prevention studies in which age at implementation, program design, and frequency and duration of follow-up have been thought through in this detail. Prevention researchers and peer reviewers are becoming increasingly sophisticated, however, and this level of detail will soon become the norm, rather than the exception, in journal articles and proposal reviews.

Peer Influence and Susceptibility to Peer Pressure

The importance of peer influences on AAUM was confirmed in the AMPS 1 study through the test of the original version of our structural equation model. In this model, exposure to peers who used or misused alcohol was a significant and important predictor of adolescent alcohol use (Dielman et al., 1989). In addition, the newly developed construct of susceptibility to peer pressure was established as an important mediating variable (Dielman, Butchart, & Shope, 1992; Dielman et al., 1989; Dielman et al., 1993; Dielman, Kloska, Leech, Schulenberg, & Shope, 1992). The students' susceptibility to peer pressure has been hypothesized to be an important intervening variable since we proposed our original model in 1983. This construct is hypothesized to intervene between the students' exposure to peer AAUM, with the associated pressure on the student to use and misuse alcohol, and the students' adoption of AAUM behavior patterns. In our first structural equation model test with the longitudinal data, this hypothesis received substantial support (Dielman et al., 1989). In an analysis of the Grades 7 and 8 follow-up data, we found the interventions direct effect on susceptibility to peer pressure to be significant. Furthermore, the intervention's indirect effect on AAUM, through susceptibility to peer pressure, was significant and greater than the direct effect of the intervention on AAUM. On the basis of these direct and indirect effects of the intervention, we concluded that the intervention was quite effective, among students who had begun experimenting with alcohol in unsupervised settings, in reducing the rate of increase in AAUM, and also that the intervention was effective, in large part, through its success in reducing adolescents' susceptibility to peer pressure (Dielman, Kloska, Leech, Schulenberg, & Shope, 1992). A thorough search of the literature indicated that this is the first time the construct of susceptibility to peer pressure has been systematically assessed and included as an intervening variable in a substance use prevention program.

Parental Influences

The importance of parental influences, in addition to the effects of peer influences, has been confirmed during the AMPS 2 study, 1988 to present, during which time the theoretical model was extended to include parental constructs (Dielman, Butchart, & Shope, 1992). A comprehensive literature search was conducted for each major conceptual area included in the revised theoretical model, which served as the current starting point. On the basis of these reviews, and analyses conducted on the data from the AMPS 1 project (Dielman et al., 1990–1991; Dielman, Shope, & Butchart, 1989b), new items were selected, revised as deemed necessary for the age range of the students in the current study, or created when no existing items were available. The data-collection instrument was revised twice on the basis of small pilot tests, and a large pilot study was conducted in 1988 with 1,340 students in Grades 6, 8, 10, and 12 from a school district that was not a part of the AMPS 1 or AMPS 2 studies. Factor analyses were conducted on two randomly split half samples at each grade level and for the total sample. The items that loaded congruent factors across samples were used to construct indices within each major conceptual area. These data served as the basis of a cross-sectional test of the revised theoretical model. As a result of the testing of the revised theoretical model, after many iterative tests and revisions, new measures were developed for the family constructs of parental alcohol use, parental approval of adolescents' alcohol use, parental nurturance, parental permissiveness, and sibling alcohol use, and also for a new intrapersonal construct of adolescent deviant self-image. The result of adding these constructs and their interrelationships to the previously used constructs in the structural equation model was an increase in the percentage of the cross-sectional true score variance explained in adolescent alcohol misuse from 45% in the earlier model to approximately 60% in the revised model.

Further, sibling use of alcohol, parental approval of adolescent alcohol use, parental nurturance, and parental permissiveness were all significantly predictive of adolescent susceptibility to peer pressure, thereby providing additional targets for the design of future interventions. Parental nurturance was also a significant (negative) predictor of the adolescent's deviant self-image, which in turn accounted for a significant, independent fraction of the variance in AAUM (Dielman, Butchart, & Shope, 1992). The results of this structural equation model analysis are shown in Fig. 7.2. These results are now in the process of a longitudinal model validation on an independent sample.

SUMMARY, CONCLUSIONS, AND FUTURE DIRECTIONS

In this chapter, I have attempted to summarize the problems encountered by earlier prevention researchers, the solutions that have thus far been applied to these problems, and recent studies that are indicative of a promising future for prevention research. Throughout, the intended emphasis has been on the need to think through problems that are encountered rather than prematurely concluding that "prevention does not work." In view of the accumulated evidence from numerous investigations, my opinion is that prevention does work and can probably work better if researchers familiarize themselves with recent work in the area and think carefully about the issues outlined in this article and others cited herein as well as other problems that are bound to be encountered in future endeavors. It has been pointed out that recent research in the refusal skills/social skills and realistic norms perception approaches to school-based alcohol misuse prevention have been successful when those conducting the studies were aware of difficulties encountered in the past and took care not to repeat past mistakes. The promise of family-based intervention approaches is just beginning to be explored. Advances in macro-level intervention research is well summarized elsewhere. Advances in methodological and statistical

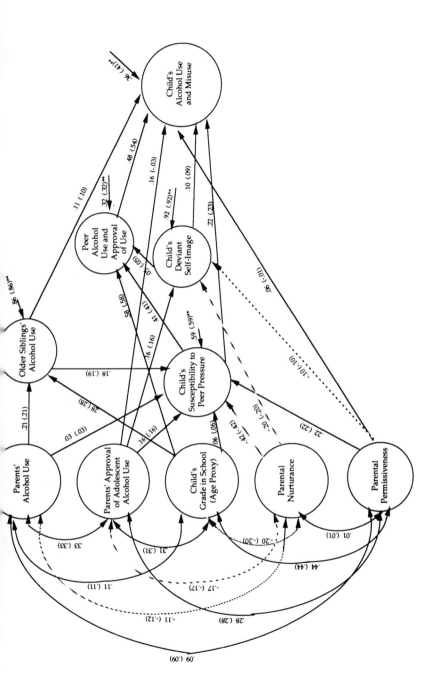

FIG. 7.2. Results of structural equation analysis standardized solution predicting AAUM. Coefficients in parentheses are from the model predicting misuse; those not in parentheses refer to use. Two asterisks represent unexplained variance, or the square of the EQS output "disturbance" value. $N = 1,340$ (1,340); $c2 = 4798.40$ (4765.09); $df = 1006$ (1006); $c2/df = 4.77$ (4.74); Bentler-Bonett nonnormed fit index = .83 (.83); Bentler-Bonett normed fit index = .83 (.83). Percent variance explained in alcohol use (misuse) = 64 (59). Solid lines indicate positive relationships; broken lines indicate negative relationships.

141

techniques are providing researchers in this area, as well as others, powerful new techniques with which to approach the design and analysis of studies. New directions for those conducting research in prevention are constantly presenting themselves. There is still room for the modification and improvement of school-based prevention approaches, and the field of family-based prevention approaches is just beginning to be opened. The development of more complete theories and the development of better measures of the theoretical constructs are important areas needing attention. The techniques currently used for parameter estimation and decision making in structural equation modeling need refinement, and new techniques must be developed to deal more adequately with the types of measurement used and the distributions encountered in conducting studies of the prevention of adolescent alcohol (or other drug) use and misuse.

More on the applied side, efforts need to be made to educate the consumers of prevention approaches. At present, the most widely used programs are those with slick packages and large marketing staffs (and consequently of higher cost), but absolutely no proven efficacy, rather than inexpensive (in many cases available at cost) programs with efficacy claims founded on sound research. There is a great need for health educators and/or school-based research coordinators to enlighten those who make decisions concerning the acquisition of prevention programs on the issue of proven efficacy claims. And last, but by no means least, as prevention approaches are developed and undergo adequate testing in small, regional populations, there will be an increasing need for research-oriented practitioners to conduct generalizability studies in larger groups and different populations, employing program implementors who are practitioners (e.g., teachers, counselors, or social workers), rather than members of a research staff.

ACKNOWLEDGMENTS

This work was supported by Grants AA06324 and AA08447 from the National Institute on Alcohol Abuse and Alcoholism.

REFERENCES

Bandura, A. (1977). *Social learning theory.* Englewood Cliffs, NJ: Prentice-Hall.
Bangert-Drowns, R. (1988). The effects of school-based substance abuse education: A

meta-analysis. *Journal of Drug Education, 18,* 243–264.

Bartlett, E. (1981). The contribution of school health education to community health promotion. What can we reasonably expect? *American Journal of Public Health, 71,* 1384–1391.

Berberian, R., Gross, C., Lovejoy, J., & Paparella, S. (1976). The effectiveness of drug education programs. A critical review. *Health Education Monographs, 4,* 377–398.

Blyth, D. A., Simmons, R. G., & Carlton-Ford, S. (1983). The adjustment of early adolescents to school transitions. *Journal of Early Adolescence, 3,* 105–120.

Bollen, K. A. (1987). *Structural equation modeling with latent variables.* New York: Wiley.

Botvin, G. (1983a). *Life skills training: Teacher's manual guide.* New York: Smithfield.

Botvin, G. (1983b). Prevention of adolescent substance abuse through the development of personal and social competence. In T. Glynn, C. Leukefeld, & J. Ledford (Eds.), *Preventing adolescent drug abuse: Intervention strategies* (Research Monograph No. 47, pp. 115–140). Rockville, MD: National Institute on Drug Abuse.

Botvin, G. (1986). Substance abuse prevention research: Recent developments and future directions. *Journal of School Health, 56,* 369–374.

Botvin, G., Baker, E., Botvin, E., Filazzola, A., & Millman, R. (1984). Prevention of alcohol misuse through the development of personal and social competence: A pilot study. *Journal of Studies on Alcohol, 45,* 550–552.

Botvin, G. J., Baker, E., Dusenbury, L., Tortu, S., & Botvin, E. M. (1990). Preventing adolescent drug abuse through a multimodel cognitive-behavioral approach: Results of a 3-year study. *Journal of Consulting and Clinical Psychology, 58,* 437–446.

Botvin, G., Baker, E., Renick, N., Filazzola, A., & Botvin, E. (1984). A cognitive-behavior approach to substance abuse prevention. *Addictive Behavior, 9,* 137–147.

Bukoski, W. J. (1991). A framework for drug abuse prevention research. In C. G. Leukefeld & W. J. Bukoski (Eds.), *Drug abuse prevention intervention research: Methodological issues* (PHHS Publication No. ADM 91–1761, pp. 7–28). Washington, DC: U.S. Government Printing Office.

Campanelli, P. C., Dielman, T. E., Shope, J. T., Butchart, A. T., & Renner, D. S. (1989). Pretest and treatment effects in an elementary school-based alcohol misuse prevention program. *Health Education Quarterly, 16,* 113–130.

Campbell, D. T. (1957). Factors relevant to the validity of experiments in social settings. *Psychological Bulletin, 54,* 297–312.

Campbell, D. T., & Fiske, D. W. (1959). Convergent and discriminant validation by the multitrait-multimethod matrix. *Psychological Bulletin, 56,* 81–105.

Crockett, L. J., Petersen, A. C., Graber, J. A., Schulenberg, J. E., & Ebata, A. (1989). School transitions and adjustment during early adolescence. *Journal of Early Adolescence, 9,* 181–210.

DiCicco, L. M. (1978). Evaluating the impact of alcohol education. *Alcohol Health and Research World, 3*(2), 14–20.

Dielman, T. E. (in press). Correction for the design effect in school-based substance use and abuse prevention research: Sample size requirements and analysis considerations [NIDA Monograph]. *Scientific Methods for Prevention Intervention Research.*

Dielman, T. E., Butchart, A. T., & Shope, J. T. (1993). Structural equation model tests of patterns of family interaction, peer alcohol use, and intrapersonal predictors of adolescent alcohol use and misuse. *Journal of Drug Education, 23*(3), 273–316.

Dielman, T. E., Butchart, A. T., Shope, J. T., Campanelli, P. C., & Caspar, R. A. (1989). A covariance structure model test of antecedents of adolescent alcohol misuse and a prevention effort. *Journal of Drug Education, 19*(4), 337–361.

Dielman, T. E., Butchart, A. T., Shope, J. T., & Miller, M. (1990–1991). Environmental correlates of adolescent substance use and misuse: Implications for prevention programs. *International Journal of the Addictions, 7A/8A*, 857–882.

Dielman, T. E., Kloska, D., Leech, S., Schulenberg, J., & Shope, J. T. (1992). Susceptibility to peer pressure as an explanatory variable for the differential effectiveness of an elementary school-based alcohol misuse prevention program. *Journal of School Health, 62*, 233–237.

Dielman, T. E., Kloska, D. D., Leech, S. L., & Shope, J. T. (1993). *Differential effectiveness of a school-based alcohol misuse prevention program: Treatment condition, prior drinking experience, and grade level at program delivery.* Manuscript submitted for publication.

Dielman, T. E., Lorenger, A. T., Leech, S. L., Lyons, A. L., Klos, D. M., & Horvath, W. J. (1985). Resisting pressures to smoke: Fifteen-month follow-up results of an elementary school based smoking prevention project. *Hygie, 4*, 28–35.

Dielman, T. E., Schulenberg, J. E., Leech, S. L., & Shope, J. T. (1991, August). *Reduction of susceptibility to peer pressure and alcohol use/misuse through a school-based prevention program.* Paper presented at the meeting of the Society for Research on Adolescence, Atlanta.

Dielman, T. E., Shope, J. T., & Butchart, A. T. (1989a, October). Differential effectiveness of an elementary school-based alcohol misuse prevention program by type of prior drinking experience. *Journal of School Health, 59*(6), 255–263.

Dielman, T. E., Shope, J. T., & Butchart, A. T. (1989b). *Risk factors for adolescent alcohol misuse.* Paper presented at the ADAMHA Conference on Treatment of Adolescents with Alcohol, Drug Abuse and Mental Health Problems, Alexandria, VA.

Dielman, T. E., Shope, J. T., Butchart, A. T., & Campanelli, P. C. (1986). Prevention of adolescent alcohol misuse: An elementary school program. *Journal of Pediatric Psychology, 11*, 259–281.

Dielman, T. E., Shope, J. T., Campanelli, P. C., & Butchart, A. T. (1987). Elementary school based prevention of adolescent alcohol misuse. *Pediatrician: International Journal of Child and Adolescent Health, 14*, 70–76.

Donner, A., Birkett, N., & Buck, C. (1981). Randomization by cluster: Sample size requirements and analysis. *American Journal of Epidemiology, 114*, 906–914.

Duryea, E. (1983). Utilizing tenets of inoculation theory to develop and evaluate a preventive alcohol education intervention. *Journal of School Health, 53*, 250–256.

Duryea, E., Mohr, P., Newman, I., Martin, G., & Egwaoje, E. (1984). Six-month follow-up results of a preventive alcohol education intervention. *Journal of Drug Education, 14*, 97–104.

Evans, R. (1976). Smoking in children. Developing a social psychological strategy of deterrence. *Preventive Medicine, 5*, 122–127.

Evans, R., Henderson, A., Hill, P. & Raines, B. (1979). Smoking in children and adolescents: Psychosocial determinants and prevention strategies. *Smoking and Health: A Report of the Surgeon General, 26*, 69–96.

Evans, R., Rozelle, R., Mittlemark, M., Hansen, W., Bane, A., & Havis, J. (1978). Deterring the onset of smoking in children. Knowledge of immediate physiological effects and coping with peer pressure, media pressure, and parent modeling. *Journal of Applied Social Psychology, 8*, 126–135.

Festinger, L.(1957). *A theory of cognitive dissonance.* Stanford, CA: Stanford University Press.

Forman, S. G., & Linney, J. A. (1991). School-based social and personal coping skills training. In L. Donohew, H. E. Sypher, & W. J. Bukoski (Eds.), *Persuasive communication and drug abuse prevention* (pp. 263–282). Hillsdale, NJ: Lawrence Erlbaum Associates.

Goodstadt, M. (1986). School-based drug education in North America: What is wrong? What can be done? *Journal of School Health, 56,* 278–281.

Hansen, W. B. (1992). School-based substance abuse prevention: A review of the state of the art in curriculum, 1980–1990. *Health Education Research, 7,* 403–430.

Hansen, W. B., & Graham, J. W. (1991). Preventing alcohol, marijuana, and cigarette use among adolescents: Peer pressure resistance training versus establishing conservative norms. *Preventive Medicine, 20,* 414–430.

Hansen, W. B., Johnson, C. A., Flay, B. R., Graham, J. W., & Sobel, J. (1988). Affective and social influences approaches to the prevention of multiple substance abuse among seventh grade students: Results from Project SMART. *Preventive Medicine, 17,* 135–154.

Hayduk, L. A. (1987). *Structural equation modeling with LISREL: Essentials and advances.* Baltimore, MD: Johns Hopkins University Press.

Johnson, C. A., Pentz, M. A., Weber, M. D., Dwyer, J. H., Baer, N., MacKinnon, D. P., & Hansen, W. B. (1990). Relative effectiveness of comprehensive community programming for drug abuse prevention with high-risk and low-risk adolescents. *Journal of Consulting and Clinical Psychology, 58,* 447–456.

Johnston, L. D., O'Malley, P., & Bachman, J. (1991). *Drug use among American high school seniors, college students, and young adults, 1975–1990* (DHHS Publication No. ADM 91–1813). Washington, DC: U.S. Government Printing Office.

Kinder, B., Pape, N., & Walfish, S. (1980). Drug and alcohol education. A review of outcome studies. *International Journal of the Addictions, 15,* 1035–1054.

Kish, L. (1965). *Survey sampling.* New York: Wiley.

Long, J. S. (Ed.) (1988). *Common problems/proper solutions: Avoiding error in quantitative research.* Newbury Park, CA: Sage.

Mauss, A. L., Hopkins, R. H., Weisheit, R. A., & Kearney, K. A. (1988). The problematic prospects for prevention in the classroom: Should alcohol education programs be expected to reduce drinking by youth? *Journal of Studies on Alcohol, 49,* 51–61.

McAlister, A., Perry, C., Killen, J., Slinkard, L., & Maccoby, N. (1980). Pilot study of smoking, alcohol and drug abuse prevention. *American Journal of Public Health, 70,* 719–721.

McGuire, W. (1969). The nature of attitudes and attitude change. In G. Lindzey & E. Aronson, *Handbook of social psychology: Vol. 3. The individual in a social context* (2nd ed.; pp.136–314). Reading, MA: Addison-Wesley.

Moskowitz, J. M. (1989). The primary prevention of alcohol problems: A critical review of the research literature. *Journal of Studies on Alcohol, 50,* 54–88.

Murray, D. M., & Hannan, P. J. (1990). Planning for the appropriate analysis in school-based drug-use prevention studies. *Journal of Consulting and Clinical Psychology, 58,* 458–468.

National Institute on Drug Abuse. (1991). *National household survey on drug abuse: Highlights 1990* (DHHS Publication No. ADM 91–1789). Washington, DC: U.S. Government Printing Office.

Newcomb, M. D., & Bentler, P. M. (1988). *Consequences of adolescent drug use: Impact on the lives of young adults.* Newbury Park, CA: Sage.

O'Malley, P. M., Bachman, J. G., & Johnston, L. D. (1988). Period, age, and cohort effects on substance use among young Americans: A decade of change, 1976–1986. *American Journal of Public Health, 78,* 1315–1321.

Oetting, E. P., & Beauvais, F. (1990). Adolescent drug use: Findings of national and local surveys. *Journal of Consulting and Clinical Psychology, 58,* 385–394.

Pentz, M. A., Dwyer, J. H., MacKinnon, D. P., Flay, B. R., Hansen, W. B., Wang, E. Y. I., & Johnson, C. A. (1989). A multi-community trial for primary prevention of adolescent drug abuse: Effects on drug use prevalence. *Journal of the American Medical Association, 261,* 3259–3266.

Rachal, J., Guess, L., Hubbard, R., Maisto, S., Cavanaugh, E., Waddell, R., & Benrud, C. (1980). *The extent and nature of adolescent alcohol and drug use: The 1974 and 1978 national sample studies.* Rockville, MD: National Institute on Alcohol Abuse and Alcoholism. (NTIS No. PB81199267)

Saffer, H., & Grossman, M. (1987). Drinking age laws and highway mortality rates: Cause and effect. *Economic Inquiry, 25,* 403–417.

Schaie, K. W., & Hertzog, C. (1985). Measurement in the psychology of adulthood and aging. In J. Birren & K. W. Schaie (Eds.), *Handbook of the psychology of aging* (2nd ed.; pp. 61–94). New York: Van Nostrand Reinhold.

Simmons, R. G., & Blyth, D. A. (1987). *Moving into adolescence: The impact of pubertal change and school context.* Hawthorne, NJ: Aldine.

Staulcup, H., Kenward, K., & Frigo, D. (1979). A review of federal primary alcoholism prevention projects. *Journal of Studies on Alcohol, 40,* 943–968.

Tobler, N. S. (1987). Meta-analysis of 143 adolescent drug prevention programs: Quantitative outcome results of program participants compared to a control or comparison group. *Journal of Drug Issues, 17,* 489.

Treno, A. J., Parker, R. N., & Holder, H. D. (1993). Understanding U.S. alcohol consumption with social and economic factors: A multivariate time series analysis, 1950–1986. *Journal of Studies on Alcohol, 54,* 146–156.

Young, M. (1968). Review of research and studies related to health education practice (1961–1966). School health education. *Health Education Monograph, 28,* 1–97.

8

Preventing Alcohol Abuse in College Students: A Harm-Reduction Approach

G. Alan Marlatt
John S. Baer
Mary Larimer
University of Washington

Excessive consumption of alcohol by young people is a challenging problem for society. According to the law, it is illegal for Americans under the age of 21 to drink alcohol. School-based primary prevention programs have adopted a "Just Say No" policy to underage drinking and other drug use. Alcohol prevention programs with an exclusive abstinence-only message fail to respond to older adolescents who have already initiated alcohol use (Baer, 1993). College students represent a unique population of adolescents and young adults at risk for alcohol problems. In this chapter, we provide an overview of our research program designed to develop effective secondary prevention programs for high-risk drinkers in the college population.

How many college students drink, and what are the problems they experience with alcohol? A random survey conducted with 1,595 students at the University of Washington (Lowell, 1993) provides illustrative data from a large public west coast university with a population of over 35,000 students. More than half the students were light or nondrinkers, but undergraduates tended to be more extreme in their drinking patterns than graduate/professional students. Although there were more abstainers (28.6%) among undergraduates than graduate students (19.0%), among undergraduates there was a higher proportion (31%) of *binge drinkers*[1] (defined as drinking five or more drinks on a single occasion) than among graduate students (17%). A significant minority of undergraduate students (11.4%) reported drinking more than eight drinks on a single occasion. Drinking rates for University of Washington students may be lower due to the high percentage of Asian-American students (who tend to drink less than other ethnic groups) in the undergraduate population.

Binge drinking rates among undergraduate students may be even higher on other campuses. In one survey of drinking practices among freshman class students at 14 colleges in Massachusetts, Wechsler and Issac (1992) found that 56% of the men and more than 35% of the women reported binge drinking. More than 33% of the male and 25% of the female binge drinkers reported engaging in unplanned sexual activity, compared with only 10% of nonbinge drinkers. Binge drinkers were six times as likely to drive after consuming large quantities of alcohol and were twice as likely as nonbinge drinkers to ride with an intoxicated driver (Wechsler & Issac, 1992).

National surveys reveal that U.S. college students have a slightly higher annual prevalence of any alcohol use (88%) compared to their age peers who do not attend college (85%); 43% of college students report at least one episode of binge drinking in the last 2 weeks, compared to 34% of their age peers (Johnston, O'Malley, & Bachman, 1992). Other surveys indicate that heavy alcohol use is associated with a wide range of adjustment problems for college students, including school failure, relationship difficulties, vandalism, aggression, and date rape (Berkowitz & Perkins, 1986; Engs & Hanson, 1985). Alcohol-related accidents and injuries are the leading cause of death in this age group (National Institute on Alcohol Abuse and Alcoholism, 1984).

Adolescent drinking patterns change over time (Grant, Harford, & Grigson, 1988). Although drinking rates show a significant increase in the transition from high school to the college freshman year (Baer, Kivlahan, & Marlatt, in press), heavy drinking declines as students get older and assume increased adult responsibilities (Fillmore, 1988; Jessor, Donovan, & Costa, 1991; Zucker, in press). Although the majority of young adults show this "maturing out" pattern over time, longitudinal studies show a continuity of drinking problems for a subset

---

[1]The term *binge drinking* has been used to describe both the rapid drinking behavior of adolescents and young adults (drinking five or more drinks in a single episode or "drinking to get drunk") and alcoholic drinking patterns (drinking heavily because of an inability to stop or "loss of control" drinking). In this chapter, binge drinking is used as a descriptive term that refers to rapid consumption of alcohol leading to acute intoxication (blood-alcohol levels of at least .10%).

(approximately 30%) of heavy drinkers (Fillmore, 1988; Zucker, in press). Among identified risk factors for continued alcohol problems in this age population, environmental factors such as residence (Larimer, 1992) and "party" settings (Geller & Kalsher, 1990; Geller, Russ, & Altomari, 1986), along with personal dispositional factors such as family history of alcoholism (Sher, 1991) and history of conduct disorder (Jessor, 1984) have all been identified in the literature.

Students who drink excessively are at risk not only for the immediate problems associated with binge drinking and *alcohol abuse*, defined in the *DSM-IV* as "recurrent use in situations in which use is physically hazardous" (American Psychiatric Association, 1994), some are also at risk of developing increased levels of *alcohol dependence*, or "impaired control of...use and continued use of the substance despite adverse circumstances" (American Psychiatric Association, 1994). Our prevention efforts described here are designed with these two goals in mind: (a) to reduce the harm of alcohol abuse in adolescents who show a pattern of binge drinking, and (b) to prevent the development of alcohol dependence among high-risk drinkers.

In this chapter, we first discuss background research on determinants of drinking and the development of our initial prevention programs for high-risk college drinkers. Preliminary results from a longitudinal study of a "stepped care" secondary prevention program that targeted high-risk students are presented next. Our preliminary work with students living in the "Greek community" (fraternities and sororities) is then outlined, followed by a concluding discussion of the harm-reduction approach to the prevention of alcohol abuse.

BACKGROUND RESEARCH AND PRELIMINARY STUDIES

Determinants of College Student Drinking

We developed our first alcohol prevention programs based on past research conducted in our laboratory on determinants of college student drinking. With our background and theoretical orientation in behavioral psychology and social cognitive theory, we were initially interested in psychosocial and environmental influences on drinking in this young population. Over the past two decades, our laboratory group conducted a series of studies in which college students consumed alcohol under controlled experimental conditions.

In several studies, we assessed student drinking with an ad-lib analogue measure, the taste-rating task (Marlatt, 1978). In this task, subjects are told that they will be making comparative taste ratings for several different types of alcoholic beverages (e.g., comparisons among three different wines). Because subjects are told to drink as much as they need to in order to make their ratings, we were able to use this task as an unobtrusive dependent measure of alcohol consumption. Using the taste-rating task, we first found that male college students increased their drinking significantly when they thought they were being evaluated for personal attractiveness by a group of female students (Higgins & Marlatt, 1975). In our current college student programs, we continue to see students, particularly males, who use alcohol as a "social lubricant" to reduce interpersonal tension and potentiate personal attractiveness.

Drinking is sometimes motivated by negative emotional states such as anxiety and anger. Alcohol may appear attractive to young people because it is seen as a means of reducing or escaping from tension or conflict. In a related study (Marlatt, Kosturn, & Lang, 1975), we found that college students who were angered (by an experimental confederate) drank significantly more than nonangered controls in a taste-rating task; angered subjects in a third group who were given the opportunity to express their anger prior to drinking consumed significantly less than students in the control conditions (nonangered control and no-retaliation groups). These results suggested that engaging in an alternative coping response (expressing anger) could lead to reduced drinking—thus providing empirical support for the inclusion of skill training (e.g., assertiveness training) in prevention programs for alcohol abuse. In other studies exploring more global lifestyle coping strategies, we showed that by training students who were heavy drinkers to engage in a regular program of exercise and/or meditation, alcohol consumption could be significantly reduced (Marlatt, Pagano, Rose, & Marques, 1984; Murphy, Pagano, & Marlatt, 1986).

Peer pressure and social influence are often described as powerful forces in shaping drinking behavior in adolescents and young adults (Collins & Marlatt, 1981). To investigate the impact of peer-drinking models, we conducted several seminaturalistic studies in BARLAB, a simulated tavern setting located on our college campus. In our first study (Caudill & Marlatt, 1975), exposure to a heavy-drinking model (a confederate subject) significantly enhanced alcohol consumption in a taste-rating task for students who were drinking in the company of the model, whereas exposure to a light-drinking model had the opposite effect. In a subsequent taste-rating task study, we found this peer influence effect to be particularly strong for males with a history of heavy drinking, compared to heavy-drinking females or light drinkers of either gender (Lied & Marlatt, 1979). Subsequent research showed that the nature of the social interaction (e.g., friendly vs. unfriendly) was an important mediator of the modeling influence (Collins, Parks, & Marlatt, 1985). In our current prevention programs, we attempt to teach students peer communication and negotiation skills and to inform them of the impact of social and peer-based norms on student drinking behavior.

Our laboratory was among the first to demonstrate the impact of expectancy and placebo effects in drinking behavior (Marlatt, Demming, & Reid, 1973; Rohsenow & Marlatt, 1981). In one study, for example, college students who were administered placebo drinks they thought contained alcohol were as likely as subjects who actually received alcohol to aggressively retaliate in an analogue aggression task (Lang, Goeckner, Adesso, & Marlatt, 1975). Subsequent research examined the specific content of alcohol outcome expectancies in college student drinkers (Fromme, Kivlahan, & Marlatt, 1986; Goldman, Brown, & Christiansen, 1987; Southwick, Steele, Marlatt, & Lindell, 1981). Assessment of alcohol expectancies may provide a means of developing a measure of psychological dependency, with implications for early detection and prevention of alcohol problems in adolescent and other high-risk groups (Marlatt, 1987). The modification of unrealistic or overly positive expectancies about alcohol's transformative properties is an essential component of our prevention efforts.

Preliminary Prevention Programs for High-Risk Drinkers

Based on the background research studies just described, we developed a comprehensive prevention program for college student drinkers called the Alcohol Skills-Training Program (ASTP). We then conducted a controlled clinical trial to evaluate the impact of ASTP, presented in the form of an 8-week class (Kivlahan, Marlatt, Fromme, Coppel, & Williams, 1990). The design of this study called for random assignment of student drinkers ($N = 43$) to one of three conditions: the ASTP experimental group, a comparison group called the Alcohol Information School, or an assessment-only control group. Students were followed for a period of 1 year; a brief description of the study and the results follows.

Student volunteers were recruited to participate in the study by flyers, campus newspaper advertisements, and class announcements asking for participants who wanted to better understand or change their drinking patterns. Subjects who qualified were paid for their time and effort for participation. To qualify, subjects needed to be heavy social drinkers who reported at least one negative consequence of drinking and who indicated no more than mild physical dependence on the Alcohol Dependence Scale (ADS; Skinner & Horn, 1984). The sample of students who completed the study was 58% male and averaged 23 years of age. On average, baseline drinking averaged 15 drinks per week and subjects reported for the prior year an average of 7.5 occasions of driving after consuming 4 or more drinks.

Students assigned to ASTP completed an 8-week course (each weekly class was 2 hours long). Groups of eight students were led by male and female co-leaders. Each weekly session focused on a specific topic:

1. Models of addiction and effects of drinking.
2. Estimation of blood-alcohol levels and setting drinking limits.
3. Relaxation training and lifestyle balance.
4. Nutritional information and aerobic exercise.
5. Coping with high-risk drinking situations.
6. Assertiveness training and drink refusal skills.
7. An expectancy challenge in which students consumed placebo beverages in BARLAB, and
8. Relapse prevention strategies for maintaining drinking behavior changes.

In each class, a cognitive–behavioral psychoeducational model was adopted, with didactic presentations and small group discussions.

In the Alcohol Information School control condition, students received an 8-week course required by the State of Washington for those convicted of underage possession of alcohol or driving under the influence of alcohol. The program content was purely informational, and no new coping skills were taught. Lecture topics included physical and behavioral effects of alcohol, dispelling myths about alcohol, alcoholism problems, and legal aspects of alcoholism. In the assessment-only control group, students participated in all assessment and follow-up measures, but received no prevention program until after the completion of the 1-year follow-up period. This control group provided data to assess the effects of completing the assessment forms and self-monitoring drinking.

The impact of the prevention programs was assessed by student evaluations, self-monitored drinking rates, and estimates of weekly drinking rates. Self-monitored drinking rates (daily drinking diaries) were scored by computer to yield standard drinks per week and the peak (maximum) blood-alcohol level reached each week. At baseline, prior to program entry, students reported an average of 15 drinks per week and a peak weekly blood-alcohol level of 0.13% (0.10% or above defines legal intoxication in most states). At the 1-year follow-up, ASTP subjects reported 6.6 drinks per week and a maximum blood-alcohol level of 0.07%, compared to 12.7 drinks per week and a maximum blood-alcohol level of 0.09% for students in the Alcohol Information School, and 16.8 drinks per week and 0.11% blood-alcohol maximum for assessment-only controls. Measures of self-perceived drinking patterns (in which subjects reported their drinking over a 90-day period) showed students in the ASTP to have reduced their drinking significantly more than the other two groups when assessed at the 1-year follow-up.

The results of this preliminary pilot study were encouraging. Students involved in the research project reported that they significantly reduced their drinking and subjects in our ASTP condition showed the greatest changes at each follow-up period. Limitations included the small sample size, the use of only volunteer subjects, and the lack of collateral reports to validate self-report measures of drinking (the issue of the validity of self-report and the use of collaterals is discussed further later). In addition, subject recruitment was difficult; as expected, students failed to respond to an invitation to participate in an "alcohol program." Once engaged, however, the evaluation feedback indicated that the ASTP was perceived as just as helpful as typical alcohol education programs.

The second trial of our alcohol skills-training approach was designed to evaluate the effectiveness of the ASTP program presented in different formats (Baer et al., 1992). Students ($N = 134$) were randomly assigned to one of three conditions: a classroom program (a replication of the ASTP program but reduced to six sessions from the original eight), a "correspondence course" (the ASTP program content presented in a written six-lesson format), and a single session of "professional advice" consisting of individual feedback and advice presented to the student. Although this third condition could be considered a minimal-contact control group, other studies indicated that even a single session of advice or motivational enhancement can have a significant impact on subsequent drinking behavior, even for those with serious alcohol problems (Edwards et al., 1977; Miller & Rollnick, 1991).

Student volunteers were again recruited from the campus population via flyers and newspaper ads, offering participation in a skills-training program to learn more about or change personal drinking patterns. As in the first study, subjects were offered monetary compensation for the time and effort involved in participating in a research program with multiple assessment periods. To qualify, students needed to report at least one significant alcohol problem and at least 2 days drinking on an average week with blood-alcohol levels approaching 0.10% or above.

The sample of 134 students who enrolled in the program was slightly younger (average age = 21) than those in the first study. Over half the sample consisted of females. Drinking patterns included an average of six alcohol problems; students reported drinking an average of 20 drinks per week spread over four drinking occasions (average drinks per occasion = five, the lower cut-off for binge-level drinking). Estimated peak blood-alcohol levels for weekly drinking averaged 0.14%. Students assigned to the correspondence course format were least likely to complete the assignment; less than half completed all six assignments. Drop-outs were less likely in the classroom group condition, perhaps because of the peer support available in this format. The classroom condition was rated highest in the evaluation forms.

As in the first study, all students significantly reduced their alcohol consumption during the course of the intervention program. Average drinks per week declined overall from 12.5 to 8.5, and peak blood-alcohol levels dropped from 0.14% to 0.10%. Reported reductions in drinking levels were maintained significantly over the 2-year follow-up period. At each assessment, subjects in the classroom condition drank the least, although differences between the conditions only approached statistical significance. It is noteworthy that the single session of professional advice showed results comparable to that of the more extensive prevention programs. On the basis of this finding, we decided to begin with a single session of advice as the first of a series of "stepped-care" options. Our major study investigating the effectiveness of a stepped-care prevention model is described next.

OVERVIEW OF THE LIFESTYLES '94 PROJECT

Rationale for Stepped Care and Study Design

The Lifestyles '94 project was designed to replicate and extend our earlier studies of brief, skills-based prevention programs with college student heavy drinkers. The Lifestyles '94 study differed in several ways from our earlier studies. First, we did not wish to bias the sample by advertising for volunteers for a research program, but rather to apply this prevention to a cross-section of heavy drinkers in the college population. As a result, we screened all students in an entering college class and directly invited the heavier drinkers into a longitudinal study. Second, as we wished to test our interventions in a more preventive context, when students are younger and before problems develop, we focused on the first year in college (average age = 19) as the time for intervention (our previous samples were 3 to 4 years older on average). Third, we wished to test if our brief, 1-hour feedback interview could be used as the first step in a graded program of interventions.

Our previous success with brief interventions suggested that motivational interventions such as feedback and advice may be sufficient to reduce harm associated with drinking among the college population. However, for those who did not respond, more intensive treatments were available. What is not clear is how to move students into more intensive and focused services. We felt that a brief, nonconfrontational feedback session might be the best "first step" in gaining rapport and access to students, hence facilitating the use of other, more intensive treatments as needed. Finally, the Lifestyles '94 study included specific research design improvements (from our earlier studies) including a much larger sample size, longer term (4-year) follow-up, the use of collateral reporters to confirm self-reports of alcohol consumption, and the assessment and analysis of individual differences that may explain differential response to treatment. These individual difference measures included gender, family history of alcoholism, history of conduct-disordered behavior, and type of student residence.

Subjects, Procedures, and Measures

Screening and Recruitment.   In the spring of 1990, we mailed a questionnaire to all students who were accepted and had indicated an intention to enroll at the University of Washington the following autumn term (by sending in a $50 deposit), who were matriculating from high school, and who were not more than 19 years of age. Each student was offered $5 and entrance into a drawing for prizes for return of the questionnaires. Of 4,000 questionnaires sent, 2,179 completed forms were returned. Of these 2,179, 2,041 students provided usable questionnaires and indicated a willingness to be contacted for future research.

From the screening pool a high-risk sample was selected. Students were considered high risk if they reported drinking at least monthly and consuming five to six drinks on one drinking occasion in the past month, or reported the experience of three alcohol related problems on three to five occasions in the past 3 years on the Rutgers Alcohol Problem Inventory (RAPI; White & Labouvie, 1989). These criteria identified approximately 25% of the screening sample ($n = 508$). An additional control sample was randomly selected from the pool of 2,041 responders to provide a normative comparison group ($n = 151$). As this sample was selected to represent normative practices, it was not restricted to those not previously screened as high risk. As a result, 33 individuals were selected both as high risk and as representing a normative comparison.

When they arrived on campus, students selected for the study were invited into a 4-year longitudinal study of alcohol use and other lifestyle issues via letter. Phone calls were used to assure the receipt of the letter and to respond to questions. Students were asked to agree to be interviewed for approximately 45 minutes and to fill out questionnaires for a $25 payment during the autumn academic term. Students in the high-risk group also agreed to be randomly assigned to receive or not receive individualized feedback the following academic quarter. All subjects agreed to additional questionnaire assessments annually for payment. Of the 508 high-risk students invited, 366 were successfully recruited for the current study; 115 of 151 randomly selected subjects were similarly recruited (26 students were in both groups). Comparisons on screening measures between those subjects successfully recruited for the project and those not recruited revealed no significant differences in drinking rates (quantity and frequency), alcohol-related problems (RAPI scores), or gender.

Baseline and Follow-Up Assessments.   The initial or baseline assessment was used to guide individual feedback sessions for those in the experimental group. The interview protocol was based on three standardized interviews; the Brief Drinker Profile (Miller & Marlatt, 1984), the Family Tree Questionnaire (Mann, Sobell, Sobell, & Pavan, 1985), and the Diagnostic Interview Schedule–Child (DIS–C; Helzer & Robins, 1988). From these protocols we assessed typical drinking quantity and frequency, alcohol-related life problems, history of conduct disorder, *DSM-III-R* alcohol dependency criteria, and family history of drinking problems and other psychopathology. Interviewers were trained members of our research staff. In addition, students completed questionnaires at baseline that included indices of the type of living situation, alcohol expectancies, perceived risks, psychiatric symptomotology (BSI; Derogatis & Spencer, 1982), perceived norms for alcohol consumption, and sexual behavior.

Students completed follow-up assessments through mailed questionnaires in the spring of the first year in college, and every autumn thereafter throughout college. At the time of this writing (March 1994) we analyzed data from the junior year assessment, 2 years after baseline assessment. Note that the 2- year assessment takes place in the junior year for those students who pursued their college education continuously (all subjects were followed regardless of enrollment or academic status). At each follow-up assessment, students reported their typical drinking patterns, drinking problems, alcohol dependency, in addition to measures of alcohol expectancies, life events, psychiatric symptomatology. Details of these assessments are described here.

Measures

Drinking Rates.   At all assessments, students used 6-point scales to report their typical drinking quantity, frequency, and the single greatest amount of alcohol consumption (peak consumption) over the past month. For the assessment of drinking frequency, response options and associated labels were: *less than once a month* (0), *about once a month* (1), *two or three times a month* (2), *once or twice a week* (3), *three or four times a week* (4), *nearly everyday* (5). For the assessment of typical drinking quantity and most recent peak consumption, the response options and associated labels were: *0 drinks* (0), *1–2 drinks* (1), *3–4 drinks* (2), *5–6 drinks* (3), *7–8 drinks* (4), *more than 8 drinks* (5). A second measure of drinking quantity and frequency was obtained at each follow-up assessment using the Daily Drinking Questionnaire (Collins et al., 1985).

Alcohol-Related Problems and Dependence.   Alcohol-related problems were assessed with two different methodologies at each assessment. Students completed the RAPI (White & Labouvie, 1989), rating the frequency of occurrence of 23 items reflecting alcohol's impact on social and health functioning over the past 6 months. Sample items include "Not able to do homework or study for a test," "Caused shame or embarrassment," "Was told by friend or neighbor to stop or cut down drinking." The scale is reliable and accurately discriminates between clinical and normal samples (White & Labouvie, 1989). Students also completed the ADS (Skinner & Horn, 1984), a widely used assessment of severity of dependence symptoms.

Other Risk Factors.   Students were classified as family history positive if they reported either natural parent or a sibling as being an alcoholic or problem drinker and reported at least two identifiable problem drinking symptoms for that individual. History of conduct problems was assessed from fourteen items on the DIS–C that reflect common adolescent conduct problems, excluding alcohol or drug use (i.e., truancy, fighting, stealing, school misconduct). These were coded as present or absent prior to age 18 and summed to form a scale, with alpha = .65. College residence was coded as living off campus, in the dormitory system, or in a fraternity or sorority (Greek house).

Subjects. A description of this samples' drinking during high-school and the transition into college has been presented elsewhere (Baer et al., 1994). Of the 366 high-risk students recruited, 11 were removed from randomization due to extreme levels of drinking and drinking-related problems. These individuals were given our clinical intervention (described later) and referred for additional treatment. In addition, 7 subjects returned questionnaires too late for the randomiza-tion. The final sample of 348 subjects were randomly assigned to re-ceive or not receive intervention. At baseline, prior to randomization, the sample of high-risk drinkers (188 females and 160 males) reported a drinking frequency of 2.6 (SD = 1.04) on our 6-point scale, with over 63% reporting drinking at least *one to two times a week*. Drinking quan-tity was reported at an average of 2.6 (SD = 1.42) on our 6-point scale, with 52.2% reporting drinking as many as *3–4 drinks* on a typical weekend evening of drinking; 61.4% reported binge-drinking at least *5–6 drinks* on a single drinking occasion during the previous month. Using the RAPI, the sample reported an average of 7.5 (SD = 5.86) alcohol-related problems as having occurred at least once over the 6 months prior to the first year autumn assessment; these students re-ported an average of 2.2 (SD = 2.83) problems occurring at least three to five times over this same period. Students reported an average of 2.5 (SD = 1.94) conduct incidents during childhood, although the distribu-tion was predictably skewed. Most high-risk subjects reported be-tween zero and three previous conduct incidents (72.1%). Fifty-three subjects (12.9%) reported significant drinking problems in a first-de-gree relative (parent or sibling).

Procedures for Motivational Interviewing

The motivational intervention provided in the winter of the first year of college was based on prior research with brief interventions among the college students described earlier (see also Baer et al., 1992) and motivational interviewing more generally (Miller & Rollnick, 1991). Students assigned to receive an intervention were contacted first by phone and subsequently by mail to schedule a feedback interview (based on the data obtained the previous autumn term). Students were provided with alcohol-consumption monitoring cards and asked to track their drinking for 2 weeks prior to their scheduled interview.

In the feedback interview, a professional staff member met individ-ually with the students, reviewed their self-monitoring, and gave them concrete feedback about their drinking patterns, risks, and beliefs about alcohol effects. Drinking rates were compared to college aver-ages, and risks for current and future problems (grades, blackouts, accidents) were identified. Beliefs about real and imagined alcohol effects were addressed through discussions of placebo effects and the nonspecifics of the effects of alcohol on social behavior. Biphasic effects of alcohol were described and the students were encouraged to question if "more alcohol is better." Suggestions for risk reduction were outlined.

The style of the interview was based on techniques of motivational interviewing. Confrontational communications, such as "you have a problem and you are in denial" are thought to create a defensive response in the client and were specifically avoided. Instead, we simply placed the available evidence to the client and side-stepped arguments. We sought to allow the students to evaluate their situation and begin to contemplate the possibility of change. "What do you make of this?" and "Are you surprised?" were common questions raised to students in an effort to facilitate conversations about risk and the possibility of behavior change. The technique is quite flexible. Issues of setting (life in a fraternity), peer use, prior conduct difficulties, and family history were addressed only if applicable.

From a motivational interviewing perspective (Miller & Rollnick, 1991), students are assumed to be in a natural state of ambivalence, and must come to their own conclusion regarding the need to change behavior and reduce risks. Thus, the goals of subsequent behavior changes were left to the student and not outlined or demanded by the interviewer. This style leaves responsibility with the client and hence treats all clients as thoughtful adults. Each student left the interview with a "personalized feedback sheet" (that compared their responses with college norms and listed reported problems), and a "tips" page that described biphasic responses to alcohol, placebo effects, and provided suggestions for reducing the risks of drinking. Each student was encouraged to contact the Lifestyles '94 project if they had any further questions or were interested in any additional services throughout college.

Results to Date

Early results of this brief intervention with college freshman have been reported previously (Baer, 1993). Summarizing, those receiving the feedback interview reported less drinking than those in the control group at 3 months follow-up. Longer term outcomes are described briefly here; a more thorough report of 2- and 3-year outcomes is currently being prepared. We have been generally successful in retaining the sample of students with more than 88% providing data at the 2-year follow-up assessment.

Multivariate analyses completed on 1- and 2-year postbaseline follow-up points revealed that, although all students on average reported reduced drinking over time, significantly greater reductions were continually reported by those given the brief advice intervention. Further, two different measures of alcohol-related problems (RAPI and ADS) revealed statistically significant differences between treatment and control groups, with results favoring the treatment group. Despite a general developmental trend of reporting fewer problems over time, examination of mean RAPI scores indicates that those given the brief intervention in the freshman year report on average 3.3 negative consequences from alcohol use by the junior year, compared to 4.7 for the high-risk control group. Our random group, which serves as a normative comparison for high risk students, reports on average 2.4 problems at the junior year assessment (see Fig. 8.1). Thus, these differences, if reliable, reflect meaningful risk reduction among those receiving the motivational intervention.

Analysis of individual differences that might relate to treatment response are complex: There are simply too many factors to analyze simultaneously and retain power to test all possible interactions. Therefore, a series of multivariate repeated measures analyses of variance was completed to evaluate each individual difference factor (i.e., family history of alcoholism, conduct problem history, type of univer-

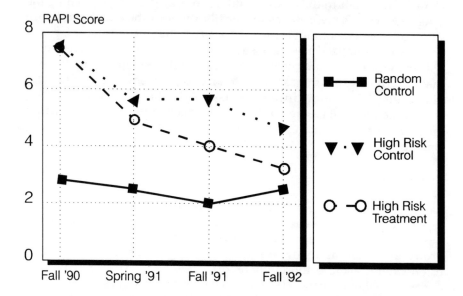

FIG. 8.1.   RAPI scores over 2 years for high-risk and normative groups.

sity residence) as main effects and in interaction with gender and treatment in the prediction of drinking trends. Both alcohol-use rates and alcohol-related problems were evaluated as dependent measures. Analyses completed to date can be summarized by describing a few consistent trends in the data pertaining to the report of alcohol-related problems. None of the individual difference factors studied consistently interacted with treatment response: Our treatment seems effective for all students regardless of risk status. However, several trends in our data suggested that not all students are equally at risk, and therefore treatment may be more important for certain individuals.

First, a family history of alcohol problems did not relate in any consistent fashion to changes to the self-report of drinking problems (no main effects or interactions). However, those with a history of conduct problems or delinquent behaviors reported more alcohol-related problems at all points in time (main effect). In addition, men living in fraternities reported more alcohol-related problems than women or those living elsewhere at all points in time (gender × residence interaction). Finally, compared to men, women reported greater decreases in problems over the 2-year follow-up time period (gender × time interaction).

The treatment effects just described and the individual differences in developmental trends sum or compile to create a risky picture for certain individuals, in particular men with conduct histories living in the fraternity system. For women, our prevention program appeared to enhance a downward developmental trend for drinking problems, regardless of residence. For men, a different and more troubling picture emerged. Men living in the fraternity system reported more problems on average, and all men reported more consistent problems over time. Further, all of these trends were exacerbated by a history of conduct difficulties and roughly two thirds of those reporting conduct histories were men. As a result, individuals with multiple risk profiles (men living in fraternities who also have a history of conduct problems) showed the most severe pattern of drinking problems over time and the least decline. These individuals, therefore, may benefit the most from our preventive programming. For example, in this study, men in the fraternity system who did not receive treatment represented our only subgroup in which alcohol dependence scores actually increased during the first 2 years of college.

Use of Collateral Data

Our studies of college student drinking described here potentially are limited by the self-report nature of the data pertaining to alcohol use and estimates of blood-alcohol levels. Although often criticized, self-reports of drinking behavior often show considerable reliability and validity under conditions of confidentiality and safety (Babor, Stephens, & Marlatt, 1987). We emphasized repeatedly to participants the confidential and nonevaluative nature of our data. Nevertheless, we cannot control completely for possible increases in the social desirability of reporting drinking reductions among those receiving treatment (and developing relationships with program staff) compared to those in the control condition. As a result of this concern, we have spent considerable effort in our latest study collecting confirmatory data from collateral reporters. Collateral data serve two general purposes. First, the procedure communicates to the subject an emphasis on accuracy and a check on self-report. A long history of research on "bogus pipeline" effects in social psychology suggests that this procedure should promote accurate reporting by subjects (Jones & Sigall, 1971). Second, collateral reports constitute a separate data source. With collateral reports we can check if others perceive changes in our subjects' drinking.

In our current longitudinal study, collateral data has provided support for our self-report data even though it has also created some practical, analytic, and interpretive problems. First, we encountered difficulty routinely collecting collateral data from all participants at all points in time. Collaterals have proven to be less compliant than the subjects; for some subjects we have two collateral reports and for some subjects we have none. As a result, complete collateral data is available to confirm treatment effects for only a subsample of the study. We asked collaterals to rate fairly specific aspects of subjects' drinking and the presence of low-level problems. Reliability with subjects' reports was lower (roughly $r = .45-.50$) than we expected. Collateral data from early follow-ups (3 and 9 months postintervention) did not reflect the changes in drinking that subjects were reporting.

Later follow-up assessments, however, have resulted in more reliable collateral assessments (both within collaterals and between subjects and collaterals); reliability for some responses are above $r = .70$. Further, these reports begin to confirm some behavioral differences based on self-report between treatment and control groups. In particular, collaterals perceive those in the treatment group as drinking less frequently and drinking to intoxication less often compared to those in the control condition. These trends appear most evident when collaterals report on female subjects, and less so with men. Treatment group subjects are also more likely to be seen as having decreased their drinking than are control subjects. These data offer one important source of confirmatory evidence that our brief preventive intervention resulted in decreased drinking behavior.

OVERVIEW OF THE GREEK SYSTEM
PREVENTION PROJECT

Overview and Rationale

Considerable evidence suggests that men residing in college fraternities are at increased risk for alcohol-related problems as compared to their nonfraternity peers. Although women residing in sororities have been studied less frequently (as have all women), anecdotal reports of heavy drinking by sorority women abound. Several studies have indicated fraternity men consume considerably more alcohol than other male college students (Johanson, Baer, Kivlahan, Collier, & Marlatt, 1988a, 1988b; Johanson & Marlatt, 1989; Klein, 1989). A comparison of 329 students residing in fraternities, sororities, dormitories, and off-campus residences (Johanson & Marlatt, 1989) indicated fraternity residents on average consumed nearly twice as much alcohol as other male on-campus residents (M = 22.4 drinks per week for fraternity men, on 4.1 drinking occasions per week), and experienced significantly more alcohol-related problems (average Michigan Alcoholism Screening Test score [MAST] = 6.4) than did all other student groups. Although sorority residents did not differ from male or female dormitory residents in alcohol consumption (M = 10 drinks per week for sorority women, 10.7 for dormitory men, 7.6 for dormitory women), they drank significantly more than all off-campus residents (M = 3.1 drinks per week for men, 3.5 for women). An additional study (Johanson et al., 1988a, 1988b), showed men residing in two fraternities consumed large amounts of alcohol (15.7 drinks per week, 5.6 drinks per occasion), had numerous alcohol-related problems (89% reported blackouts on the MAST), but reported very low motivation to change. A three-session version of the ASTP failed to affect changes in drinking behavior with these men, even though similar programming had been successful for other heavy-drinking college student populations.

Perceived organizational or environmental norms regarding the acceptability, prevalence, and importance of heavy alcohol use play a role in fraternity system alcohol abuse, especially for men residing in fraternities (Faulkner, Alcorn, & Garvin, 1989; Goodwin, 1989; Larimer, 1992). When 10 subjects from each of the 32 fraternities and 18 sororities at a large west coast university were asked to rate the top and bottom five fraternities and three sororities in terms of reputation for alcohol use, they demonstrated remarkable reliability for this ambiguous task, with 98% of subjects in agreement on the top alcohol use fraternity (Larimer & Marlatt, 1991). In addition, houses ranked as low alcohol use houses in this survey were also ranked by subjects as being at the bottom of the fraternity system in social status. A heavy emphasis on social status within this system may therefore serve to exert pressure on members within each house to involve alcohol in their social functions as a means of improving or maintaining house social standing within the fraternity system.

Judgments of the importance of alcohol to the social reputation of the fraternity house may in fact be a strong predictor of individuals' behavior. Faulkner et al. (1989) studied the drinking behavior of freshman pledges from five fraternities at a southern university, and found that alcohol use during the first month of pledge training could be best predicted by subjects' perceptions of the socialization value of alcohol within their house; subjects who believed alcohol was "very highly involved" or "highly involved" in house social functions drank more than other subjects. This socialization value was a better predictor of consumption than were such previously studied variables as prior drinking habits, familial drinking habits and familial norms, and religiosity. Because women were not included in the Faulkner et al. (1989) study, it is unclear whether perceptions of alcohol's socialization value would similarly predict drinking by sorority members. In fact, in a recent study of perceived organizational norms regarding alcohol (Larimer, 1992), women in sororities appeared to be less influenced by these environmental factors than men.

False norms regarding quantity and frequency of alcohol use within the fraternity system do appear to be a factor influencing heavy drinking (Larimer, 1992). Data regarding biases in the perception of drinking norms among college students (Baer, Stacy, & Larimer, 1991; Berkowitz & Perkins, 1986; Goodwin, 1989), suggest individuals in heavy-drinking fraternities or sororities view the normative quantity and frequency of drinking within their house to be higher than their own self-reported drinking, and higher than the observed norm based on the average of these self-reports. This type of bias may lead individuals to drink more in an effort to live up to the perceived norm of their organization. Interestingly, in the Larimer (1992) study, subjects in fraternities with reputations for the heaviest drinking accurately reported heavy-drinking norms within their house, consistent with their own self-reported drinking. It may be that this type of very heavy drinking (the *Animal House* tradition) is viewed as an ideal by both men and women within the fraternity system. Both men and women in this study accurately perceived their observer-rated reputation for heavier alcohol use compared to their peers, and houses with reputations for heavy drinking were also viewed as more popular and more positive along a number of dimensions.

Perceived norms regarding the acceptability of engaging in heavy alcohol use have also been found to be related to drinking by fraternity system members. Goodwin (1989) investigated the relationships between fraternity/sorority member's estimates of the acceptability of intoxication in various social situations, their perceptions of normative drinking behavior in their fraternities or sororities, and their current drinking habits. Results indicated perceptions of the acceptability of intoxication, as well as perceptions of normative drinking, were related to self-reported drinking habits for both men and women. Similarly, Larimer (1992) found that members of houses with reputations for heavy alcohol consumption perceived heavy alcohol use and other high-risk behaviors to be more acceptable within their house than did members of houses with low alcohol use reputations.

On the basis of these findings regarding the role of perceived norms and other environmental factors on the high-risk drinking behavior of fraternity men, we are currently extending our work to target entire fraternities and sororities. The use of nonconfrontational, motivational enhancement strategies, including the provision of accurate group feedback regarding drinking practices and problems within the house, is hypothesized to increase individual and organizational motivation to change risky drinking behavior. Although women in sororities appear to have somewhat different factors related to their drinking, they are included in the present study due to the fact that the majority of drinking within this system takes place in mixed-gender social functions. In addition to using group motivational feedback, our current study was designed to represent a true collaboration with the individual houses, allowing subjects to guide and direct the intervention to meet the specific health-risk reduction needs of their organizations.

The Greek project utilizes a quasi-experimental design, with random assignment of houses, rather than individuals, to immediate or 1-year delayed intervention. Sixteen house presidents (8 fraternities, 8 sororities) out of 48 responded to a letter and telephone call requesting volunteer houses to participate. From these, two matched sets were created (two fraternity–sorority pairs per set) based on membership size and drinking rates. One matched set was randomly selected to participate. Within this set, one pair was randomly assigned to the immediate intervention condition, and members of all four houses were recruited to participate. Of the 290 eligible members, 220 agreed to participate. Participation rates were somewhat higher in the sororities (82% and 85%) than in the fraternities (64% and 68%).

All subjects completed baseline assessment measures during the fall quarter of 1993, including the Drinking Norms Rating Form (Baer et al., 1991) for assessment of typical weekly drinking as well as perceived normative drinking by house members and other target groups, the RAPI (White & Labouvie, 1989), the ADS (Skinner & Horn, 1984), and a variety of other measures. Analyses at baseline indicated no differences in self-reported alcohol consumption between the two fraternities (drinks per week = 16.6 intervention, 16.5 control; average drinks per occasion = 5.5 intervention, 4.5 control) nor between the two sororities (drinks per week 7 intervention, 7.8 control; average drinks per occasion 2.9 intervention, 2.9 control). Compared to a systemwide survey of 1,391 fraternity members conducted 2 years prior, the selected houses were very representative of the system (systemwide average for men 16.5 drinks per week, for women 8.6 drinks per week).

Both men and women were experiencing significant consequences of their drinking; men reported an average of six alcohol-related consequences occurring at least once in the past 3 months on the RAPI; women averaged five alcohol-related consequences. There was no significant difference between men and women on the number of problems experienced. The most commonly reported alcohol-related problems for men included getting into fights (41.6%), neglecting responsibilities (53.2%), missing school or work (58.4%), blackouts (31.2%), passing out (27.3%), and tolerance (41.6%). For women, reported problems included failure to do homework (44.7%), neglecting responsibilities (51.8%), change in personality related to drinking (37.7%), missing work or school (41.2%), fights or arguments with friends (28.9%), tolerance (30.7%), blackouts (21.1%), and passing out (19.3%). In addition, 33.8% of men and 10.5% of women reported driving after more than four drinks at least once in the past 3 months.

Following completion of baseline measures, Alcohol Awareness Committees were formed in the intervention houses, consisting of one to two members of the project staff and three to five interested house members. These committees initially served as focus groups, providing information on house-specific needs and interests relating to alcohol use and other lifestyle and health issues. For both the fraternity and sorority, these initial meetings served to generate hypotheses regarding the issues most salient to the house membership and therefore most likely to serve as motivation-enhancing foci. Specific areas that were of concern for women included assertiveness in addressing problem behaviors observed within the house, risk of acquaintance rape, and disordered eating. For men, alcohol-related violence was a primary issue, as were the short- and long-term health consequences of drinking. Financial costs of heavy drinking and time-management problems were also areas that were of interest to the men.

During the winter quarter of 1994, both the fraternity and the sorority received one session of house-specific feedback based on their survey responses, tailored to address their specific concerns as generated by the Alcohol Awareness Committees. In addition to feedback on quantity and frequency of alcohol use, prevalence of problems, and estimated BALs, men received more detailed information regarding alcohol and aggression, whereas women received feedback regarding alcohol's role in women's sexuality , as well as alcohol and assertiveness. Both the content and process of these feedback sessions were very similar to the brief intervention utilized in the Lifestyle '94 project, with the exception that the feedback was about house risks, rather than individual risks. In addition, the Alcohol Awareness Committees, in conjunction with the membership of each intervention house, generated ideas for future interventions, including a planned assertiveness training workshop for the women, a second feedback session for the men focusing on a greater variety of short- and long-term consequences of drinking and an economic cost–benefit analysis of drinking. Additional assessments are planned in spring and fall of 1994 as well as spring of 1995, to assess short- and long-term response to the interventions. In addition, the control houses will begin the intervention process following the fall 1994 assessment. The results of the Greek project will tell us whether the individual motivational interviewing approach we found to be successful in the Lifestyles '94 project will be effective when administered to an entire high-risk group.

HARM REDUCTION AND THE PREVENTION OF ALCOHOL ABUSE

Our work on the prevention of alcohol problems with college students is best conceptualized as a *harm-reduction* approach (Marlatt, Larimer, Baer, & Quigley, 1993). The terms *harm reduction* and *harm minimization* are often used interchangeably in the literature, but both refer to policies and programs designed to reduce or minimize the harm associated with ongoing or active addictive behaviors. Interest in this approach began in Europe (particularly in the United Kingdom and the Netherlands) in response to two particular pressures: the problem of HIV injection among injecting drug users and the growing accumulation of data showing that the criminal-justice approach to controlling drug use was exacerbating the problem rather than reducing or eliminating it (Engelsman, 1989; Heather, Wodak, Nadelmann, & O'Hare, 1993; Marks, 1992; O'Hare, Newcombe, Matthews, Buning, & Drucker, 1992).

We believe that harm reduction provides a conceptual umbrella that covers a variety of previously unrelated programs and techniques in the addictive behaviors field, including needle-exchange programs for injection drug users, methadone maintenance for opiate users, nicotine replacement methods for smokers, weight management and eating behavior change programs for the obese, and safe-sex programs (e.g., condom distribution in high schools) to reduce the risk of HIV infection and AIDS (Marlatt & Tapert, 1993). Our work in the prevention of alcohol abuse in college students fits well within this domain.

Harm-reduction methods are based on the assumption that habits can be placed along a continuum of harmful consequences. The goal of harm reduction is to move the individual with alcohol problems along this continuum: to begin to take "steps in the right direction" to reduce harmful consequences. It is important that the harm-reduction model accepts abstinence as the ideal or ultimate risk-reduction goal. But the harm-reduction model promotes any movement in the right direction along this continuum as progress, even if total abstinence is not attained.

Clearly, the excessive use of alcohol is associated with increasingly harmful consequences as consumption increases. Harm reduction is based on the assumption that by reducing the level of drinking, the risk of harm will drop in a corresponding manner. By this logic, total abstinence from alcohol would seem to be associated with the lowest level of harmful consequences. In some areas, however, the benefits of moderate drinking may outweigh the harm-reduction advantages offered by abstinence.

Moderate drinking can have both harmful and helpful consequences. Moderate to heavy drinking is reported to increase the risk associated with motor vehicle crashes, birth defects, and harmful interactions with certain medications; yet it is also associated with reduced risk of cardiovascular disease (National Institute on Alcoholism and Alcohol Abuse, 1992). Given the mixed risks associated with moderate drinking, arguments have been presented on both sides concerning whether abstinence or moderation should be recommended to the public concerning their use of alcohol (Peele, 1993; Shaper, 1993).

Harm-reduction approaches are not limited to the type of individual clinical approaches or self-management training programs described in this chapter. Changes in the physical and social environment can also be implemented, along with public policy changes designed to minimize harm (e.g., legalization of needle-exchange programs). The best results occur when all three methods are combined. For example, to reduce the harm associated with automobile accidents it is possible to develop better driver training programs (individual self-management or autoregulation), to construct safer automobiles and highways (changing the environment), as well as to introduce safety-enhancing public policies (e.g., reduced speed limit or enhanced enforcement programs). To reduce the harm of drunk driving, it is again possible to combine these three elements: programs mandated for the drunk driver (e.g., programs designed to modify drinking and avoid intoxicated driving), physical and social environmental changes (e.g., use of car ignition systems that are designed to foil the intoxicated driver; designated driver selection), and policy changes (e.g., reducing the blood-alcohol minimum for legal intoxication while driving).

As documented in the present review, harm reduction can be applied to the secondary prevention of alcohol problems with moderation as the goal. In sharp contrast to the disease model and Twelve-Step programs that insist on abstinence as the "First Step" in dealing with any alcohol problem, harm reduction encourages a gradual "step-down" approach to reduce the harmful consequences of alcohol or other drug use. By stepping down the harm incrementally, drinkers can be encouraged to pursue proximal subgoals along the way to either moderation or abstinence. When the "Just Say No" message no longer applies for people who have already said "Yes," harm reduction provides answers to the next question: "Just Say How?"

ACKNOWLEDGMENTS

This research was supported in part by a Research Scientist Award and a MERIT award (Grants #AA00113 and #AA05591) awarded to the senior author and by a research grant (Grant #AA08632) awarded to the second author, all from the National Institute on Alcohol Abuse and Alcoholism. Research in the Greek system was supported in part by two grants from the Alcoholic Beverage Medical Research Foundation.

REFERENCES

American Psychiatric Association. (1994). *Diagnostic and statistical manual of mental disorders* (4th ed.). Washington, DC: Author.

Babor, T. F., Stephens, R. S., & Marlatt, G. A.(1987). Verbal report methods in clinical research on alcoholism: Response bias and its minimization. *Journal of Studies on Alcohol, 48*, 410–424.

Baer, J. S. (1993). Etiology and secondary prevention of alcohol problems with young adults. In J. S. Baer, G. A. Marlatt, & R. J. McMahon (Eds.), *Addictive behaviors across the lifespan* (pp. 111–137). Newbury Park, CA: Sage.

Baer, J. S., Kivlahan, D. R., & Marlatt, G. A. (in press). High-risk drinking across the transition from high school to college. *Alcoholism: Clinical and Experimental Research.*

Baer, J. S., Marlatt, G. A., Kivlahan, D., Fromme, K., Larimer, M., & Williams, E. (1992). An experimental test of three methods of alcohol risk reduction with young adults. *Journal of Consulting and Clinical Psychology, 60,* 974–979.

Baer, J. S., Stacy, A., & Larimer, M. (1991). Biases in the perception of drinking norms among college students. *Journal of Studies on Alcohol, 52,* 580–586.

Berkowitz, A. D., & Perkins, H. W. (1986). Problem drinking among college students: A review of recent research. *Journal of American College Health, 35,* 1–28.

Caudill, B. D., & Marlatt, G. A. (1975). Modeling influences in social drinking: An experimental analogue. *Journal of Consulting and Clinical Psychology, 43,* 405–415.

Collins, R. L., & Marlatt, G. A. (1981). Social modeling as a determinant of drinking behavior: Implications for prevention and treatment. *Addictive Behaviors, 6,* 233–240.

Collins, R. L., Parks, G. A., & Marlatt, G. A. (1985). Social determinants of alcohol consumption: The effects of social interaction and model status on the self-administration of alcohol. *Journal of Consulting and Clinical Psychology, 53,* 189–200.

Derogatis, L. R., & Spencer, P. M. (1982). *The Brief Symptom Inventory (BSI): Administration, scoring, procedures manual-I.* Baltimore, MD: Johns Hopkins University of Medicine.

Edwards, G., Orford, J., Egert, S., Guthrie, S., Hawker, A., Hensman, C., Mitcheson, M., Oppenheimer, E., & Taylor, C. (1977). Alcoholism: A controlled trial of "treatment" and "advice." *Journal of Studies on Alcohol, 38,* 1004–1031.

Engelsman, E. L. (1989). Dutch policy on the management of drug-related problems. *British Journal of Addiction, 84,* 211–218.

Engs, R. C., & Hanson, D. J. (1985). The drinking-patterns and problems of college students: 1983. *Journal of Alcohol and Drug Education, 31,* 65–82.

Faulkner, K. K., Alcorn, J. D., & Garvin, R. B. (1989). Prediction of alcohol consumption among fraternity pledges. *Journal of Alcohol and Drug Education, 34,* 12–20.

Fillmore, K. M. (1988). *Alcohol use across the life course.* Toronto: Alcoholism and Drug Addiction Research Foundation.

Fromme, K., Kivlahan, D. R., & Marlatt, G. A. (1986). Alcohol expectancies, risk identification, and secondary prevention with problem drinkers. *Advances in Behavior Research and Therapy, 8,* 237–251.

Geller, E. S., & Kalsher, M. J. (1990). Environmental determinants of party drinking: Bartenders vs. self-service. *Environment and Behavior, 22*(1), 74–90.

Geller, E. S., Russ, N. W., & Altomari, M. G. (1986). Naturalistic observations of beer drinking among college students. *Journal of Applied Behavior Analysis, 19*(4), 391–396.

Goldman, M. S., Brown, S. A., & Christiansen, B. A. (1987). Expectancy theory: Thinking about drinking. In H. T. Blaine & K. E. Leonard (Eds.), *Psychological theories of drinking and alcoholism* (pp. 181–226). New York: Guilford Press.

Goodwin, L. (1989). Explaining alcohol consumption and related experiences among fraternity and sorority males. *Journal of College Student Development, 30,* 448–458.

Grant, B. F., Harford, T. C., & Grigson, M. B. (1988). Stability of alcohol consumption among youth: A national longitudinal study. *Journal of Studies on Alcohol, 49,* 253–260.

Heather, N., Wodak, A., Nadelmann, E., & O'Hare, P. (Eds.). (1993). *Psychoactive drugs and harm reduction: From faith to science.* London: Whurr Publishers.

Helzer, J. E., & Robins, L. N. (1988). The diagnostic interview schedule: Its development, evolution, and use. *Social Psychiatry and Psychiatric Epidemiology, 23*(6), 6–16.

Higgins, R. L., & Marlatt, G. A. (1975). Fear of interpersonal evaluation as a determinant of alcohol consumption in male social drinkers. *Journal of Abnormal Psychology, 84,* 644–651.

Jessor, R. (1984). Adolescent development and behavior health. In J. D. Matarazzo, S. M. Weiss, J. A. Herd, and N. E. Miller (Eds.), *Behavior health: A handbook of health enhancement and disease prevention* (pp. 69–90). New York: Wiley.

Jessor, R., Donovan, J. E., & Costa, F. M. (1991). *Beyond adolescence: Problem behavior and young adult development.* New York: Cambridge University Press.

Johanson, M. E., Baer, J. S., Kivlahan, D., Collier, W., & Marlatt, G. A. (1988a, June). *Drinking behavior in college fraternities.* Paper presented at the Research Society on Alcoholism, Wild Dunes, SC.

Johanson, M. E., Baer, J. S., Kivlahan, D., Collier, W., & Marlatt, G. A. (1988b, September). *Assessment of drinking practices and intervention within American college fraternities.* Paper presented at the World Congress on Behavior Therapy, Edinburgh, Scotland.

Johanson, M. E., & Marlatt, G. A. (1989, June). *Drinking behavior in university residences.* Paper presented at the Research Society on Alcoholism, Beaver Creek, CO.

Johnston, L. D., O'Malley, P. M., & Bachman, J. G. (1992). *Smoking, drinking, and illicit drug use among American secondary school students, college students, and young adults, 1975-1991.* Washington DC: National Institute on Drug Abuse, U.S. Department of Health and Human Services.

Jones, E. E., & Sigall, H. (1971). The bogus pipeline: A new paradigm for measuring affect and attitude. *Psychological Bulletin, 76,* 349–364.

Kivlahan, D. R., Marlatt, G. A., Fromme, K., Coppel, D. B., & Williams, E. (1990). Secondary prevention with college drinkers: Evaluation of an alcohol skills training program. *Journal of Consulting and Clinical Psychology, 58,* 805–810.

Klein, H. (1989). Helping the college student problem drinker. *Journal of College Student Development, 30,* 323–331.

Lang, A. R., Goeckner, D. J., Adesso, V. J., & Marlatt, G. A. (1975). The effects of alcohol on aggression in male social drinkers. *Journal of Abnormal Psychology, 84,* 644–651.

Larimer, M. E. (1992). *Alcohol abuse and the Greek system: An exploration of fraternity and sorority drinking.* Unpublished doctoral dissertation, University of Washington, Seattle.

Larimer, M. E., & Marlatt, G. A. (1991, November). *Booze, sex, and the Greek system: Examining community reinforcement of high-risk behavior.* Poster presented at the 25th Annual Association for the Advancement of Behavior Therapy convention, New York.

Lied, E. R., & Marlatt, G. A. (1979). Modeling as a determinant of alcohol consumption: Effect of subject sex and prior drinking history. *Addictive Behaviors, 4,* 47–54.

Lowell, N. (1993, December). *University life and substance abuse: 1993 survey* (Office of Educational Assessment, Rep. 93-4). Seattle: University of Washington.

Mann, R. E., Sobell, L. C., Sobell, M. B., & Pavan, D. (1985). Reliability of a family tree questionnaire for assessing family history of alcohol problems. *Drug and Alcohol Dependence, 15,* 61–67.

Marks, J. (1992). The practice of controlled availability of illicit drugs. In N. Heather, W. R. Miller, & J. Greeley (Eds.), *Self-control and the addictive behaviors* (pp. 304–316). Botany Bay, Australia: Maxwell MacMillan.

Marlatt, G. A. (1978). Behavioral assessment of social drinking and alcoholism. In G. A. Marlatt & P. E. Nathan (Eds.), *Behavioral approaches to alcoholism* (pp. 35–37). New Brunswick, NJ: Rutgers Center of Alcohol Studies.

Marlatt, G. A. (1987). Alcohol, the magic elixir: Stress, expectancy, and the transformation of emotional states. In E. Gottheil, K. A. Druly, S. Pashko, & S. P. Weinstein (Eds.), *Stress and addiction* (pp. 302–322). New York: Brunner/Mazel.

Marlatt, G. A., Demming B., & Reid, J. B. (1973). Loss of control drinking in alcoholics: An experimental analogue. *Journal of Abnormal Psychology, 81,* 233–241.

Marlatt, G. A., Kosturn, C. F., & Lang, A. R. (1975). Provocation to anger and opportunity for retaliation as determinants of alcohol consumption in social drinkers. *Journal of Abnormal Psychology, 84,* 652–659.

Marlatt, G. A., Larimer, M. E., Baer, J. S., & Quigley, L. A. (1993). Harm reduction for alcohol problems: Moving beyond the controlled drinking controversy. *Behavior Therapy, 24,* 461–504.

Marlatt, G. A., Pagano, R. R., Rose, R. M., & Marques, J. K. (1984). Effects of meditation and relaxation training upon alcohol use in male social drinkers. In D. H. Shapiro & R. N. Walsh (Eds.), *Meditation: Classic and contemporary perspectives* (pp. 105-120). New York: Aldine.

Marlatt, G. A., & Tapert, S. F. (1993). Harm reduction: Reducing the risks of addictive behaviors. In J. S. Baer, G. A. Marlatt, & R. J. McMahon (Eds.), *Addictive behaviors across the lifespan: Prevention, treatment, and policy issues* (pp. 243-273). Newbury Park, CA: Sage.

Miller, W. R., & Marlatt, G. A. (1984). *The Brief Drinker Profile.* Odessa, FL: Psychological Assessment Resources.

Miller, W. R., & Rollnick, S. (1991). *Motivational interviewing: Preparing people for change.* New York: Guilford.

Murphy, T. J., Pagano, R. R., & Marlatt, G. A. (1986). Lifestyle modification with heavy alcohol drinkers: Effects of aerobic exercise and meditation. *Addictive Behaviors, 11,* 175–186.

National Institute on Alcohol Abuse and Alcoholism. (1984). *Report of the 1983 Prevention Planning Panel.* Rockville, MD: Author.

National Institute on Alcohol Abuse and Alcoholism. (1992). *Alcohol alert* (p. 2). Rockville, MD: Author.

O'Hare, P. A., Newcombe, R., Matthews, A., Buning, E. C., & Drucker, E. (1992). *The reduction of drug-related harm.* London: Routledge.

Peele, S. (1993). The conflict between public health goals and the temperance mentality. *American Journal of Public Health, 83,* 805–810.

Rohsenow, D. J., & Marlatt, G. A. (1981). The balanced placebo design: Methodological considerations. *Addictive Behaviors, 6,* 107–122.

Shaper, A. G. (1993). Editorial: Alcohol, the heart, and health. *American Journal of Public Health, 83,* 799–800.

Sher, K. J. (1991). *Children of alcoholics: A critical appraisal of theory and research.* Chicago: University of Chicago Press.

Skinner, H. A., & Horn, J. L. (1984). *Alcohol Dependence Scale* (ADS). Toronto, Ontario, Canada: Addiction Research Foundation.

Southwick, L., Steele, C., Marlatt, G. A., & Lindell, M. (1981). Alcohol-related expectancies: Defined by phase of intoxication and drinking experience. *Journal of Consulting and Clinical Psychology, 49,* 713–721.

Wechsler, H., & Issac, N. (1992). "Binge" drinkers at Massachusetts Colleges. *Journal of the American Medical Association, 267,* 292–293.

White, H. R., & Labouvie, E. W. (1989). Towards the assessment of adolescent problem drinking. *Journal of Studies on Alcohol, 50,* 30–37.

Zucker, R. A. (in press). Alcohol involvement over the life span: A developmental perspective on theory and course. In L. S. Gaines & P. H. Brooks (Eds.), *Alcohol studies: A lifespan perspective.* New York: Springer.

9

Parental Participation in Drug Abuse Prevention: Results from the Midwestern Prevention Project

Louise Ann Rohrbach
University of Southern California

Carol S. Hodgson
University of California, Los Angeles

Benjamin I. Broder
Susanne B. Montgomery
University of Southern California

Brian R. Flay
University of Illinois at Chicago

William B. Hansen
Wake Forest University

Mary Ann Pentz
University of Southern California

Since the 1980s, numerous studies have shown that school-based smoking prevention programs that teach youths peer pressure resistance and social competence skills can delay the onset of tobacco use in youth (Flay, 1985). Recent evidence demonstrates that psychosocial-based approaches also delay the onset of alcohol and marijuana use (G. J. Botvin, Baker, Dusenbury, Tortu, & E. M. Botvin, 1990; G. J. Botvin, Baker, Filazzola, & E. M. Botvin, 1990; G. J. Botvin, Baker, Renick, Filazzola, & E. M. Botvin, 1984; Ellickson & Bell, 1990; Graham, Johnson, Hansen, Flay, & Gee, 1990; Hansen & Graham, 1991; Hansen, Johnson, Flay, Graham, & Sobel, 1988; Hansen & Graham, 1991; Pentz, Dwyer, et al., 1989). However, the effectiveness of psychosocial-based drug abuse prevention programs in producing significant and sustained changes in drug use behavior has been questioned (Moskowitz, 1989). Reported effects have been minimal and moderate and, in some cases, short lived (Ellickson, Bell, & McGuigan, 1993; Flay et al., 1989; Murray, Davis-Hearn, Goldman, Pirie, & Luepker, 1988; Murray, Pirie, Luepker, & Pallonen, 1989; Tobler, 1986).

It has been suggested that the effectiveness of school-based drug abuse prevention programs might be enhanced by addressing contextual factors that provide normative expectations for adolescents' behavior, such as the family environment. Numerous studies have documented the relationship between family environment and adolescent drug use. Use of alcohol by one or more parents is associated with adolescent alcohol use and initiation into alcohol use (Braucht, Brakarsh, Follingstad, & Berry, 1973; Grube & Morgan, 1986; Kandel, Kessler, & Margulies, 1978). Parental use of drugs other than alcohol predicts adolescents' use of legal and illegal drugs (Johnson, Schoutz, & Locke, 1984; Kandel et al., 1978). In addition to parental influences, modeling of drug use by older siblings is associated with younger siblings' use (J. S. Brook, Whiteman, Gordon, & D. W. Brook, 1988).

Risk factors that may be as important as parental modeling of substance use include parental attitudes toward drug use and overall parenting practices. Permissive parental attitudes toward alcohol and other drugs have been positively associated with adolescents' alcohol (Barnes & Welte, 1986; Grube & Morgan, 1986; Kandel, 1980) and other drug use (J. S. Brook, Gordon, Whiteman, & Cohen, 1986). Similarly, perceived parental disapproval for alcohol and other drug use has been negatively associated with adolescent drug use (Grube & Morgan, 1986). Young people are also more apt to experiment with substances when their parents fail to set clear rules and consequences for violation of those rules (Kandel & Andrews, 1987; Kaplan, Johnson, & Bailey, 1986; Penning & Barnes, 1982).

Despite these findings, most drug abuse prevention programs have paid little attention to involving parents and other family members in the educational process. Traditionally, parent-focused prevention approaches have targeted parents of adolescents who are at risk or have a history of drug abuse (e.g., Dishion, Kavanagh, & Reid, 1989; Rose, Battjes, & Leukefeld, 1984; Szapocznik, Santisteban, Rio, Perez-Vidal, & Kurtines, 1989). Another approach has been to provide parenting education to drug abusers who are participating in treatment (e.g., DeMarsh & Kumpfer, 1986).

A few primary prevention approaches to reducing smoking among youth have included brief or minimal parent involvement components. The school-based, smoking prevention program implemented by Flay et al. (1987), for example, included parent–child homework exercises and television programs that students were encouraged to view with their parents. Student self-reports of participation indicated that 94% completed homework exercises and 43% viewed one or more television segments with parents. The results suggested that parental involvement may have influenced program impact. No data were collected directly from parents, however, and the effects of parental involvement were inconsistent.

Perry and her colleagues (Perry, Pirie, Holder, Halper, & Dudovitz, 1990) evaluated a correspondence-type smoking prevention program for adolescents and their parents involving the use of an activity package. In telephone interviews with target parents, they found that 80% of parents were aware of the program and more than 70% reported that their child had brought the program materials home. The program appeared to have a stronger effect on parents' attitudes regarding smoking in homes without smokers than in homes with smokers.

A few studies have evaluated the effects of drug abuse prevention programs aimed directly at parents, focusing on parenting skills training in conjunction with school-based prevention programs (Grady, Gersick, & Boratynski, 1985; Klein & Swisher, 1983). Although such training programs appear to be effective in improving parental communication skills in the short term, the evidence regarding effects on children is inconclusive because of the methodological limitations. Furthermore, little has been reported about how parents who attend skills training programs differ from parents who did not attend. Grady et al. (1985) reported that they were able to recruit only one third of eligible parents even though they offered a stipend for participation, suggesting that recruitment to parent training programs in the school setting is difficult.

During the past decade, there has been a proliferation of grass-roots parent groups devoted to the prevention of alcohol and other drug use among adolescents. A recent evaluation of the effects of these parent group activities, which primarily include drug education, rule setting, and communication skills training, suggested that they had a positive impact on family relations and parental control of children's social activities. Program participation did not appear to change patterns of substance use in youth, although results were inconclusive because of weaknesses in the research design (Klitzner, Gruenewald, & Bamberger, 1990; Klitzner, Vegega, & Gruenewald, 1988).

In sum, previous research suggests that parents do participate in primary prevention interventions, particularly those that are home-based, and that participation may have a positive effect on parent–child communication about substance use. Several limitations of existing studies should be noted, however. First, little is known about how parent program participation affects use of alcohol and other drugs among children, although there is some evidence that parental participation may reduce smoking among youth (Brannon et al., 1989; Flay et al., 1987). Second, studies have not examined the effects of parental involvement relative to other significant risk factors for drug use, such as use by an adolescent's friends. Association with drug-using peers has consistently been found to be one of the strongest predictors of adolescent substance use (Barnes & Welte, 1986; Kandel & Andrews, 1987). Newcomb and Bentler (1986) found that the influence of peers on substance use was stronger than that of parents. Third, our understanding of correlates of parental participation in drug abuse prevention programs is limited, although it appears that parents of high-risk adolescents may not be as likely to participate in and benefit from parent-focused interventions. Finally, each of the existing studies has addressed a single strategy for parent involvement in drug abuse prevention; none has evaluated a multiple-component parent-focused program.

OVERVIEW OF THE STUDY

In this article, we investigate relationships between parental participation in the multicomponent Midwestern Prevention Project (MPP) parent program and adolescent use of alcohol and cigarettes. The influence of parental participation is examined relative to other risk factors for adolescent drug use, including alcohol and cigarette use by parents, siblings, and peers.

The MPP is a comprehensive, community-based substance abuse prevention intervention that integrates a parent education program with four other intervention components, including a school-based social influence resistance curriculum, mass-media programming, community organization, and health policy change (Pentz, Dwyer, et al., 1989; Pentz, Johnson, et al., 1989; Pentz, MacKinnon, Dwyer, et al., 1989; Pentz, MacKinnon, Flay, et al., 1989). The intervention strategy has been described in detail elsewhere (Pentz, 1986; Pentz, Dwyer, et al., 1989). The scope of the intervention is considerably wider than previous social influence programs in that it focuses on the reduction of multiple individual, interpersonal, and contextual (i.e., social environmental) risk factors for adolescent substance abuse.

Previous research on the parent component of the MPP has focused on the effects of parent–child homework exercises on parents. Results have demonstrated that parents of students in program groups were more likely to be aware of prevention activities in the community, to rate parent involvement in prevention as important, and to engage in discussion about drug use avoidance with their children than parents of students in control groups (Pentz, Johnson, et al., 1989; Rohrbach, Hansen, & Pentz, 1992).

METHOD

MPP

The MPP has been implemented in two large metropolitan areas: (a) Kansas City, Kansas and Missouri, and (b) Indianapolis and Marion County, Indiana. In this article, we focus on the Indianapolis site. The program is referred to as Indiana Students Taught Awareness and Resistance (I–STAR). The intervention comprised five program components (i.e., school, mass media, parent education, community organization, and policy change), which were introduced sequentially, beginning with the school and mass-media components.

The school-based social influence resistance curriculum consisted of 13 sessions focusing on peer and environmental pressure resistance skills training; problem solving for difficult situations that involve drug use; correction of misperceptions regarding social norms; information about the consequences of substance use; recognition and counteraction of adult, media, and community influences on drug use; and statement of public commitment to avoid drug use. Preliminary results of effects of the school program on students, analyzed through 18-month follow-up, have shown modest net declines in weekly prevalence rates of alcohol use (2.9% vs. 4.6% increase in program vs. control groups, or a net decline of 37%) and marijuana use (1.8% vs. 4.2% increase, or a net decline of 57%; Pentz et al., 1991).

Parent Education Program

The parent education program of I–STAR consisted of parent–child homework exercises, parent organization at school sites, parenting skills training workshops, and parent participation in broader-based community organization activities. The objectives of the component were to: (a) increase parents' understanding of the causes of adolescent substance abuse, (b) obtain parents' assistance in the I–STAR prevention effort, (c) facilitate creation of drug-free schools and neighborhoods, and (d) gain parents' support of school administrators who are promoting nonuse of substances among youth.

The program component that was expected to reach the largest number of parents was a packet of parent–child homework exercises that were linked to key sessions in the social influence curriculum. Students were instructed to complete each exercise with one or both parents. The exercises were designed to reinforce lesson objectives and to increase parent–child communication about alcohol and other drugs. In one exercise, for example, students demonstrated the "techniques to say 'no'" presented in the lesson, and they practiced the techniques in role-playing situations with their parents.

The second component of the parent program was school-based parent organization. A program implementation committee was formed at each school, consisting of the school principal, a school staff member, two to four student peer leaders, and four to six parents identified by the principal as being active in school affairs. The objectives of the committee were to: (a) organize and implement parenting skills training and (b) coordinate ongoing parent involvement in prevention activities at the school. Before implementing the parent skills program, committee members participated in a full-day training session conducted by I–STAR program staff.

The parenting skills training program consisted of two sessions that were conducted at the school site by trained parent committee members. The sessions were designed to: (a) teach parents how to support their child's practice of drug-free behaviors, (b) increase parent–child communication regarding the selection of non-drug-using friends, (c) facilitate the development of effective family rules and expectations, and (d) establish positive communication skills between parent and child. Parents and their children participated in both sessions.

The parent program implementation committee members were also trained to implement supplemental activities, including coordinating active support of school policies about drug use, promoting drug-free neighborhoods, educating merchants about reducing sales of cigarettes and alcohol to minors, and organizing parent friendship circles.

Parents were also encouraged to participate in ongoing community-wide activities for drug abuse prevention. Community leaders and other community representatives in the Indianapolis area were recruited to develop a community coalition devoted to supporting drug abuse prevention activities. The coalition included parent representatives and subcommittees that addressed parent–child program issues (Pentz & Montgomery, 1993).

Project Design

The research design of the MPP at the Indianapolis site, which is presented in Table 9.1, involved three cohorts of students at 57 schools in 12 school districts throughout the metropolitan area (Pentz, Alexander, Cormack, & Light, 1990; Pentz et al., 1991). Beginning in the fall of 1986, middle and junior-high schools within each school district were randomly assigned to intervention or delayed intervention control conditions on the basis of high-school feeder patterns. The school and media components of the intervention were implemented beginning in fall, 1987. The school-site parent education, policy change, and community organization components were implemented city-wide beginning in the 1988–1989 school year.

This article focuses on the third cohort of students and their parents, who were exposed to all components of the I–STAR student and parent education program concurrently.

Sample

The target sample comprised students who were present at both baseline and 18-month follow-up and whose parents returned a completed

TABLE 9.1
Research Design for I-STAR School and Parent Programs

	School Year						
Program	1986–1987	1987–1988	1988–1989	1989–1990	1990–1991	1991–1992	1992–1993
Cohort 1							
All control[a]	$O_{6,7}$	$O_{7,8}$	$O_{8,9}$	$O_{9,10}$	$O_{10,11}$	$O_{11,12}$	O_{12}
Cohort 2							
Program[b]		$O_{6,7}X_{C1,HW}$	$X_{C2,PP}O_{7,8}$	$X_{PP}O_{8,9}$	$O_{9,10}$	$O_{10,11}$	$O_{11,12}$
Delayed program[c]		$O_{6,7}$	$X_{PP}O_{7,8}$	$X_{PP}O_{8,9}$	$O_{9,10}$	$O_{10,11}$	$O_{11,12}$
Cohort 3							
All program[d]			$O_{6,7}X_{C1,HW,PP}$	$X_{C2,PP}O_{7,8}$	$O_{8,9}$	$O_{9,10}$	$O_{10,11}$

Note. O = assessment, X = school-based program. The subscripts indicate the grade and/or school program components, including: C1 = social influences curriculum, Part 1; C2 = social influences curriculum, Part 2; HW = parent/child homework exercises linked to curriculum, Part 1; PP = school-based parent program (parent skills training, school-site committees).
[a]n = 3,177 at 57 schools. [b]n = 1,700 at 32 schools. [c]n = 1,700 at 25 schools. [d]n = 3,528 at 57 schools.

parent survey. During the 1988–1989 school year, the social-influences curriculum was implemented in sixth or seventh grade classrooms (depending on transition year) in all public ($n = 29$) and private ($n = 28$) middle or junior-high schools in the greater Indianapolis metropolitan area. At baseline (Fall 1988), a 25% sample ($n = 3,528$) was randomly selected by classroom from each school to participate in the program evaluation. Students were assessed 18 months later (Spring 1990). At both measurement points, multiple attempts were made to survey absentees. A total of 2,649 students were present at both baseline and follow-up measurement sessions (i.e., a 75% retention rate).

Parents were randomly selected to participate in an evaluation of the parent program at the 18-month follow-up. A 70% sample of parents of students who were present at baseline ($n = 2,500$) was selected, 28% minority and 72% White, to represent the ethnic composition of the greater Indianapolis metropolitan area.

Parents were surveyed by mail. The first survey was mailed in the early spring of 1990, with a reminder or thank-you card sent 1 week later. One month after the first mailing, a second survey was sent to nonresponders. A total of 1,262 parents returned the survey (i.e., a 50.5% overall response rate). Of the 2,649 students with data at both measurement points, 2,213 were randomly selected to be sent the parent survey. Of the 2,213 parents of those students, a total of 1,001 returned a completed survey (i.e., a 45.2% response rate). In summary, the analysis sample included 1,001 students who were present at baseline and 18-month follow-up and whose parents returned a completed parent survey.

Measurements

Student Questionnaires.   Students completed a 100-item questionnaire in the classroom at baseline and follow-up. The survey assessed frequency and amounts of alcohol, cigarette, marijuana, smokeless tobacco, and other illicit drug use; psychosocial variables; and demographic characteristics.

Use of alcohol and cigarettes in the student's lifetime, in the past 30 days, and in the past 7 days was measured using seven response categories. Responses to cumulative lifetime alcohol use, for example, included (a) none, (b) sips only, (c) part or all of 1 drink, (d) 2 to 4 drinks, (e) 5 to 10 drinks, (f) 11 to 20 drinks, and (g) more than 20 drinks. Similar scales were constructed for each alcohol and tobacco item. Students also reported the number of times they had been drunk in their lifetime and in the past 30 days, using five response categories:

(a) never, (b) once, (c) two or three times, (d) four or five times, and (e) more than five times.

Composite indices of alcohol and cigarette use were created by averaging statistically standardized items (Hansen & Graham, 1991). The alcohol-use index was a composite of use in the student's lifetime, during the last 30 days, and during the last 7 days, and drunkenness in lifetime and during the last 30 days. Cronbach's alphas for the baseline and follow-up alcohol-use indices were .86 and .88, respectively. The cigarette use index was a composite of use in the student's lifetime, during the last 30 days, and during the last 7 days. Cronbach's alphas for the baseline and follow-up cigarette use indices were .85 and .87, respectively.

Three of the psychosocial items in the survey measured parent–child communication about substance use. First, students were asked how easy it would be to talk to their parents about an alcohol or other drug problem (i.e., communication). Responses were rated on a 4-point scale ranging from *very hard* (1) to *very easy* (4). Second, students were asked how their parents would react if they turned down a chance to use alcohol or other drugs (i.e., parents' reaction). Responses were rated on a 4-point scale ranging from *not at all pleased* (1) to *very pleased* (4). Third, students were asked how much they cared about how their parents would act if they used alcohol or other drugs (i.e., care about parents). Responses were rated on a 4-point scale ranging from *not at all* (1) to *very much* (4).

Peer use of cigarettes and alcohol was measured by asking students how many of their close friends used each substance. Response categories ranged from *none* to *more than 10*. Three additional items assessed how often they were around young people who smoked cigarettes, drank alcohol, and got drunk; the scale ranged from *never* (1) to *often* (4). A composite friends' use index was created by standardizing and averaging the five items (Cronbach's α = .82 at baseline and .85 at follow-up). Siblings' smoking was assessed by asking students how many of their older brothers or sisters smoked.

Demographic variables included sex, grade, socioeconomic status (SES), and ethnicity. Grade at baseline was six or seven, depending on which represented the transition grade to middle or junior-high school. To assess SES, students were asked to describe the occupation of their father or other male guardian. Their responses were categorized into 1 of 10 occupation types, based on Hollingshead (1975).[1] For

---

[1]Preliminary analyses of MPP data indicated a high correlation between students' reports of mother's and father's occupation. To reduce coding in the intervention trial, we measured and coded only father's occupation.

the analyses comparing students who were present and absent at follow-up, a dichotomous SES variable was created: professional or managerial occupations (coded *high SES* [1]) or other (coded *low SES* [0]). Ethnicity was recoded to create a dichotomous variable (coded *White* [1] or *Black/other* [0]).

Student Biochemical Measure of Cigarette Smoking. Measurement of carbon monoxide concentration in expired air was used in a "pipeline" procedure to increase accuracy of self-reported cigarette use (Bauman & Dent, 1982; Evans, Hansen, & Mittlemark, 1977; Freier, Bell, & Ellickson, 1991; Pechacek et al., 1984).

Parent Questionnaire. The 68-item parent survey measured use of cigarettes, alcohol, and other drugs; exposure to I–STAR parent prevention program activities; level of support for community-wide prevention; and demographic characteristics.

Respondents were asked whether they and their spouse currently smoked cigarettes. For each item, responses were framed in terms of numbers of cigarettes ranging from *none* (1) to *more than 1 pack per day* (6). A composite index of parental smoking was created by standardizing and averaging both items (Cronbach's α = .52). To measure alcohol use, respondents indicated how often they and their spouse drank alcohol ranging from *never* (1) to *five or more times per week* (5). A composite index of parental alcohol use was created by standardizing and averaging both items (Cronbach's α = .60).

Participation in the parent program was measured with five items regarding whether parents had participated in the following activities during the preceding 18-month period: (a) helping their child with Project I–STAR homework, (b) participating in the Project I–STAR parent program implementation committee, (c) attending one or more Project I–STAR parenting skills training sessions, (d) participating in any community activities or meetings for drug prevention, and (e) participating in any committee meetings or other activities of the Project I–STAR Community Advisory Council. A total parental participation score was created by summing positive responses.

Parent SES was assessed with three items: (a) total household income in the previous year, (b) highest grade in school completed by the respondent, and (c) highest grade in school completed by the respondent's spouse. A composite parent SES index was created by standardizing and averaging the three items. Cronbach's alpha was .75. Parent marital status was recoded as *married* (1) or *other* (0).

Data Analysis

A multiple regression procedure was used to evaluate linear relationships between parental participation in the I–STAR program and seven indicators of program impact: children's use of alcohol and cigarettes, substance use by children's friends and siblings, and the three measures of parent–child communication about substance use at followup. For each model, the following covariates were entered: demographic variables (child's sex, ethnicity, and grade, and parent's marital status and SES); family drug use variables (parental use of cigarettes and alcohol, child's baseline use of cigarettes and alcohol, and siblings' baseline use of cigarettes); baseline friends' substance use; and baseline parent–child communication variables (ease in talking with parents about drugs, perceived parents' reaction to drug use, and extent of caring about parents' reaction).

RESULTS

Characteristics of Parent Sample

The characteristics of parent survey respondents are presented in Table 9.2. The majority of the respondents were mothers of the adolescents. Most were White, married, and between 31 and 50 years old; they had obtained education beyond a high-school diploma; and they had a family income of $40,000 or more per year.

Population Representativeness of
Parent/Student Sample

Two sets of analyses were performed to determine the representativeness of the parent/student study sample. First, comparisons on demographic and drug use variables were made between students (n = 1,001) who were present at baseline and 18-month followup and whose parents completed a survey and students (n = 2,527) present at baseline measurement only. The results indicated that students who were present at both measurement points were more likely to have high SES, $\chi^2(1, N = 3,118) = 47.5, p < .0001$, and be White, $\chi^2(1, N = 3,527) = 60.0, p < .0001$); they also had a lower prevalence of lifetime alcohol use, $\chi^2(1, N = 3,507) = 9.9, p < .01$), lifetime cigarette use, $\chi^2(1, N = 3,505) = 46.9, p < .0001$, 30-day cigarette use, $\chi^2(1, N = 3,510) = 35.0, p < .0001$, and 30-day alcohol use, $\chi^2(1, N = 3,519) = 6.4, p < .05$.

TABLE 9.2
Characteristics of Parent Survey Respondents[a]

Characteristic	%
Relationship to child	
Mother/stepmother	80.8
Father/stepfather	17.9
Grandparent	1.1
Other	0.2
Age	
21–30 years	1.2
31–40 years	5.2
41–50 years	51.5
51–60 years	40.6
Greater than 60 years	1.0
Ethnicity	
White	82.5
Black	15.5
Asian	0.8
Latino	0.4
Other	0.8
Marital status	
Married	76.1
Divorced	16.9
Separated	1.7
Widowed	1.4
Never married	3.9
Education	
Grade 8 or less	1.3
Some high school	6.4
High-school graduate	28.9
Some college or vocational school	30.6
College graduate	14.5
Graduate/professional school	18.3
Total family income	
$20,000 or less	16.6
$20,001–$40,000	31.8
More than $40,000	51.6

[a]$N = 1,001$.

The second set of analyses compared two groups of students with complete baseline and follow-up data: (a) those whose parents completed a survey ($n = 1,001$) and (b) those whose parents did not ($n = 1,215$). Students whose parents returned the survey were more likely to be from high SES families, $\chi^2(1, N = 1,966) = 63.9$, $p < .0001$, and White $\chi^2(1, N = 2,216) = 85.9$, $p < .0001$, and they had a lower prevalence of lifetime cigarette use, $\chi^2(1, N = 2,202) = 58.9$, $p < .0001$, lifetime alcohol use, $\chi^2(1, N = 2{,}201) = 13.9$, $p < .0001$, 30-day cigarette use, $\chi^2(1, N = 2{,}204) = 35.5$, $p < .0001$, and 30-day alcohol use, $\chi^2(1, N = 2{,}210) = 6.2$, $p < .05$.

Parental Participation in I–STAR Activities

The majority of parent respondents (72.9%) reported participation in at least one program component during the 18-month period before assessment. Most respondents (66.3%) helped their children with the homework exercises that were linked to the I–STAR curriculum. Over one fifth of respondents (23.0%) participated in the parenting skills training workshops and 23.1% participated in community drug prevention meetings. As was expected, because of the nature of the activities, participation was lower in the school site parent program implementation committee (9.2%) and the I–STAR Community Advisory Council (7.2%). The mean score on the parental participation scale was 1.29 ($SD = 1.16$).

Correlates of Parent Participation

The correlations among parent and child demographic, drug use, and communication variables are presented in Table 9.3. The strongest correlate of parent program participation was parents' SES ($r = .25$, $p < .0001$). Significant correlations indicated Whites were more likely to participate than Blacks/others ($r = .10$, $p < .05$), married individuals were more likely to participate than others ($r = .07$, $p < .05$), and current smokers were less likely to participate ($r = -.09$, $p < .05$). Participation was negatively associated with child's cigarette use at baseline ($r = -.12$, $p < .0001$) and follow-up ($r = -.14$, $p < .0001$), child's alcohol use at follow-up ($r = -.11$, $p < .05$), friends' drug use at baseline ($r = -.14$, $p < .0001$) and follow-up ($r = -.15$, $p < .0001$), and siblings' smoking at baseline ($r = -.12$, $p < .0001$) and follow-up ($r = -.13$, $p < .0001$). There was a positive association between parental participation and parent–child communication ($r = .07$, $p < .05$).

Relationships Between Parental Participation and Program Outcomes

Table 9.4 presents the results of four multiple regressions in which a set of 15 variables was used to predict Time 2 alcohol and cigarette use, friends' substance use, and siblings' cigarette use. In each model, independent variables included demographic characteristics, parental smoking and drinking, students' baseline cigarette and alcohol use,

TABLE 9.3

Intercorrelations Among Variables in the Multiple Regression Models

Variable	1	2	3	4	5	6	7	8	9	10	11	12	13	14	15	16	17	18	19
1. SES	—																		
2. Marital status	.38**	—																	
3. Ethnicity (C)	.23**	.21**	—																
4. Sex (C)	.04	.05	.03	—															
5. Grade (C)	-.16**	-.01	-.04	-.01	—														
6. Parental smoking	-.31**	-.11*	.05	-.02	.08*	—													
7. Parental alcohol use	.23**	.02	.20**	.02	-.10*	.03	—												
8. Time 1 cigarette use (C)	-.14**	-.11*	.03	.03	.14**	.14**	-.01	—											
9. Time 2 cigarette use (C)	-.17**	-.12**	.12**	.01	.11*	.18**	.01	.53**	—										
10. Time 1 alcohol use (C)	-.05	-.01	.06*	.08*	.14**	.08*	.07	.51**	.31**	—									
11. Time 2 alcohol use (C)	-.11*	-.05	.08*	.08*	.13**	.08*	.08*	.37**	.60**	.42**	—								
12. Time 1 friends' use (C)	-.25**	-.15**	-.08*	-.01	.14**	.16**	-.06*	.51**	.39**	.55**	.41**	—							
13. Time 2 friends' use (C)	-.22**	-.13**	.01	-.01	.16**	.20**	.01	.35**	.64**	.31**	.66**	.53**	—						
14. Time 1 sibling cigarette use (C)	-.17**	-.11*	-.02	-.08*	.07*	.13**	-.04	.18**	.20**	.05	.14**	.17**	.17**	—					
15. Time 2 sibling cigarette use (C)	-.10*	-.05	.03	-.04	.04	.11*	-.05	.15**	.21**	.07	.17**	.15**	.21**	.74**	—				
16. Time 1 communication (C)	.04	.01	-.05	-.03	-.03	-.02	-.02	-.15**	-.14**	-.14**	-.14**	-.20**	-.17**	-.02	-.04	—			
17. Time 1 parents' reaction (C)	.09*	.10*	.08*	-.04	-.05	-.01	.07*	-.10*	-.09*	-.10*	-.08*	-.16**	-.10*	-.03	-.01	.07*	—		
18. Time 1 care parents (C)	.02	.02	.05	-.05	-.05	.04	.01	-.20**	-.17**	-.24**	-.19**	-.21**	-.18**	-.01	-.03	.13**	.20**	—	
19. Parental participation	.25**	.07*	.10*	-.01	-.02	-.09*	.04	-.12**	-.14**	-.05	-.11*	-.14**	-.15**	-.12**	-.13**	.07*	.02	.05	—

Note. Sex is coded *female* (0) or *male* (1). SES is coded *low SES* (0) or *high SES* (1). Ethnicity is coded *Black/other* (0) or *White* (1). Marital status is coded *not married* (0) or *married* (1). (C) = Child measure.

*p < .05. **p < .0001.

TABLE 9.4

Multiple Regression Analyses Predicting Time 2 Alcohol Use, Cigarette Use,
Friends' Use, and Siblings' Use[a]

Variable	Time 2 Alcohol Use	Time 2 Cigarette Use	Time 2 Friends' Use	Time 2 Siblings' Use
Demographic				
SES (parent)	−.027	−.053	−.044	.038
Marital status	−.026	−.046	−.034	.006
Ethnicity (child)	.072*	.143**	.054	.040
Sex (child)	.059*	−.002	.005	.030
Grade (child)	.060*	.008	.062*	−.016
Substance use				
Parental smoking	−.025	.061*	.090*	.021
Parental alcohol use	.068*	.017	.030	−.048*
Time 1 cigarette use (child)	.113*	.424**	.063	−.018
Time 1 alcohol use (child)	.201**	−.032	−.019	.016
Time 1 friends' use (child)	.209**	.128*	.446**	.043
Time 1 siblings' smoking (child)	.069*	.071*	.046	.739**
Parent/child relationship				
Time 1 communication (child)	−.024	−.024	−.038	−.015
Time 1 parents' reaction (child)	−.007	−.016	−.002	.022
Time 1 care about parents (child)	−.066*	−.061*	−.074*	−.022
Program				
Parental participation	−.053[†]	−.056*	−.063*	−.050*
Adjusted R^2	.261	.339	.326	.554

[a]$N = 947$.
*$p < .05$. **$p < .01$. [†]$p < .10$.

siblings' baseline smoking, friends' baseline substance use, parent–child communication variables, and parental participation.

The results of the first model indicated that the sex, grade, and ethnicity of the child; parental alcohol use; the child's Time 1 cigarette and alcohol use; Time 1 siblings' smoking; and Time 1 friends' substance use were positively associated with Time 2 alcohol use. Alcohol use was higher among males than females, and it was higher among Whites than Blacks/others. The extent to which adolescents cared about their parents' reaction to drug use was negatively associated with Time 2 alcohol use. Parental participation in the I–STAR program was a marginally significant negative correlate of adolescents' Time 2 alcohol use, after controlling for the covariates. The set of variables accounted for 26.1% of the variance in follow-up alcohol use.

As indicated in Table 9.4, there was also a negative association between parental participation and Time 2 cigarette use among students. Parental participation was also negatively associated with the fourth dependent variable—siblings' smoking at Time 2—after controlling for covariates.[2]

In the third model, parental participation in the program was negatively associated with friends' substance use at Time 2. Other correlates included grade, parental smoking, Time 1 friends' use, and caring about parent's reaction to use. Substance use was higher among friends of seventh graders than friends of sixth graders. The set of variables accounted for 32.6% of the variance in Time 2 friends' substance use.

Because the increases from baseline to follow-up in the magnitude of zero-order correlations between parental participation and siblings' use ($r = -.12$ to $r = -.13$), friends' use ($r = -.14$ to $r = -.15$), and students' smoking ($r = -.12$ to $r = -.14$) were small, one might suggest that the effects of parental participation on these variables were present before as well as after the program. That is, an alternative explanation for the observed associations between parental participation and these outcome variables might be that participation was related to other parent characteristics that were not controlled statistically. To investigate this possibility, we tested three models in which Time 1 students' cigarette use, Time 1 siblings' use, and Time 1 friends' use were regressed on parental participation and the set of covariates. In all three models, parental participation was not a significant correlate of Time 1 substance use when covariates were controlled.[3]

Finally, relationships between parental participation and parent–child communication were examined by testing three multiple regression models in which the dependent variables were Time 2 communication, Time 2 parents' reaction, and Time 2 care about parents. Independent variables included parental participation and the 14 covariates shown in Table 9.4. The results of these models (not shown) indicated that parental participation was not associated with Time 2 communication, but associations between participation and Time 2 parents' reaction and between participation and Time 2 care about parents were marginally significant ($p < .10$).

---

[2]The pattern of results was similar in models in which dichotomous alcohol- and cigarette-use variables were regressed on parental participation and the covariates.

[3]For each of the Time 1 dependent variables, two models were tested; one that included the Time 2 variable as a covariate and one that did not. For example, the first model for Time 1 cigarette use included Time 2 cigarette use as a covariate and the second model did not include Time 2 cigarette use. In all cases, parental participation was not associated with the Time 1 dependent variable.

DISCUSSION

In this study, we evaluated parental participation in a multicomponent community-based drug abuse prevention program. The program approach was unique in that it combined home-based parent–child exercises, school-based parenting skills training, and community-wide activities to involve parents in prevention. Seventy-three percent of parent respondents reported that they participated in one or more components of the I–STAR intervention over an 18-month period. Two thirds completed parent–child homework exercises. The rate of participation in parenting skills training (23%) was similar to the rate reported by Grady et al. (1985). As was expected, fewer parents participated in community-wide prevention activities than in school-based programs.

Our findings indicate that participation in the parent program was negatively associated with students' follow-up cigarette use, and marginally associated with alcohol use, after controlling for demographic variables, substance use by parents, siblings, and friends, and parent–child communication variables. Consistent with previous studies (e.g., Newcomb & Bentler, 1986), peer influences were stronger predictors of alcohol and cigarette use than were parent influences. Nevertheless, parental participation, parental substance use, and the degree to which adolescents cared about their parents' expectations were significantly associated with adolescent substance use, which provides support for programmatic efforts to involve parents in drug abuse prevention.

Parental participation in the program was also negatively associated with follow-up substance use among students' friends, suggesting that parental participation may have influenced young people's selection of non-drug-using friends. The role of parents in mediating children's selection of friends was emphasized in the parent program.

Although enhancing parent–child communication about drugs was one of several objectives of the parent program, there were marginally significant associations between parental participation and two of the three parent–child communication variables. It is possible that our measures of communication were not sufficiently sensitive. On the other hand, more intensive communication-skills building exercises may be needed. Although parent–child communication-skills training appears to be a promising programmatic strategy, more research is needed to determine whether and how such training affects participants and their children.

One of the strengths of this study is the inclusion of parental measures of substance use and program participation. Much of the research on family risk factors for drug abuse has relied exclusively on adolescents' reports of these variables. The use of a longitudinal design is an additional strength that makes a valuable contribution to the literature.

Several limitations of the study should be noted. First, parents were not randomly assigned to program or control conditions. This study is, therefore, not a test of whether the program changed parental behavior vis-à-vis their children, but it is an analysis of associations among parental participation or exposure to the program, and changes in adolescent drug use. Second, the parent/student analysis sample was self-selected, and students in the analysis sample differed from other students in the intervention trial with regard to demographic characteristics and substance use prevalence. Furthermore, analyses of data from students whose parents did not respond suggest that parent respondents and nonrespondents may have differed on variables in addition to demographic characteristics and their children's drug use. These findings are consistent with previous studies, which have shown that students who drop out of prevention studies are more likely to be gateway substance users than students who remain (Hansen, Collins, Malotte, Johnson, & Fielding, 1985). Furthermore, parent self-selection has been a methodological limitation of previous parent prevention program evaluations (e.g., Grady et al., 1985; Klein & Swisher, 1983). This self-selection of the sample compromises the external validity of the study, and the findings may not be generalizable to all adolescents who are at risk, including children in low-income families.

Parents in the sample also self-selected the extent of their participation. An alternative explanation for the negative associations between amount of participation and children's drug use is that parent participants might have differed from nonparticipants prior to the program. Differences in ethnicity, marital status, SES, alcohol use, and smoking were controlled in the analyses. It is possible, however, that other parent characteristics, such as parenting style, were responsible for the apparent associations between parental participation and drug use. It is important that future research on parent prevention programs incorporate quasi-experimental designs that allow the researcher to separate effects due to the program from those due to initial noncomparability between program and comparison groups. In applied settings, however, it is very difficult to control for parent self-selection when parent training programs require participants to leave their homes. One strategy is to provide incentives to randomly selected parent samples for participation in both the intervention and assessments (e.g., Grady et al., 1985).

The findings of this study support the importance of including a parental involvement component in comprehensive drug abuse prevention programs. Researchers have emphasized that prevention programs are most successful when a comprehensive, integrated approach with multiple strategies is used to reach multiple target audiences (Becker et al., 1989; Johnson et al., 1990; Perry et al., 1988). In Project I–STAR, parental involvement was enhanced by the use of formats that included roles for both parents and children, the implementation of a variety of community-based prevention activities, and the support of community activities through mass-media coverage.

Second, the findings suggest that parents may be more likely to participate in home-based prevention activities that are linked to school curricula than to attend skills training programs at their child's school. Although process evaluations indicated a positive response from parents to the I-STAR parent skills training workshops, they were attended by a relatively small proportion (23%) of parents. Given the difficulties in recruiting and maintaining parental participation in skills training classes (Grady et al., 1985; Perry, Crockett, & Pirie, 1987), it may be more cost-effective to reach parents through such innovative home-based formats as videos, mass-media programs linked to school programs (e.g., Flay et al., 1987), and family games (e.g., Perry et al., 1990). Although our study was not designed to test the relative effectiveness of the different components of the I–STAR parent program, future researchers would make a valuable contribution if they examined whether home-based formats are sufficient to produce a preventive effect or whether more intensive involvement is necessary.

ACKNOWLEDGMENTS

This research was supported by National Institute on Drug Abuse Grant R01 DA03976–08 to Mary Ann Pentz (principal investigator), James H. Dwyer, Brian R. Flay, William B. Hansen, C. Anderson Johnson, and David MacKinnon (co-principal investigators) and by a grant from the Eli Lilly Endowment.

We express our gratitude to the participants in Project I–STAR, as follows: Charles Roach and Dr. John Light, former Executive Directors; Karen Showalter, Jan Weigle, and Beth Troxell, Program Specialists; Roselyn Cole, Program Manager; Barb Bishop, Research Coordinator; Marion Martin, Bernice Overholt, Julie Matlock, and Ron Lucich, research staff; Sharon Barnett, Pat Smith, and Kennetha Tooley, volunteers; Bebe Courtney, Administrative Assistant; and the superintendents, faculty, and staff members of school districts in the Indianapolis metropolitan area.

192   ROHRBACH ET AL.

REFERENCES

Barnes, G. M., & Welte, J. W. (1986). Patterns and predictors of alcohol use among 7–12th grade students in New York State. *Journal of Studies on Alcohol, 47,* 53–62.

Bauman, K., & Dent, C. (1982). Influence of an objective measure on self-reports of behavior. *Journal of Applied Psychology, 67,* 623–628.

Becker, S. L., Burke, J. A., Arbogast, R. A., Naughton, M. H., Backman, I., & Spohn, E. (1989). Community programs to enhance in-school anti-tobacco efforts. *Preventive Medicine, 18,* 221–228.

Botvin, G. J., Baker, E., Dusenbury, L., Tortu, S., & Botvin, E. M. (1990). Preventing adolescent drug abuse through a multimodal cognitive-behavioral approach: Results of a 3-year study. *Journal of Consulting and Clinical Psychology, 58,* 437–446.

Botvin, G. J., Baker, E., Filazzola, A. D., & Botvin, E. M. (1990). A cognitive-behavioral approach to substance abuse prevention: One year follow-up. *Addictive Behavior, 15,* 47–63.

Botvin, G. J., Baker, E., Renick, N., Filazzola, A. D., Botvin, E. M. (1984). A cognitive-behavioral approach to substance abuse prevention. *Addictive Behavior, 9,* 137–147.

Brannon, B. R., Dent, C. W., Flay, B. R., Smith, G., Sussman, S., Pentz, M. A., Johnson, C. A., & Hansen, W. B. (1989). The television, school, and family project: 5. The impact of curriculum delivery format on program acceptance. *Preventive Medicine, 18,* 492–502.

Braucht, G. N., Brakarsh, W. D., Follingstad, D., & Berry, K. L. (1973). Deviant drug use in adolescence: A review of psychosocial correlates. *Psychological Bulletin, 79,* 92–106.

Brook, J. S., Gordon, A. S., Whiteman, M., & Cohen, P. (1986). Some models and mechanisms for explaining the impact of maternal and adolescent characteristics on adolescent stage of drug use. *Developmental Psychology, 22,* 460–467.

Brook, J. S., Whiteman, M., Gordon, A. S., & Brook, D. W. (1988). The role of older brothers in younger brothers' drug use viewed in the context of parent and peer influences. *Journal of Genetic Psychology, 151,* 59–75.

DeMarsh, J., & Kumpfer, K. L. (1986). Family-oriented interventions for the prevention of chemical dependency in children and adolescents. In S. Griswold-Ezekoye, K. L. Kumpfer, & W. J. Bukoski (Eds.), *Childhood and chemical abuse: Prevention and intervention* (pp. 117–151). New York: Haworth.

Dishion, T. J., Kavanagh, K., & Reid, J. B. (1989, November). *Childrearing vs. peer interventions in the reduction of risk for adolescent substance use and adjustment problems: A secondary prevention strategy.* Paper presented at the Conference for the Advancement of Applied Behavior Therapy, Washington, DC.

Ellickson, P. L., & Bell, R. M. (1990) Drug prevention in junior high: A multi-site longitudinal test. *Science, 247,* 1299–1305.

Ellickson, P. L., Bell, R. M., & McGuigan, K. (1993). Preventing adolescent drug use: Long-term results of a junior high program. *American Journal of Public Health, 83*(6), 856–861.

Evans, R., Hansen, W. B., & Mittlemark, M. (1977). Increasing the validity of self-reports of smoking behavior in children. *Journal of Applied Psychology, 62,* 521–523.

Flay, B. R. (1985). Psychosocial approaches to smoking prevention: A review of findings. *Health Psychology, 4,* 449–488.

Flay, B. R., Hansen, W. B., Johnson, C. A., Collins, L. M., Dent, C. W., Dwyer, K. M., Grossman, L., Hockstein, G., Rauch, J., Sobel, J., Sobol, D. F., Sussman, S., & Ulene, A. (1987). Implementation effectiveness trial of a social influences smoking prevention program using schools and television. *Health Education Research, 2,* 385–400.

Flay, B. R., Koepke, D., Thomson, S. J., Santi, S., Best, J. A., & Brown, K. S. (1989). Six-year follow-up of the first Waterloo school smoking prevention trial. *American Journal of Public Health, 79*(10), 1371–1376.

Freier, M. C., Bell, R. M., & Ellickson, P. L. (1991). *Do teens tell the truth? The validity of self-reported tobacco use by adolescents* (Report No. N–3291–CHF). Santa Monica, CA: RAND.

Grady, K., Gersick, K. E., & Boratynski, M. (1985). Preparing parents for teenagers: A step in the prevention of adolescent substance abuse. *Family Relations, 34,* 541–549.

Graham, J. W., Johnson, C. A., Hansen, W. B., Flay, B. R., & Gee, M. (1990). Drug use prevention programs, gender, and ethnicity: Evaluation of three seventh-grade Project SMART cohorts. *Preventive Medicine, 19,* 305–313.

Grube, J. W., & Morgan, M. (1986). *Smoking, drinking and other drug use among Dublin post-primary school pupils.* Dublin: Economic and Social Research Institute.

Hansen, W. B., Collins, L. M., Malotte, C. K., Johnson, C. A., & Fielding, J. E. (1985). Attrition in prevention research. *Journal of Behavioral Medicine, 8*(3), 261–275.

Hansen, W. B., & Graham, J. W. (1991). Preventing alcohol, marijuana, and cigarette use among adolescents: Peer pressure resistance training versus establishing conservative norms. *Preventive Medicine, 20,* 414–430.

Hansen, W. B., Johnson, C. A., Flay, B. R., Graham, J. W., & Sobel, J. (1988). Affective and social influences approaches to the prevention of multiple substance abuse among seventh grade students: Results from Project SMART. *Preventive Medicine, 17,* 135–154.

Hollingshead, A. B. (1975). *Four factor index of social status.* Unpublished manuscript, Yale University, Department of Sociology, New Haven, CT.

Johnson, C. A., Pentz, M. A., Weber, M. D., Dwyer, J. H., MacKinnon, D. P., Flay, B. R., Baer, N. A., & Hansen, W. B. (1990). The relative effectiveness of comprehensive community programming for drug abuse prevention with high-risk and low-risk adolescents. *Journal of Consulting and Clinical Psychology, 58,* 447–456.

Johnson, G. M., Schoutz, F. C., & Locke, T. P. (1984). Relationships between adolescent drug use and parental drug behaviors. *Adolescence, 19,* 295–299.

Kandel, D. B. (1980). Drug and drinking behavior among youth. *Annual Review of Sociology, 6,* 235–285.

Kandel, D. B., & Andrews, K. (1987). Processes of adolescent socialization by parents and peers. *International Journal of the Addictions, 22,* 319–342.

Kandel, D. B., Kessler, R. C., & Margulies R. Z. (1978). Antecedents of adolescent initiation into stages of drug use: A developmental analysis. *Journal of Youth and Adolescence, 7,* 13–40.

Kaplan, H. B., Johnson, R. J., & Bailey, C. A. (1986). Self-rejection and explanation of deviance: Specification of the structure among latent constructs. *American Journal of Sociology, 92,* 384–411.

Klein, M. A., & Swisher, J. D. (1983). A statewide evaluation of a communication and parenting skills program. *Journal of Drug Education, 13*(1), 73–82.

Klitzner, M., Gruenewald, P. J., & Bamberger, E. (1990). The assessment of parent-led prevention programs: A preliminary assessment of impact. *Journal of Drug Education, 20*(1), 77–94.

Klitzner, M., Vegega, M. E., and Gruenewald, P. (1988). An empirical examination of the assumptions underlying youth drinking/driving prevention programs. *Evaluation and Program Planning, 11,* 219–235.

Moskowitz, J. M. (1989). The primary prevention of alcohol problems: A critical review of the research literature. *Journal of Studies on Alcohol, 50*(1), 54–88.

Murray, D. M., Davis-Hearn, M., Goldman, A. I., Pirie, P., & Luepker, R. V. (1988). Four- and five-year follow-up results from four seventh-grade smoking prevention strategies. *Jour-

nal of Behavioral Medicine, 11(4), 395–405.

Murray, D. M., Pirie, P., Luepker, R. V., & Pallonen, U. (1989). Five- and six-year follow-up results from four seventh-grade smoking prevention strategies. *Journal of Behavioral Medicine, 12*(2), 207–218.

Newcomb, M. D., & Bentler, P. M. (1986). Substance use and ethnicity: Differential impact of peer and adult models. *Journal of Psychology, 120,* 83–95.

Pechacek, T. F., Murray, D. M., Luepker, R. V., Mittelmark, M. B., Johnson, C. A., & Shutz, J. M. (1984). Measurement of adolescent smoking behavior: Rationale and methods. *Journal of Behavioral Medicine, 7*(1), 123–140.

Penning, M., & Barnes, G. E. (1982). Adolescent marijuana use: A review. *International Journal of Addictions, 17,* 749–791.

Pentz, M. A. (1986). Community organization and school liaisons: How to get programs started. *Journal of School Health, 56,* 382–388.

Pentz, M. A., Alexander, P., Cormack, C., & Light, J. (1990). Issues in the development and process of community-based alcohol and drug prevention: The Midwestern Prevention Project (MPP). In N. Giesbrecht, P. Conley, R. W. Denniston, L. Gliksman, H. Holder, A. Pederson, R. Room, & M. Shain (Eds.), *Research, action, and the community: Experiences in the prevention of alcohol and other drug problems* (OSAP Prevention Monograph No. 4, pp. 136–143). Washington, DC: Department of Health and Human Services.

Pentz, M. A., Dwyer, J. H., MacKinnon, D. P., Flay, B. R., Hansen, W. B., Wang, E. Y. I., & Johnson, C. A. (1989). A multi-community trial for primary prevention of adolescent drug abuse: Effects on drug use prevalence. *Journal of the American Medical Association, 261*(22), 3259–3266.

Pentz, M. A., Johnson, C. A., Dwyer, J. H., MacKinnon, D. P., Hansen, W. B., & Flay, B. R. (1989). A comprehensive community approach to adolescent drug abuse prevention: Effects on cardiovascular disease risk behaviors. *Annals of Medicine, 21*(3), 219–222.

Pentz, M. A., Johnson, C. A., Hansen, W. B., Flay, B. R., Dwyer, J. H., & MacKinnon, D. P. (1991, November). *Effects of community-based drug abuse prevention for adolescents.* Paper presented at the annual meeting of the American Public Health Association, Atlanta, GA.

Pentz, M. A., MacKinnon, D. P., Dwyer, J. H., Wang, E. Y. I., Hansen, W. B., Flay, B. R., & Johnson, C. A. (1989). Longitudinal effects of the Midwestern Prevention Project (MPP) on regular and experimental smoking in adolescents. *Preventive Medicine, 18,* 304–321.

Pentz, M. A., MacKinnon, D. P., Flay, B. R., Hansen, W. B., Johnson, C. A., & Dwyer, J. H. (1989). Primary prevention of chronic disease in adolescence: Effects of the Midwestern Prevention Project on tobacco use. *American Journal of Epidemiology, 130*(4), 713–724.

Pentz, M. A., & Montgomery, S. B. (1993). *Research-based community coalitions for drug abuse prevention: The Midwestern Prevention Project.* Unpublished manuscript, University of Southern California, Institute for Prevention Research, Los Angeles.

Perry, C. L., Crockett, S. J., & Pirie, P. (1987). Influencing parental health behavior: Implications of community assessments. *Health Education, 18*(5), 68–77.

Perry, C. L., Luepker, R. V., Murray, D. M., Kurth, C., Mullis, R., Crockett, S., & Jacobs, D. R. (1988). Parent involvement with children's health promotion: The Minnesota Home Team. *American Journal of Public Health, 78,* 1156–1160.

Perry, C. L., Pirie, P., Holder, W., Halper, A., & Dudovitz, B. (1990). Parent involvement in cigarette smoking prevention: Two pilot evaluations of the "Unpuffables Program." *Journal of School Health, 60*(9), 443–447.

Rohrbach, L. A., Hansen, W. B., & Pentz, M. A. (1992, November). *Strategies for involving parents in drug abuse prevention: Results from the Midwest Prevention Program.* Paper presented at the annual meeting of the American Public Health Association, Washington, DC.

Rose, M., Battjes, R., & Leukefeld, C. (1984). *Family life skills training for drug abuse prevention* (DHHS Publication No. ADM 84–1340). Washington, DC: U.S. Government Printing Office.

Szapocznik, J., Santisteban, D., Rio, A., Perez-Vidal, A., & Kurtines, W. M. (1989). Family effectiveness training: An intervention to prevent drug abuse and problem behaviors in Hispanic adolescents. *Hispanic Journal of Behavioral Sciences, 11*(1), 4–27.

Tobler, N. S. (1986). Meta-analysis of 143 adolescent drug prevention programs: Quantitative outcome results of program participants compared to a control or comparison group. *The Journal of Drug Issues, 16*(4), 537–567.

10

Community Strategies for the Reduction of Youth Drinking: Theory and Application

Alexander C. Wagenaar
Cheryl L. Perry
University of Minnesota

In this chapter, we have four objectives. First, we briefly review several theories on alcohol consumption in young people that are particularly important for the design of community action efforts on youth drinking. Second, we present elements of an integrated meta-theory of drinking behavior, drawing on concepts from many social science theories. Third, we discuss implications of those theories for the design of community efforts to affect the use of alcohol by underage youth and reduce harmful consequences of youth drinking. Fourth, we summarize the objectives and implementation strategies of two large-scale randomized community trials currently in progress that are designed to reduce youth drinking.

A POPULATION-WIDE APPROACH IS REQUIRED

Youth alcohol use is a social behavior that is primarily determined by social structures, norms, and other dimensions of the social environment in which people live (Akers, 1992). Widespread patterns of alcohol use by young people are not reflective of addictive or psychopathological behavior, but, rather, are "normal" or expected results of social policies, institutional structures, and social norms concerning alcohol in our society. Prevention efforts and public action strategies must be based on an understanding of the factors that affect patterns of alcohol use across the whole population of young people rather than just the smaller sample of those identified as problem drinkers. Predicting with great sensitivity and selectivity why a given individual will drink and understanding the nature of the consequences of individual drinking may be important in a clinical setting in which a small set of individuals with alcohol-related problems is the focus of attention. Applying such an individual focus to the development of population-wide prevention efforts is, however, not fruitful.

A population-wide focus on how the social environment fosters youth drinking is necessary for several reasons (Syme, 1986). First, the magnitude of the problem is such that even if we had a perfect "cure," we most likely would not have the resources to apply it to all who are at risk. Second, because more than half of high-school seniors drink and one third become intoxicated at least once in 2 weeks (Johnston, O'Malley, & Bachman, 1991), it is evident that many youths are at significant risk for a car crash, assault, rape, injury, or another serious problem associated with drinking. Third, there is constant turnover in the high-risk population. Turnover is most obvious for youth because most high-risk, heavy-drinking youth are at substantially lower risk when they reach age 30, and new entrants replace them in the high-risk pool of teenagers. Thus, even if we cure the current incumbents of the high-risk pool, in a short period of time turnover is such that little long-term benefit is achieved.

The fourth reason a population-wide focus is necessary is that the majority of alcohol-related death and disability is attributable to moderate drinkers, not those who are alcohol dependent. The heaviest drinkers are clearly at highest risk of problems, but there are so many more people in the lower risk "moderate" drinking group that a lower individual risk still results in a larger aggregate burden to society.[1] This is the classic *population attributable risk* concept in epidemiology (A. M. Lilienfeld & D. E. Lilienfeld, 1980), which is so frequently overlooked when prevention programs are designed solely focusing on "high-risk" youth.[2]

---

[1]Moreover, moderate-drinking youth are by no means at low risk for alcohol-related problems. At a blood alcohol concentration of .03g/dl (i.e., two drinks for most teenagers), for example, the risk of traffic crash involvement is nine times higher than for youths who have not been drinking (Farris, Malone, & Lilliefors, 1976).

[2]In a humane society, we should of course do whatever we can to assist and treat those who are identified as alcohol dependent or as being in the highest risk category. Early intervention with such individuals may well prevent further serious alcohol problems. We argue strongly, however, that primary prevention requires efforts focused on the entire population and the communities and environments that affect drinking and related behaviors. Without broader political and social change, without efforts to change the conditions that create the (high) risk in the first place, long-term success can only be limited.

THEORY: WHY YOUTH DRINK

We need to understand why the overwhelming majority of teenagers use alcohol on a regular basis and how the amount and frequency of such drinking can be reduced, with a consequent reduction in those social and health problems for which alcohol use is a contributing factor. To understand the many factors that may contribute to youth drinking, and to identify potential action strategies to reduce youth drinking, a broad range of theoretical approaches might be considered. Many of these theories use concepts that may have different labels but reflect conceptually similar underlying constructs.

Many etiological theories provide elements for a comprehensive meta-theory of population-wide drinking patterns, including: genetic theories (Hrubec & Omenn, 1981; Cloninger, 1983; Gilligan, Reich & Cloninger, 1987; Kendler, Heath, Neale, Kessler, & Eaves, 1992); tension-reduction theory (Cappell & Greeley, 1987; Corcoran & Parker, 1991; Orcutt & Harvey, 1991); psychoanalytic theory (Fenichel, 1945); cognitive theories (Lewin, Dembo, Feslinger & Sears, 1946; Bandura, 1977); labeling theory (Schur, 1971); selective interaction/differential association theory (Sutherland & Cressey, 1974); problem behavior theory (Jessor & Jessor, 1977; Jessor, 1987); stage theory (Kandel, 1975, 1988; Kandel, Yamaguchi & Chen, 1992; Bailey, 1992); economic theories (Ornstein, 1980; Becker & Murphy, 1988; Coate & Grossman, 1988); classical conditioning theory (Klein & Mowrer, 1989; Gormezano, Prokasy, & Thompson, 1987); operant conditioning theory (Skinner, 1953); social learning theory (Bandura, 1986); symbolic interactionism theory (Blumer, 1969; Cooley, 1962; Mead, 1934); social control theories (Clinard & Meier, 1989); anomie theory (Merton, 1968); bonding theory (Krohn & Massey, 1980); and availabiliity theory (Bruun, Edwards, Lumio, Mäkelä, Pan, Popham, Room, Schmidt, Skog, Sulkunen, & Österberg, 1975; Holder, 1987; Wagenaar & Farrell, 1989). Dimensions of all these theories are reflected in our model of drinking behavior shown in Fig. 10.1. A comprehensive review of all these theoretical approaches is beyond the scope of this article, but we briefly review the core propositions from those theories that most influence our approach to youth drinking.[3]

Cognitive theories focus on the central role of expectancies concerning the effects of alcohol (Bandura, 1977; Lewin, Dembo, Feslinger, &

---

[3]For specific references for the theories cited, contact the authors.

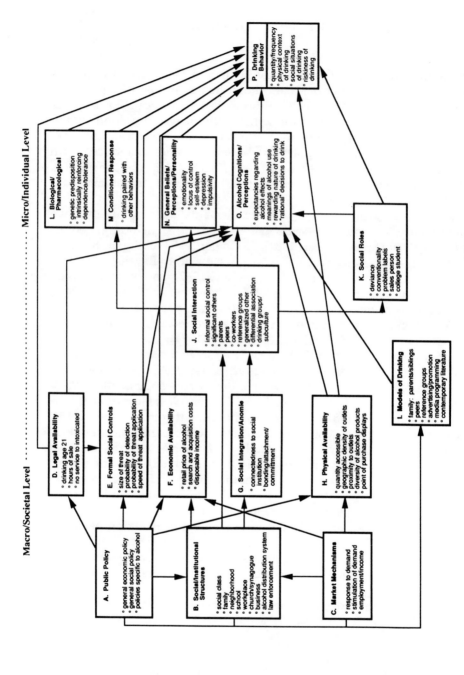

FIG. 10.1. An integrated theory of drinking behavior.

Sears, 1946). If one believes that consuming alcohol will give pleasure, reduce tension, make one more attractive, or achieve other positively valued states, then one is more likely to consume alcohol. The actual pharmacological effects of alcohol are therefore not as important as what one believes about those effects. Adolescents learn to expect that alcohol use is functional, helping them achieve desired ends. Advertising, promotion, television programming, parents, peers, and other dimensions of the social environment all can lead to the expectation that alcohol makes one attractive, powerful, mature, and happy. Prevention implications include cognitive "reprogramming" so that the outcomes of drinking are not perceived as positive and providing alternative methods to achieve valued states.

Problem behavior theory is a social-psychological theory of youth "problem" behavior, including alcohol use (Jessor, 1987; Jessor & Jessor, 1977). The theory postulates intercorrelations among a series of specific problem behavior areas (e.g., drug use, sexual intercourse, and other deviant behaviors) and indicators of conventional behaviors (e.g., academic achievement, church attendance) such that higher levels of problem behaviors and lower levels of conventional behaviors are associated with increased drinking. In addition, a variety of personal belief variables (e.g., values, locus of control), perceptions of parents' and friends' behaviors and support, and demographic/socialization background variables are postulated to affect youth drinking. Suggestions for prevention include the promotion of conventional behaviors and perceptions or beliefs that alcohol use is unacceptable and unsupported by significant others.

Stage theory of alcohol use focuses on the sequence of initiation of various drugs (Bailey, 1992; Kandel, 1975, 1988; Kandel, Yamaguchi, & Chen, 1992). Youth drug users typically begin with drugs that are legal for adults and for which social norms and meanings are less negative, such as tobacco and alcohol. A subset of tobacco and alcohol users then progresses to the least socially objectionable illegal drugs, such as marijuana. A further subset of the population moves on to the "hardest" drugs that have the strongest social proscriptions on use, such as heroin or crack cocaine. Adolescent alcohol use can therefore be considered a "gateway" drug. Efforts to prevent drug problems would focus ideally on delaying or preventing the onset of alcohol use—not just because of the consequences of alcohol use alone, but also because of its potential for increasing the acceptability of other licit and illicit drugs.

Economic theories of alcohol use state that individuals make rational decisions to consume products in which they find utility (Becker &

Murphy, 1988).[4] Consumers do not consume an infinite amount of alcohol, but rather they make decisions on whether to consume a drink on the basis of a balance of the expected utility from consuming it and the costs of doing so. Thus, consumption of alcohol is tied to the costs of the product in relation to the amount of disposable income available. Econometric studies have established that alcohol consumption is price elastic (Ornstein, 1980) and that young people are the most responsive to an increase in price by reducing consumption (Coate & Grossman, 1988).

Clearly, adolescents (like all people) frequently make decisions that do not appear rational to an outside observer. They do not know all alternatives avaiable to them, do not fully understand the expected consequences of each alternative, and do not always choose the action that optimizes their gain at minimum cost. Yet, for the most part, adolescent behavior, as all human behavior, is functional, and not arbitrary or capricious. Adolescents take many things into account in making decisions to drink, and many of those considerations are related to social expectations and influences concerning alcohol use, not just direct economic costs and benefits. Prevention efforts based on such an economic or decision-making model must recognize the functionality of alcohol use from an adolescent's perspective and encourage a broader awareness of the negative consequences of use and of normative expectations that not drinking has positive outcomes. Finally, an important way to reduce youth alcohol use may be to increase its direct cost through increased taxes and prices as well as to increase its indirect cost by reducing its accessibility to youths.

Operant conditioning theory postulates that people consume alcohol because it is reinforcing to do so. Behavior that is rewarded tends to be repeated (Skinner, 1953). The most direct reinforcement accrues from the pharmacological effects of ingesting alcohol. Adolescent alcohol use is notable for single sessions of overconsumption, during which these pharmacological reinforcers are learned rapidly. For young people, however, reinforcement for consuming alcohol may also be socially determined. For example, drinkers may receive more attention and enjoy more conviviality after drinking. Such rewards are a result of the socially shared meanings attached to alcohol use in various situations.

Social learning theory builds directly on operant conditioning in pos-

---

[4]Economic theory is related to exchange theory in sociology, which argues that exchanges are the foundation of all social behavior (I'll do X and you are expected to do Y in return).

tulating that alcohol use is a socially acquired, learned behavior resulting from antecedent cues to drink and reinforcements that are a consequence of drinking, with the cues and reinforcements mediated by learned cognitive beliefs and expectancies about alcohol (Bandura, 1986). In short, people base their actions on what they find rewarding. In addition, people behave like significant role models and learn reinforcements from observing the consequences of others' behaviors. What is perceived or experienced as rewarding is also, at least in part, socially learned. Thus, the position a person occupies in relevant social structures, and patterns of social interaction, influence what is rewarding for any given person. For adolescents, acquiring or learning a behavior such as alcohol use is not only a result of directly experienced cues and reinforcements but also of observing the response to cues and the reinforcements received by models, either directly observed or learned through the mass media, second-hand stories, and so forth.

Prevention implications of social learning theory include emphasis on negative social consequences of alcohol use, appropriate modeling by such key adult role models as parents, employing popular peer role models to discourage alcohol use, and limiting the presentation of drinking models in media to which youth are exposed. The depiction of inappropriate drinking models in television programming, for example, can be substantially reduced through organized efforts with the writers and producers of television programs (Breed & DeFoe, 1982, 1984; Lowery, 1980; Rychtarik, Fairbank, Allen, Foy, & Drabman, 1983; Wallack, Grube, & Madden, 1990). Exposure to drinking models in advertising can be reduced by regulating or prohibiting advertising in media with a substantial underage audience (e.g., television, outdoor billboards, in sports stadiums; Gerbner, 1990; Postman, Nystrom, Strate, & Weingartner, 1987).

Symbolic interactionism theory posits that people respond to events and objects in terms of the meanings they attribute to them (Blumer, 1969; Cooley, 1962; Mead, 1934). Socialization (both childhood and lifelong) is the process of learning the socially shared sets of meanings attached to events, objects, and language. Humans have the capacity for role taking—for imagining the attitudes and perceptions of others and being able to anticipate how they will respond to specific actions. One's behavior is directly affected by such anticipated actions on the part of others. The meanings attached to specific behaviors are acquired from society as a whole (i.e., the *generalized other*), as well as specific reference others or reference groups. Social norms affecting drinking are derived from interaction with individuals and groups in society, as well as from role models for appropriate behavior in specific settings. Role models and other dimensions of the social environment that define norms around drinking are not only reflected in interactions between individuals, they are also reflected in a wide range of community and societal structures and practices related to alcohol. The presence and active marketing of alcohol throughout the social environment experienced by youth through family, friends, advertising, and media programming therefore help define socially shared meanings that alcohol consumption is an expected behavior. This theory suggests that efforts to reduce alcohol use must involve multiple social structures and an array of agents, including the youths themselves, that are both proximal and distal to the adolescent, including the family, local community, mass media, marketing practices, and institutional and public policies related to alcohol.

Social control theories focus on nonnormative or deviant behavior, noting that deviance is a result of insufficient social controls to restrict behaviors that individuals are presumably motivated to perform (Clinard & Meier, 1989). Such controls may be informal, using social pressure as the control mechanism to discourage deviant behavior. Social controls may also be formal, using laws, public policy, organizational policies, regulations, or procedure specifications to limit deviant behavior. General deterrence theory focuses on formal social controls. Deviant behavior such as adolescent alcohol use is restricted by a threat of penalties that potential offenders perceive as swift, certain, and severe (Ross, 1992). The clear prevention implication is to enact public policies that deter alcohol use among young people rather than relying on their individual values or decisions or the operation of informal social norms.

Anomie theory suggests that social disorganization, lack of social integration, and lack of normative consensus lead to alcohol use (Merton, 1968). The core notion is that a healthy society with healthy individuals is characterized by young people who feel connected to society, feel they have a stake in society, and are active participants whose views and energies are taken seriously by others. Individuals who are integrated into society have a reciprocal relationship with that society such that they give of their energies in support of society and they receive benefits in return. The implications of anomie theory are clear, but implementation of prevention strategies is complex. Efforts should include active support for social changes that would facilitate the integration of youths into communities and society as a whole. At a minimum, prevention programs must incorporate youth as active participants and decision makers in efforts to address alcohol use, not only focusing on narrowly defined youth domains but also on broader institutional and community decision making.

Strain theory is a subset of anomie theory that states that people who do not have access to legitimate means to normatively valued aspirations (e.g., money, status, and happiness) turn to illegitimate means to achieve them. Alternatively, they retreat, dropping out of conventional society. Bonding theory is also a subset of anomie theory. The core notion is that youths who are less bonded to society are more likely to consume large amounts of alcohol (Krohn & Massey, 1980). Three dimensions of bonding are frequently discussed: (a) attachment, which is reflected in emotional and affective ties to family, peer groups, school, church, workplace, and other social institutions; (b) commitment, which is reflected in the amount of time, energy, and ambitions a person invests in conventional activities; and (c) involvement, the degree to which one is regularly engaged in conventional activities such that there is less opportunity for deviant activities, including heavy drinking. Bonding and strain theories suggest that collaborating with young people and building opportunities for them to participate actively in their families, schools, and communities would reduce alcohol use. Restructuring community institutions to increase opportunities for meaningful youth participation, rather than focusing on the needs of individuals, might strengthen social bonds and preclude tendencies to engage in deviant activities.

Availability theory points out that the degree to which alcoholic beverages are accessible to people affects the amount and pattern of alcohol use (Bruun et al., 1975; Holder, 1987). There are many dimensions of alcohol availability, which can be grouped for simplicity into three categories: physical availability, economic availability, and legal availability (Wagenaar & Farrell, 1989). Physical availability is the amount, diversity, and proximity of alcoholic beverages in the environment. Economic availability is the degree to which acquisition and consumption of alcoholic beverages requires expenditure of resources in relation to resources available (e.g., the cost of obtaining alcohol in relation to disposable income). Legal availability is the degree to which purchase and consumption of alcohol is limited by law. For example, sales are typically limited by time of day (i.e., no late night sales), age of purchaser (i.e., must be 21 or over), type of alcoholic beverage (i.e., only low-alcohol beer in grocery stores), or amount of alcohol (i.e., no sales or service to intoxicated customers). The availability of alcohol directly affects opportunities to drink and is also part of the environment that shapes normative expectations about appropriate alcohol consumption. Prevention implications include creating barriers to young people's drinking by reducing access and availability through public policies, excise taxes, and physical restraints.

PUTTING IT ALL TOGETHER: AN
INTEGRATED THEORY OF DRINKING

The effort to integrate all of the diverse theories of drinking into one meta-theory is a worthwhile challenge. It serves as a start toward a broader effort of additional theory building, which examines interconnections and similarities of concepts with different labels from different theoretical traditions. Such an integrated model also points out potentially fruitful avenues for action.

In our integrated model, drinking is directly affected by personal cognitions and perceptions regarding alcohol (path O–P in Fig. 10.1). When one expects alcohol to have reinforcing positive effects, when one understands alcohol use in terms of its socially shared positive meanings, and when one perceives the expected rewards of acquiring alcohol and consuming alcohol to be high in relation to costs, one is likely to drink alcohol. Perceptions about alcohol are a direct result of social interactions with significant others in one's environment (path J–O), observation of environmental models (path I–O), and formal social controls (path E–O).

The model points out a key reason that most educational interventions have had little effect on drinking (Moskowitz, 1989). Changing beliefs and perceptions about alcohol through such programs have little long-term effect because social structures, public policies, drinking models, and other antecedent dimensions of the environment are typically left unchanged. Specific knowledge and beliefs about alcohol might be affected, but the deeper social meanings attached to alcohol use, the patterns of social interaction affecting those socially shared meanings, the models of drinking, and the availability of alcohol remain unchanged and continue to encourage youth drinking. Furthermore, factors affecting drinking do not all operate through the mediating influence of cognitive/perceptual variables; they have direct effects as well. Legal, economic, and physical availability of alcohol therefore directly affect drinking behavior; they also operate indirectly by creating perceptions.

Social structures, modified by the degree to which people are integrated into them, affect social interaction patterns (paths B–J and B–G–J) and affect exposure to drinking models (path B–I). In addition, however, exposure to drinking models is importantly affected by: (a) public policy concerning media advertising and depiction of alcohol use in media programming (path A–I) and (b) market mechanisms that respond to and stimulate demand for alcohol (path C–I). Public policy also directly affects formal social controls (A–E), as well as the legal, economic, and physical availability of alcohol (A–D, A–F, A–H, respectively), all of which in turn affect drinking directly as well as through their influence on the meanings and perceptions of alcohol use.

Biological/pharmacological factors also play a role (L–P), although such effects are minor for the majority of drinkers. Consuming alcohol, for example, may be intrinsically rewarding because of the psychopharmacological actions of alcohol in the body. The rewarding dimensions of alcohol use, however, are largely socially learned meanings rather than solely the outcome of the intrinsic biological processes resulting from alcohol ingestion (Akers, 1992).

Social roles, including those labeled as deviant or problem, as well as other widespread social roles, such as that of salesperson or college student, affect drinking directly by offering more opportunities to drink (K–P), and they affect drinking indirectly by occupying such roles on alcohol-related cognitions and perceptions (K–O–P).

General personality characteristics, such as self-esteem and locus of control, may be correlated with drinking behavior. These personality characteristics are primarily the result of the cumulation of past and current socialization; in other words, they result from past and current experience in social interactions, which are in turn influenced by a variety of social and institutional structures. We therefore view self-esteem or locus of control not as causes of drinking but rather as correlates of drinking, because both drinking and general personality characteristics are strongly influenced by common antecedent factors in the environment.

IMPLICATIONS FOR PREVENTION

The many factors shown in Fig. 10.1 are not independent causes of drinking, they interact in a web of social influences. They can be distinguished by their causal distance from drinking behavior and the degree to which they operate at the macro or socioenvironmental level versus the micro or individual level. Alcohol cognitions and perceptions are conceptually close or proximate to drinking behavior, and they would therefore be expected to have higher correlations with drinking than the more distal causal factors (i.e., those on the left half of Fig. 10.1). Distal factors are more important for long-term change, however. Changing a proximate cause of drinking has, at best, a short-term effect, because without changes in the antecedent socioenvironmental conditions, the proximate factors quickly revert to their original state. If the action program that is focused on proximate causes is temporary, those exposed typically exhibit only temporary changes in attitudes and behavior. Even if those experiencing a temporary program are permanently changed, the effect on the total population is minimal because new cohorts of youths who were not exposed to the prevention program are constantly emerging. This has already been verified in smoking prevention research, in which school-based programs had effects for up to 2 or 3 years but the same programs implemented along with a broader community intervention effort demonstrated effects up to high-school graduation, 5 years after the school-based program ended (Perry et al., 1992).

Our most intensive prevention programs that target proximate causes of drinking expose youths to program materials and no-drinking messages only a few hours a week. In contrast, young people are exposed to the broader social environment of pro-drinking messages for the remainder of their waking hours. As a result, effective efforts to reduce youth drinking require a major focus on changing the community- and societal-level factors that encourage youth alcohol use and require attention to theories of action that recognize ways all participants, including the youths themselves, can become agents in the constant re-creation of their environments.

It should be noted that etiological theories of young people's alcohol use are in some ways conceptually distinct from theories of intervention or change. Each of the theories discussed previously has specific implications for action. Each of these implications requires a theory of change to direct actual efforts, such as the systematic introduction of positive and credible role models or the process of enactment of community-wide or society-wide alcohol policies. In short, it is one thing to know that a specific dimension of the environment must be changed to reduce youth drinking, but it is another thing to know how to change that factor.

Effective intervention efforts to reduce adolescent alcohol use require simultaneous and consistent messages and actions at multiple levels in the society. If the message is that adolescent alcohol use is unacceptable, both demand and supply reduction approaches are needed. Demand reduction, such as learning to identify alcohol-use influences as well as acquiring skills to resist those influences, can be paired with actual reductions in the socioenvironmental conditions that encourage use. These conditions include peer norms around alcohol use, parental support and modeling, alcohol availability and acceptability, and alcohol advertising (Atkin, in press). The potential for success improves as more levels of the social environment provide no-use messages to young people. Because change in these influences is feasible at the personal, interpersonal, and community levels but is more difficult to achieve at the societal or global levels, the community becomes the natural unit for changing socioenvironmental conditions.

Community-change strategies can incorporate multiple objectives and multiple levels of action—through schools, parents, community ordinances, and other dimensions of public policy, institutional policies and practices, and social networks. The social world of adolescents (as represented by the norms, values, opportunities, and support provided by families, schools, and community settings) should consistently and cogently encourage reflection on the implications of alcohol use and the dimensions of social environments that encourage use. The current situation in most communities is that some elements (e.g., school health education curricula) discourage drinking whereas many other elements (e.g., low-priced alcohol readily sold or provided to youths) encourage drinking (Wagenaar et al., 1993).

Several large-scale community change projects have been implemented and carefully evaluated, including projects on alcohol (Casswell & Stewart, 1990; Ritson, 1985; Rootman & Moser, 1985; Speare & Buka, 1990; Stout, 1989; Wallack, 1985; Wallack & Barrows, 1982–1983), drinking and driving (Worden, Flynn, Merrill, Waller, & Haugh, 1989), traffic safety (Hingson, Howland, & Levenson, 1988), other drugs (Johnson et al., 1989; Pentz, Dwyer, et al., 1989), tobacco (Altman, Foster, & Rasenick-Douss Tye, 1989; Forster, Hourigan, & Weigum, 1990; Lichtenstein, Wallack, & Pechacek, 1990), and cardiovascular disease risk reduction (Blackburn, 1983; Farquhar et al., 1985; McAlister, Puska, Salonen, Tuomilehto, & Koskela, 1982; Perry, Klepp, & Shultz, 1988; Puska, Salonen, Nissinen, & Tuomilehto, 1983).

The most ambitious community-wide drug abuse prevention research program completed to date is the Midwestern Prevention Project (MPP; Pentz, Dwyer et al., 1989). The MPP includes all communities within the Kansas City (Kansas and Missouri) and Indianapolis (Indiana) metropolitan areas. Within each of these two areas, cohorts of adolescents were assigned by school to intervention or delayed-intervention control conditions, with intervention programs targeted initially at sixth- or seventh-grade students. The intervention program consisted of a 10-session school-based social skills curriculum; 10 homework assignments to be completed with parents or guardians; mass-media coverage using television, radio, and print; community organization; and policy change. In the first 2 years of the project, 22,500 adolescents participated in the school and community intervention. Analyses from students in 42 schools ($N = 5,008$) indicated a lower prevalence rate of cigarette, alcohol, and marijuana use at

1-year follow-up for those exposed to the school intervention (17% vs. 24% for cigarette smoking, 11% vs. 16% for alcohol use, and 7% vs. 10% for marijuana use in the last month; Pentz, Dwyer et al., 1989). Similar results were observed after 2 years for a longitudinal panel of students from eight schools in Kansas City (N = 1,122; Pentz, MacKinnon et al., 1989). Third-year results demonstrated sustained impact only on tobacco and marijuana use but with equivalent reductions for adolescents at lower or higher risk (Johnson et al., 1990). The MPP is particularly important because it demonstrates the feasibility of a large-scale community-wide effort focused exclusively on youth, because of its impact on those at high risk, and because it has considerable methodological strength. The program's long-term impact on tobacco and marijuana use is still to be determined. The apparent lack of long-term impact on alcohol use is noteworthy.

Our review of previous community projects provides several insights that guide our current efforts. In previous projects, educational interventions alone were inadequate to achieve a long-term change in health behavior. Repeatedly, investigators realized they were attempting a health education and behavior change intervention within a broader environment that is generally hostile to the intervention goals. Hostility as used here does not imply intentionality, only that the natural consequence of competing community interests results in segments of the environment that are opposed to successful prevention efforts, particularly when they threaten benefits that some are accruing from the status quo. The hostile environment is particularly evident when attempting to change mass behavior in a way that threatens the interests of large industries, such as tobacco and alcohol producers, distributors, and retailers (Worden, 1979). The hostile environment is also characterized by norms supporting risky behavior—or at least ambivalence about such behavior. As a result, successful interventions must directly address the environment that is permitting or encouraging risky behaviors. Previous intervention trials that began to address broader environmental contributors to health problems have often faced controversy and political conflict (Casswell & Stewart, 1990). Addressing environmental contributors to health problems leads to a significantly higher degree of unpredictability, as political forces coalesce in favor of and in opposition to interventions that may successfully affect the consumption of commercially sold products. Despite the complexity and unpredictability of interventions focused on socioenvironmental change, it is apparent that long-term reductions in youth alcohol use will require such efforts.

It is worth noting that another major community project, the Trauma Reduction Trial, is also based on the conclusion that broader social and environmental change is needed to successfully address community alcohol problems. The Trauma Reduction Trial is a quasi-experimental study of two pairs of communities in which one community in each pair implements a package of programs designed to reduce alcohol-related injury (Holder, personal communication). The project is in progress and results are not yet available.

Two large-scale community trial projects that evolved out of the theoretical framework presented here are currently in progress. Both are designed to reduce underage drinking: Project Northland focuses on initiation into alcohol use among 10- to 14-year-olds, and Communities Mobilizing for Change on Alcohol (CMCA) focuses on alcohol use and intoxication among 15- to 20-year-olds. Northland combines school curricula with peer leader, parent, and community support components, and CMCA organizes and empowers community residents to change institutional and public policies and practices regarding the accessibility of alcohol to youth. Thus, CMCA focuses more on the left two columns in Fig. 10.1, and Northland focuses more on the middle and right side of Fig. 10.1. Both projects represent the integration of concepts from multiple theoretical perspectives. Both projects are randomized trials with large numbers of communities and both collect a comprehensive series of process and outcome data. The two projects are critically different, however, in the theoretical foundation for the intervention efforts and in how the intervention is implemented. Northland has a model alcohol education curriculum, developed outside the community, that is implemented through a project coordinator in schools and with parents in each community. In contrast, CMCA has a local organizer who maps the power structure of each community, organizes a local strategy team, brokers diverse interests, and works with the full range of community sectors to develop strategies for changing the community environment, institutional practices, and public policies regarding alcohol. Each project is now reviewed in more detail.[5]

CMCA PROJECT: COMMUNITIES
MOBILIZING FOR CHANGE ON ALCOHOL

This 15-community, 5-year randomized trial is designed to: (a) develop community-based strategies, designed by community members (in-

---

[5]Both the CMCA and Northland projects are in the early phase of implementation. A full range of baseline data have been collected; information on the effect of the interventions will be available in several years, after follow-up data are collected.

cluding youth), for public action on the full range of alcohol-related social and health problems among youth; (b) reduce the availability of alcohol to young people under the legal age; (c) reduce alcohol consumption among those under age 21; and (d) reduce injury, morbidity, and other health and social problems related to alcohol use among young people.

Evaluation of intervention effectiveness will include measurement of: (a) perceived and actual degree of alcohol accessibility to youths in the study communities; (b) differential degree of access in terms of characteristics of individual purchasers, social situations, social groups, alcohol selling establishments, and communities; and (c) a range of alcohol-related behaviors and outcomes using longitudinal survey methods and time-series analyses of archival records. The project is an outgrowth of previous research demonstrating the effects of public policy and the social environment on youth alcohol use (O'Malley & Wagenaar, 1991; Wagenaar, 1983, 1986). The CMCA project is also developing new theory concerning public action on alcohol, with the participation of a broad interdisciplinary research team, including political and social theorists (Boyte, 1984, 1989). In short, the project is based on three developing streams of theory, one on the determinants of youth alcohol use, a second on the role of public and institutional policies in preventing alcohol problems, and a third on organizing communities to take collective action to alter the environment regarding alcohol, which is the subject of a forthcoming article by Wolfson et al.

Specific objectives of the CMCA organizing effort are to change community policies and procedures so as to reduce: (a) the accessibility of alcohol to youth; (b) the number and proportion of alcohol outlets selling to underage individuals; (c) accessibility of alcohol to young people, whether the source of alcohol is commercial establishments, parents, other adults, or other youths; (d) youth and adult support or tolerance of underage purchase and consumption of alcohol; (e) the prevalence, quantity, and frequency of alcohol consumption among youths 15 to 20 years of age; and (f) the incidence of alcohol-related health and social problems among young people of these ages.

The CMCA project is distinguished from most previous work in that we are collaborating with community leaders to develop locally designed strategies for action. Thus, the community is not just a site for the intervention, and it is not simply an instrument for professional manipulation or direction, but rather, it is an integral agent in project design and implementation. We are testing the effects of a theory-based process of community public action, from which new theoretical insights can be generated rather than evaluating the effects of a single intervention strategy or activity. Our objective is to enhance community capacity for public action, which should result in changes in community policies and practices. Sample action strategies are shown in Table 10.1. The exact set of strategies implemented in a given community will be the result of public deliberations by residents (both youth and adults) mobilized in each community.

The communities were selected for the organizing effort randomly, not on the basis of the existence of community coalitions, other measures of readiness for action, or the extent of problems with youth drinking. Random assignment to condition is a core dimension of our research design that very few community trials implement; it dramatically improves the internal validity of the study, permitting causal inferences with a high degree of confidence. All communities within a 235-mile radius of the Twin Cities that met our size criterion and did not already have a major externally funded youth alcohol project (e.g., Center for Substance Abuse Prevention community partnership grant) were in the pool of eligible communities. After baseline surveys were completed in 15 communities, communities were randomly assigned to treatment or control condition. Thus, the project tests the ability of the organizing theory and methods to activate randomly selected communities to address dimensions of social, policy, and institutional environments that foster underage drinking.

Evaluation of the project is multidimensional, using a wide variety of process and outcome measures collected from the full set of 15 communities. We discussed the complexity of the trade-offs between the demands of science and the demands of practice in designing such a trial in a previous article (Wagenaar & Wolfson, 1992), and a comprehensive discussion of CMCA research design, data collection, and analysis issues is also available (Wagenaar, Murray, Wolfson, Forster, & Finnegan, 1994). Outcome data are being collected through school surveys of 9th and 12th graders in each community; telephone surveys of 18- to 20-year-olds; surveys of alcohol merchants; direct youth purchase attempts at on- and off-sale alcohol outlets; content analyses of print media; monitoring of governmental and organizational meeting minutes, policies, and practices; and census, police, hospital and other records on community characteristics and alcohol-related health and social problems. In addition, continuous process evaluation data are being collected by organizers and project staff in each intervention community.

TABLE 10.1
CMCA Project Action Strategy Examples

Community enforcement actions

Enforcement of laws prohibiting provision of alcohol to minors.

Decoy operations on outlets.

Comprehensive approach to alcohol-access laws.

Police attempt to identify source of alcohol in incidents.

Police or public safety departments notify retailers of age of sale laws and enforcement policy.

Citizen monitoring of outlets selling to youth.

Enforcement of institutional policies (school, workplace).

Enforcement of community regulations regarding alcohol.

Community institutional policies

Written policies at alcohol establishments on underage sales.

   Mandatory training for new managers/servers/sellers; updated training for continuing employees.

   Check IDs of all customers who appear younger than 30.

   Employee rewards for identifying false ID.

   All beer kegs sold have purchaser's name and address recorded.

   Eliminate sales practices that encourage underage consumption (e.g., pitcher service at bars).

Alcohol-free recreational opportunities for youth.

Alcohol-free public spaces.

Eliminate alcohol ads and promotion at public events where youth are present.

Alcohol-free events and trips for youth-related associations.

Alcohol-free schools and school events.

Community-initiated regulations

Restrict sales at locations where teenagers have easy access (e.g., gas stations and convenience stores near schools).

Mandate training of all managers and servers/sellers in alcohol outlets.

Restrict sales practices that particularly encourage underage consumption (e.g., pitcher service at bars).

Zone alcohol-free public areas.

Planning and zoning ordinances.

Restrict types/numbers/placement of billboards or other advertisements.

Reduce hours of sale, early closing hours to reduce nighttime off-sale access.

Public hearings for new and renewed liquor licenses.

Restrict alcohol sales at community events.

Require outlets to have written policies and plans to prevent underage purchases.

Community information dissemination

Create social pressure against providing alcohol to youth.

Education of alcohol establishments including: management and server/seller training, identification of underage youth, and false ID.

Educate alcohol establishments and other community adults about liability laws.

Encourage news reporting of alcohol-related problems.

Media advocacy.

Speakers bureau.

Call attention to ads that appeal to youth.

Counter-ads and counter promotions.

Educate community groups (e.g., church and civic groups) on actions they can take.

Youth education.

Parent education.

PROJECT NORTHLAND: PARTNERSHIPS FOR
YOUTH HEALTH

Project Northland was designed to test the efficacy of a community-wide effort to prevent alcohol use among 10- to 14-year-olds. The aim of the project is to reduce the incidence and prevalence of alcohol use among a cohort of young adolescents, the Class of 1998, who were sixth-grade students during the 1991–1992 school year. This cohort is being exposed to 3 years of school-based skills training curricula, peer leadership, parental involvement, and community-wide policy changes around the use of alcohol by adolescents. The components of the intervention are the outgrowth of previous research of the past decade that appeared both to be effective and feasible given the aims of the study (Forster et al., 1990; Pentz, Dwyer, & MacKinnon, 1989; Perry, Klepp, & Sillers, 1989; Perry, Luepker et al., 1989).

The study sample consists of all adolescents in the Class of 1998 in 24 public-school districts from six northeastern counties of Minnesota ($N = 2,419$). These counties were selected because this area of Minnesota is at very high risk for alcohol-related problems. Among the 87 counties in Minnesota, for example, the number one and three counties for a composite of alcohol-related problems (morbidity and mortality) are in this region (National Institute on Alcohol Abuse and Alcoholism [NIAAA], 1991). The six Project Northland counties include a total population of about 235,000 people who are primarily of European ethnic composition. Adolescents from four Native-American (Ojibway) reservations in this region attend public schools in the 24 school districts, and they generally exhibit a higher prevalence of alcohol-related problems. Fourteen districts were randomly assigned to an immediate education program condition, with the other 10 serving as controls. The latter 10 school districts, assigned to the delayed program condition, will receive educational materials in 1994.

The 3-year intervention program includes planned parental involvement, peer-led school-based programs, peer leadership training, and community-wide policy changes in the 14 educational program communities. Adolescents in the Class of 1998 will be exposed to the intervention during their sixth, seventh, and eighth grades (1991–1994). In the sixth grade, the students took part in the Slick Tracy Home Team Program, in which they were given activity packets to complete at home with their parents. The packets included the Slick Tracy comic strip, a follow-up activity or game for parents to participate in with their child, questions for the sixth grader to consider, and Northland

Notes for Parents. The students returned a card to their classrooms that indicated their participation as well as that of their parents. At the end of this program, Slick Tracy Nights were held at every school at which student alcohol-related projects and posters were shared with parents and other community members. Peer leaders were elected by their classmates and trained by University of Minnesota staff to encourage participation and to lead short activities in the classroom that complemented the themes of the comic book series. Finally, community-wide task forces were convened and took part in 2-day workshops to consider community-wide activities and policy options that would be feasible within each of their communities. Each community implemented a kickoff activity for Project Northland in the spring, 1992. Similar multilevel programs, linking students, parents, school personnel, and community representatives, are now ongoing for seventh graders in the second year of intervention. These are summarized in Table 10.2.

The Project Northland intervention program is unique because of the multiple levels of programs that are being implemented simultaneously and consistently in all of the communities. Each community implements the parental involvement programs, the classroom-based resistance skills curricula, alcohol-free extracurricular events for adolescents that are directed by peers, and community-wide activities and policy changes. Significant guidance is provided by the University researchers, staff, and community coordinators who represent Project Northland and yet are members of these northern Minnesota communities. The intervention program is also unique in that it explicitly links students with parents, parents with the school, students with school activities, and students and parents with the larger community. The multiple levels of intervention are therefore not distinct, but rather, they create a web of consistent ideas and messages concerning adolescent alcohol use at a time when onset is most likely to occur.

Evaluation methods for Project Northland were selected to measure change at five levels in each community. They consist of: (a) a student survey for the Class of 1998 students, (b) a parent survey for the parents of the Class of 1998, (c) a community leader survey of five specific leaders in each of the communities adjacent to the 24 school districts, (d) an observation study of potential underage buying of alcohol in all off-sale outlets in the region, and (e) a survey of alcohol merchants. Other process measures, such as participation in activities, monitoring of local newspapers, and feedback from task force members, are being implemented so that the lessons learned through this multilevel complex study can be disseminated.

TABLE 10.2
Project Northland Program Components

Years	Program	Description
School-based and peer leadership programs		
1991–1992	The Slick Tracy Program	Four sessions of peer-led activities in class to introduce Slick Tracy Home Team concepts.
1992–1993	Amazing Alternatives!	Eight sessions of peer-led activities around resisting influences to use alcohol and normative expectations.
1992–1993	Alternatives!	Multiple extracurricular social events planned by peer leaders for all seventh-grade students.
1993–1994	Shifting Gears	Eight sessions of peer-led activities around nondrinking, safe driving, and community action.
Parent involvement programs		
1991–1992	The Slick Tracy Home Team	4 weeks of activities for sixth graders and parents to complete at home regarding adolescent alcohol use issues, presented in comic book format.
1991–1992	The Slick Tracy Night	A family night for sixth graders to share health-related projects and posters with their families.
1992–1993	The Amazing Alternatives Home Program	4 weeks of activities for seventh graders and parents to complete at home.
1992–1993	The Amazing Alternatives Awesome Autumn Party	A fall-alternatives fun night for the family.
1993–1994	Shifting Gears Parents Nights	A series of forums on adolescent health issues.
Community-wide programs		
1991–1992	Task-Force Development	Community leaders are convened by Project Northland coordinators, policy options are prioritized, and community kickoff is implemented.
1992–1993	Adolescent Alcohol-Use Access	Task forces implement education and enforcement to reduce teenage access to alcohol to create alcohol-free alternative events.
1993–1994	Policy Development	Task forces develop and plan implementation of new policies regarding adolescent alcohol use.

CONCLUSIONS

Effective efforts to reduce youth drinking and associated health and social problems must focus on change at multiple levels—family, social groups, community, and society. Attempting to change drinking behavior without direct attention to the socioenvironmental conditions generating alcohol use are of limited utility; at best, short-term changes in small segments of the population are achieved. In contrast, a focus on the broader environment that encourages drinking can lead to long-term reductions in drinking across the entire population of young people. Knowing that prevention efforts must focus on changing the broader environment is only the first step. The next step is learning how to change public policy, social and institutional structures, market mechanisms, alcohol availability, environmental drinking models, and lack of social integration in ways that reduce youth drinking. We need to move on to the development and testing of theories and strategies of planned social change (Chin & Benne, 1985; Zaltman & Duncan, 1977), applying lessons from that literature to youth alcohol use.

Effective prevention programs are fundamentally about changing society. Social change regarding alcohol use requires changes in public policy—facing the economic and political power of alcohol producers and sellers, who have a vested interest in encouraging alcohol use. It requires addressing the anomie, limited opportunity structure, and lack of social integration of large numbers of young people in our society. Prevention programs must now increase their efforts in this broader social environment to achieve continued success in reducing alcohol-related health and social problems among young people.

ACKNOWLEDGMENTS

Preparation of this chapter was supported in part by Grant R01 AA90142, to Alexander C. Wagenaar, and Grant R01 AA08596, to Cheryl Perry, from the NIAAA.

We thank all the scientists involved in the CMCA and Northland projects at the University of Minnesota for their contributions to our thinking on these issues. This chapter reflects only part of the full interdisciplinary diversity of the large group of investigators on these two projects. We also thank Jan Howard and two reviewers for their insightful comments. Views expressed here remain solely our responsibility.

REFERENCES

Akers, R. L. (1992). *Drugs, alcohol, and society: Social structure, process, and policy.* Belmont, CA: Wadsworth.
Altman, D. G, Foster, L., & Rasenick-Douss Tye, J. B. (1989). Reducing the illegal sale of

cigarettes to minors. *Journal of the American Medical Association, 261,* 80–83.

Atkin, C. K. (in press). Survey and experimental research on alcohol advertising effects. In S. E. Martin & P. Mail (Eds.), *Effects of mass media on the use and abuse of alcohol.* Rockville, MD: National Institute on Alcohol Abuse and Alcoholism.

Bailey, S. L. (1992). Adolescents' multisubstance use patterns: The role of heavy alcohol and cigarette use. *American Journal of Public Health, 82,* 1220–1224.

Bandura, A. (1977). *Social learning theory.* Englewood Cliffs, NJ: Prentice-Hall.

Bandura, A. (1986). *Social foundations of thought and action: A social cognitive theory.* Englewood Cliffs, NJ: Prentice-Hall.

Becker, G. S., & Murphy, K. M. (1988). A theory of rational addiction. *Journal of Political Economy, 96,* 675–700.

Blackburn, H. (1983). Research and demonstration projects in community cardiovascular disease prevention. *Journal of Public Health Policy, 4,* 398–421.

Blumer, H. (1969). *Symbolic interactionism: Perspective and method.* Englewood Cliffs, NJ: Prentice-Hall.

Boyte, H. (1984). *Community is possible.* New York: Harper & Row.

Boyte, H. (1989). *Commonwealth: A return to citizen politics.* New York: Free Press.

Breed, W., & DeFoe, J. R. (1982). Effecting media change: The role of cooperative consultation on alcohol topics. *Journal of Communication, 32,* 88–99.

Breed, W., & DeFoe, J. R. (1984). Drinking and smoking on television, 1950–1982. *Journal of Public Health Policy, 5,* 257–270.

Bruun, K., Edwards, G., Lumio, M., Mäkelä, K., Pan, L., Popham, R. E., Room, R., Schmidt, W., Skog, O., Sulkunen, P., & Österberg, E. (1975). *Alcohol control policies in public health perspective.* Helsinki: The Finnish Foundation for Alcohol Studies.

Cappell, H., & Greeley, J. (1987). Alcohol and tension reduction: An update on research and theory. In H. T. Blane & K. E. Leonard (Eds.), *Psychological theories of drinking and alcoholism* (pp. 15–22). New York: Guilford.

Casswell, S., & Stewart, L. (1990). Aftermath of the community action project on alcohol. In *Research, action, and the community* (Prevention Monograph No. 4, pp. 213–224). Rockville, MD: Office for Substance Abuse Prevention.

Chin, R., & Benne, K. D. (1985). General strategies for effecting changes in human systems. In W. G. Bennis, K. D. Benne, & R. Chin (Eds.), *The planning of change* (4th ed.; pp. 22–45). New York: Holt, Rinehart & Winston.

Clinard, M. B., & Meier, R. F. (1989). *Sociology of deviant behavior* (7th ed.). New York: Holt, Rinehart & Winston.

Cloninger, C. R. (1983). Genetic and environmental factors in the development of alcoholism. *Journal of Psychiatric Treatment and Evaluation, 5,* 487–496.

Coate, D., & Grossman, M. (1988). Effects of alcoholic beverage prices and legal drinking ages on youth alcohol use. *Journal of Law and Economics, 31,* 145–171.

Cohen, J., & Cohen, P. (1983). Applied multiple regression/correlation analysis for the behavioral sciences. Hillsdale, NJ: Lawrence Erlbaum Associates.

Cooley, C. H. (1962). *Human nature and the social order.* New York: Schocken.

Corcoran, K. J., & Parker, P. S. (1991). Alcohol expectancy questionnaire tension reduction scale as a predictor of alcohol consumption in a stressful situation. *Addictive Behaviors, 16,* 129-137.

Farquhar, J. W., Fortmann, S. P., Maccoby, N., Haskell, W. L., Williams, P. T., Flora, J. A., Taylor, C. B., Brown, B. W., Solomon, D. S., & Hulley, S. B. (1985). The Stanford Five-City Project. *American Journal of Epidemiology, 122,* 323–334.

Farris, R., Malone, T. B., & Lilliefors, H. (1976). *A comparison of alcohol involvement in exposed and injured drivers: Phases 1 and 2* (Tech. Rep. No. DOT–HS–801–826). Washington, DC: National Highway Traffic Safety Administration.

Fenichel, O. (1945). *The psychoanalytic theory of psychosis.* New York: Norton.

Forster, J. L., Hourigan, M., & Weigum, J. (1990, May). *The movement to restrict children's access to tobacco in Minnesota.* Paper presented at the Surgeon General's Interagency Committee on Smoking and Health, Washington, DC.

Gerbner, G. (1990). Stories that hurt: Tobacco, alcohol, and other drugs in the mass media. In H. Resnik (Ed.), *Youth and drugs: Society's mixed messages* (DHHS Publication No. ADM 90–1689, pp. 53–127). Washington, DC: Office for Substance Abuse Prevention.

Gilligan, S. B., Reich, T., & Cloninger, R. (1987). Etiologic heterogeneity in alcoholism. *Genetics Epidemiology, 4,* 395-414.

Gormezano, I., Prokasy, W. F., & Thompson, R. F. (Eds.). (1987). *Classical conditioning* (3rd ed.). Hillsdale, NJ: Lawrence Erlbaum Associates.

Hingson, R. W., Howland, J., & Levenson, S. (1988). Effects of legislative reform to reduce drunken driving and alcohol-related traffic fatalities. *Public Health Reports, 103,* 659–666.

Holder, H. D. (Ed.). (1987). *Control issues in alcohol abuse prevention: Strategies for states and communities.* Greenwich, CT: JAI.

Hrubec, Z., & Omenn, G. S. (1981). Evidence of genetic predisposition to alcoholic cirrhosis and psychosis: Twin concordance for alcoholism and its biological end points by zyosity among male veterans. *Alcoholism: Clinical and Experimental Research, 5,* 207–215.

Jessor, R. (1987). Problem-behavior theory, psychosocial development, and adolescent problem drinking. *British Journal of Addiction, 82,* 331–342.

Jessor, R., & Jessor, S. L. (1977). *Problem behavior and psychosocial development: A longitudinal study of youth.* New York: Academic.

Johnson, C. A., Pentz, M. A., Weber, M. D., Dwyer, J. H., Baer, N., MacKinnon, D. P., & Hansen, W. B. (1989). Relative effectiveness of comprehensive community programming for drug abuse prevention with high-risk and low-risk adolescents. *Journal of Consulting and Clinical Psychology, 58,* 447–456.

Johnston, L. D., O'Malley, P. M., & Bachman, J. G. (1991). *Drug use among American high school seniors, college students and young adults, 1975–1990.* (DHHS Publication No. ADM 91–1813). Washington, DC: U.S. Government Printing Office.

Kandel, D. B. (1975). Stages in adolescent involvement in drug use. *Science, 190,* 912–914.

Kandel, D. B. (1989). Issues of sequencing of adolescent drug use and other problem behaviors. *Drugs and Society, 3,* 55–76.

Kandel, D., Yamaguchi, K., & Chen, K. (1992). Stages of progression in drug involvement from adolescence to adulthood: Further evidence for the Gateway Theory. *Journal of Studies on Alcohol, 53,* 447–457.

Kendler, K. S., Heath, A. C., Neale, M. C., Kessler, R. C., & Eaves, L. J. (1992). A population-based twin study of alcoholism in women. *Journal of the American Medical Association, 268,* 1877–1882.

Klein, S. B., & Mowrer, R. R. (Eds.). (1989). *Contemporary learning theories: Pavlovian conditioning and the status of traditional learning theory.* Hillsdale, NJ: Lawrence Erlbaum Associates.

Krohn, M. D., & Massey, J. L. (1980). Social control and delinquent behavior: An examination of the elements of the social bond. *The Sociological Quarterly, 21,* 529–543.

Lewin, K., Dembo, T., Feslinger, L., & Sears, P. S. (1946). Level of aspiration. In J. Hunt

(Ed.), *Personality and the behavior disorders* (Vol. 1, pp. 333–378). New York: Ronald.

Lichtenstein, E., Wallack, L., & Pechacek, T. F. (1990). *Introduction to the Community Intervention Trial for Smoking Cessation (COMMIT).* Unpublished manuscript.

Lilienfeld, A. M., & Lilienfeld, D. E. (1980). *Foundations of epidemiology* (2nd ed.). New York: Oxford University Press.

Lowery, S. A. (1980). Soap and booze in the afternoon. *Journal of Studies on Alcohol, 41,* 829–837.

McAlister, A., Puska, P., Salonen, J. T., Tuomilehto, J., & Koskela, K. (1982). Theory and action for health promotion. *American Journal of Public Health, 72,* 43–50.

Mead, G. H. (1934). *Mind, self and society from the standpoint of a social behaviorist.* Chicago: University of Chicago Press.

Merton, R. K. (1968). *Social theory and social structure.* New York: Free Press.

Moskowitz, J. M. (1989). The primary prevention of alcohol problems: A critical review of the research literature. *Journal of Studies on Alcohol, 50,* 54–88.

National Institute on Alcohol Abuse and Alcoholism. (1991). *County alcohol problem indicators, 1979–1985: Vol. 3. U.S. Alcohol epidemiologic data reference manual.* Rockville, MD: Author.

O'Malley, P., & Wagenaar, A. C. (1991). Effects of minimum drinking age laws on alcohol use, related behaviors, and traffic crash involvement among American youth 1976–1987. *Journal of Studies on Alcohol, 52,* 478–491.

Orcutt, J. D., & Harvey, L. K. (1991). The temporal patterning of tension reduction: Stress and alcohol use on weekdays and weekends. *Journal of Studies on Alcohol, 52,* 415–424.

Ornstein, S. I. (1980). Control of alcohol consumption through price increases. *Journal of Studies on Alcohol, 41,* 807–817.

Pentz, M. A., Dwyer, J. H., MacKinnon, D. P., Flay, B. R., Hansen, W. B., Wang, E. Y., & Johnson, C. A. (1989). A multicommunity trial for primary prevention of adolescent drug abuse: Effects on drug use prevalence. *Journal of the American Medical Association, 261,* 3259–3266.

Pentz, M. A., MacKinnon, D. P., Flay, B. R., Hansen, W. B., Johnson, C. A., & Dwyer, J. H. (1989). Primary prevention of chronic diseases in adolescence: Effects of the Midwestern Prevention Project on tobacco use. *American Journal of Epidemiology, 130,* 713–724.

Perry, C. L., Kelder, S. H., Murray, D. M., & Klepp, K-I. (1992). Community-wide smoking prevention: Long-term outcomes of the Minnesota heart health program and the class of 1989 study. *American Journal of Public Health, 82,* 1210–1216.

Perry, C. L., Klepp, K-I., & Shultz, J. (1988). Primary prevention of cardiovascular disease. *Journal of Consulting and Clinical Psychology, 56,* 358–364.

Perry, C. L., Klepp, K-I., & Sillers, C. (1989). Community-wide strategies for cardiovascular health: The Minnesota heart health youth program. *Health Education Research, 4,* 87–101.

Perry, C. L., Luepker, R. V., Murray, D. M., Hearn, M. D., Halper, A., Dudovitz, B., Maile, M. D., & Smyth, M. (1989). Parent involvement with children's health promotion: A one-year follow-up of the Minnesota Home Team. *Health Education Quarterly, 16,* 171–180.

Postman, N., Nystrom, C., Strate, L., & Weingartner, C. (1987). *Myths, men, & beer: An analysis of beer commercials on broadcast television.* Falls Church, VA: AAA Foundation for Traffic Safety.

Puska, P., Salonen, J., Nissinen, A., & Tuomilehto, J. (1983). The North Karelia Project.

Preventive Medicine, 12, 191–195.

Ritson, E. B. (1985). *Community response to alcohol-related problems* (Public Health Rep. No. 81). Geneva: World Health Organization.

Rootman, I., & Moser, J. (1985). *Community response to alcohol-related problems.* Washington, DC: National Institute on Alcohol Abuse and Alcoholism.

Ross, H. L. (1992). *Confronting drunk driving: Social policy for saving lives.* New Haven, CT: Yale University Press.

Rychtarik, R. G., Fairbank, J. A., Allen, C. M., Foy, D. W., & Drabman, R. S. (1983). Alcohol use in television programming: Effects on children's behavior. *Addictive Behaviors, 8,* 19–22.

Schur, E. M. (1971). *Labeling deviant behavior: Its sociological implications.* New York: Harper & Row.

Skinner, B. F. (1953). *Science and human behavior.* New York: Free Press.

Speare, M. C., & Buka, S. L. (1990, January). *The Rhode Island alcohol/injury prevention project.* Paper presented at the conference for Evaluating Community Prevention Strategies: Alcohol and Other Drugs, San Diego.

Stout R. L. (1989). Prevention experiments in the context of ongoing community processes: Opportunities or obstacles for research. In H. D. Holder & J. M. Howard (Eds.), *Community prevention trials for alcohol problems: Methodological issues* (pp. 121–136). Westport, CT: Praeger.

Sutherland, E. H., & Cressey, D. R. (1970). *Criminology* (8th ed.). Philidelphia: Lippincott.

Syme, S. L. (1986). Social determinants of health and disease. In J. Last (Ed.), *Public health and preventive medicine* (pp. 953–970). Norwalk, CT: Appleton-Century-Crofts.

Wagenaar, A. C. (1983). *Alcohol, young drivers, and traffic accidents: Effects of minimum-age laws.* Lexington, MA: Lexington.

Wagenaar, A. C. (1986). Preventing highway crashes by raising the legal minimum age for drinking: The Michigan experience six years later. *Journal of Safety Research, 17,* 101–109.

Wagenaar, A. C., & Farrell, S. (1989). Alcohol beverage control policies: Their role in preventing alcohol-impaired driving. In U.S. Department of Health and Human Services, *Surgeon General's workshop on drunk driving, background papers* (pp. 1–14). Washington DC: Office of the Surgeon General.

Wagenaar, A. C., Finnegan, J. R., Wolfson, M., Anstine, P. S., Williams, C. L., & Perry, C. L. (1993). Where and how adolescents obtain alcoholic beverages. *Public Health Reports, 108,* 459–464.

Wagenaar, A. C., Murray, D. M., Wolfson, M., Forster, J. L., Finnegan, J. R. (1994). Communities mobilizing for change on alcohol: Design of a randomized community trial. *Journal of Community Psychology* (CSAP Special Issue), 79–101.

Wagenaar, A. C., & Wolfson, M. (1992). Trade-offs between science and practice in the design of a randomized community trial. In T. K. Greenfield & R. Zimmerman (Eds.), *Experiences with community action projects: New research in the prevention of alcohol and other drug problems* (pp. 119–129). Rockville, MD: Center for Substance Abuse Prevention. (DHHS Publication No. ADM 93-1976)

Wallack, L. A. (1985). A community approach to the prevention of alcohol-related problems. *International Quarterly of Community Health Education, 5,* 85–102.

Wallack, L. A., & Barrows, D. (1982–1983). Evaluating primary prevention. *International Quarterly of Community Health Education, 3,* 307–336.

Wallack, L. A., Grube, J. W., & Madden, P. A. (1990). Portrayals of alcohol on prime-time television. *Journal of Studies on Alcohol, 51,* 428–436.

Worden, M. A. (1979). Popular and unpopular prevention. *Journal of Drug Issues, summer,* 425–433.

Worden, J. K., Flynn, B. S., Merrill, D. G., Waller, J. A., & Haugh, L. D. (1989). Preventing alcohol-impaired driving through community self-regulation training. *American Journal of Public Health, 79,* 287–290.

Zaltman, G., & Duncan, R. (1977). *Strategies for planned change.* New York: Wiley.

11

Effects of Alcohol Price Policy on Youth: A Summary of Economic Research

Michael Grossman
City University of New York Graduate School and National Bureau of Economic Research

Frank J. Chaloupka
University of Illinois at Chicago and National Bureau of Economic Research

Henry Saffer
Kean College of New Jersey and National Bureau of Economic Research

Adit Laixuthai
University of Illinois at Chicago

Since the mid-1970s, the U.S. Federal government and various state and local governments have campaigned to reduce deaths from motor vehicle accidents by discouraging alcohol abuse. Much of this campaign has focused on teenagers and young adults. This focus has been adopted because motor vehicle accident mortality is the leading cause of death of persons under the age of 35, and alcohol is involved in over half these fatal crashes. In 1984, persons under the age of 25 accounted for 20% of all licensed drivers but 35% of all drivers involved in fatal accidents (National Highway Traffic Safety Administration, 1986). These figures are even more dramatic than they appear because members of the young driver group do not drive nearly as much as older drivers (Voas & Moulden, 1980). Moreover, there is a pronounced negative relationship between age and abuse of or dependence on alcohol (Grant et al., 1991). It is also important to focus on the young because alcohol abuse in adolescence appears to be associated with alcohol abuse in later life (Rachal et al., 1980). Policies to prevent the onset of this behavior in adolescents might therefore be the most effective means to curb it in all segments of the population.

The major element of programs to deter adolescent alcohol abuse has been the upward trend in state minimum legal ages for the purchase and consumption of alcoholic beverages. This trend began with the increase in the legal drinking age in Minnesota from 18 to 19 years of age in 1976, and an additional 27 states had increased their legal drinking age by the time Congress passed the Federal Uniform Drinking Age Act of 1984 (Public Law 98–363). This act pressured all states into raising the minimum legal drinking age to 21 by withholding part of their federal highway funding if they failed to comply. Currently, all 50 states and the District of Columbia have a minimum drinking age of 21 years.[1]

Other elements of the antidrinking campaign have been directed at all segments of the population. The Alcohol Traffic Safety Act of 1983 (Public Law 97–364), for example, provides financial incentives for states to enact and enforce new, more stringent drunk-driving laws. These measures include more severe and certain penalties for conviction of drunk driving, an easing of the standards required for conviction, and increased allocation of resources for the apprehension of drunk drivers. Approximately 500 new state and local laws resulted from this legislation (Ross, 1990). A second example, Public Law 100–690, requires that, as of November 1989, all alcoholic beverages sold in the United States must carry warning labels alerting consumers to such dangers as drunk driving and drinking during pregnancy.

Although these policies are vehicles to discourage alcohol abuse by youths and adults, increased taxation, which results in higher prices, is another policy that might significantly reduce this behavior. This vehicle, however, has been virtually ignored in the antidrinking campaign. In January, 1991, the federal excise tax rates on beer and wine were increased for the first time since November, 1951, and the federal excise tax rate on distilled spirits was raised for only the second time since 1951. The tax on beer doubled from 16¢ per six-pack to 32¢, the tax on

---

[1]The last two Surgeon Generals of United States, Antonia Novello and C. Everett Koop, have advocated policies under which beer and wine companies would stop broadcasting television and radio commercials aimed at children and adolescents, although industry leaders deny they target youth. These efforts are part of a broader strategy to curtail or ban broadcast advertising of beverage alcohol in general or to require the alcoholic beverage industry or the broadcast media to finance antidrinking advertising on radio and television. This policy is still in the discussion stage.

wine jumped from just over 3¢ per 750-ml bottle to about 21¢, and the tax on a 750-ml bottle of 80-proof distilled spirits rose from $1.98 to $2.14.

Even though the beer and wine tax hikes were substantial, they fell far short of the 25¢ tax per ounce of pure alcohol in any alcoholic beverage that was initially proposed by the Bush Administration. The actual rates are approximately 10¢, 7¢, and 21¢ for beer, wine, and distilled spirits, respectively. In addition, although Congress may have been persuaded by the health-promotion aspects of higher alcohol taxes, the increases were well below those recommended by numerous public health organizations as prevention measures.

Like the federal government, state and local governments have raised taxes on alcohol modestly and infrequently, almost always with the intent of increasing revenues rather than discouraging alcohol abuse. Due in part to the stability of these taxes, the real prices on alcoholic beverages (i.e., their prices after accounting for the effects of inflation) have declined significantly over time (see Fig. 11.1). For example, between 1975 and 1990, the real price of distilled spirits fell by 32%, the real price of wine fell by 28%, and the real price of beer fell by 20%.

The recent increases in federal taxes on beer and distilled spirits fall far short of those needed to offset the effects of inflation since 1951. In 1991, for example, the distilled spirits tax rate would have to have been 75% higher and the beer tax rate would have to have been 162% higher to reach their real values as of 1951. If alcohol abuse is sensitive to price, as economists have argued, a policy of maintaining relatively low excise tax rates would exacerbate this problem. If alcohol consumption, particularly heavy consumption, is negatively affected by price, and if alcohol problems are positively related to alcohol consumption, increasing real excise tax rates would reduce alcohol consumption and its negative consequences. As a result, drinking and driving and other public health problems related to alcohol abuse would fall.

In this article, we review the research by economists on the price sensitivity of alcohol use and abuse by youths. This review emphasizes the work by our colleagues, Douglas Coate and Gregory Arluck, and by those at the Health Economics Program at the National Bureau of Economic Research (NBER), dealing with the effects of taxes on drinking, heavy drinking, and drinking and driving among young people. In addition, we summarize related research by Donald Kenkel of Pennsylvania State University and by Philip Cook and Michael Moore of Duke University. Because the policy to raise the minimum purchasing age to 21 has played such a prominent role in the antidrinking cam-

Real Alcoholic Beverage Prices
1975 - 1992

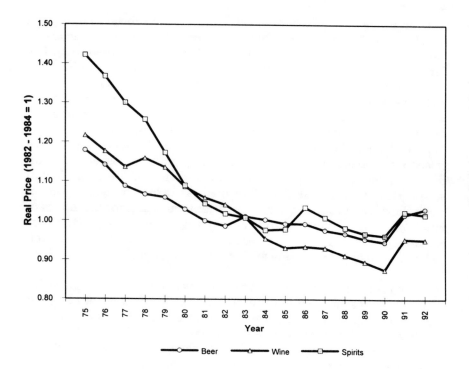

FIG. 11.1. Real alcoholic beverage prices. 1992 prices are for the first quarter. Distilled spirits prices from 1975 through 1977 are based on the whiskey price index. All data used for the figure are from Bureau of Labor Statistics, U.S. Department of Labor, *Monthly Labor Review*, various issues, and *Consumer Price Index-Detailed Report*, various issues.

paign, we compare tax or price effects with drinking-age effects in a variety of individual and state-level data sets that span the period from 1974 through 1989.

Before turning to a discussion of methods and results, we address some conceptual issues. A fundamental principle of economics is that of the downward sloping demand curve: As the price of any good rises, consumption of that good falls. Some economists have argued that the consumption of a potentially addictive good, such as alcohol, might be an exception to that rule. Numerous studies confirm, however, that this principle does apply to the demand for alcoholic beverages. (See Leung & Phelps, 1993, for a detailed review of these studies; see Manning, Blumberg, & Moulton, 1992, for the most recent estimates pertaining to all segments of the population.)

The studies just mentioned focus on the consumption of alcoholic beverages by adults or by all segments of the population. Yet there are reasons to believe that alcohol consumption by young people may be more sensitive to price than alcohol consumption by adults. One factor is that the fraction of disposable income that a youthful drinker spends on alcohol probably exceeds the corresponding fraction of an adult drinker's income. A second factor is that bandwagon or peer effects are much more important in the case of youth drinking than in the case of adult drinking (Rachal et al., 1980). Thus, a rise in price would curtail youth consumption directly and indirectly through its impact on peer consumption. Finally, youths are more likely to discount the future consequences of their current actions than adults. Becker, Grossman, and Murphy (1991) showed that this makes youths more responsive to price than adults are, and it makes adults more sensitive to changes in the perceived or actual harmful consequences that take place in the future.

Drinking-age hikes have been shown to have negative effects on alcohol consumption, alcohol abuse, and motor vehicle accident mortality (see O'Malley & Wagenaar, 1991, for the most recent of a number of studies). In comparing price or tax and drinking-age policies, we realize that the uniform drinking age of 21 is unlikely to be lowered in the future. The aim of the comparisons is to gauge the magnitude of the tax policy by contrasting its impact with that of a policy that was advocated widely in the 1980s.

Of course, an effectively enforced prohibition of alcohol consumption by persons below the age of 21 should have a larger effect on their consumption than would an increase in the excise tax rate. Because of the problem of evasion, however, the effects of the minimum-age law are diminished. Underage youths can obtain alcohol from their older siblings or friends. In addition, they can purchase fake identification cards or buy alcohol in stores that do not demand proof of age. This type of evasion simply is not possible with an excise tax hike; the responsiveness of youths to the price of alcohol determines the change in consumption.

Put differently, the "full" price of consuming alcohol equals the sum of the monetary price and the indirect price. An increase in the tax rate on alcohol raises the monetary price. From the point of view of an underage youth, an increase in the drinking age raises such indirect price components as the expected penalty for breaking the law, the financial cost of a fake identification and the value of the time required to obtain one, and the value of the time required to find a store that does not demand proof of age. Thus, tax hikes and drinking-age hikes can be treated in a symmetrical manner. A 10¢ increase in the tax rate raises the monetary price of alcohol by 10¢.[2] A 3-year increase in the drinking age from 18 to 21 raises the indirect price of alcohol for an 18-year-old by an unknown amount. In turn, this amount depends on how strictly or loosely the law is enforced. We return to the issue of enforcement and its role in the design of optimal policies to curtail alcohol abuse after reviewing the empirical evidence.

METHODS

The research on youth alcohol consumption discussed in this chapter uses five nationally representative data sets. These are the first National Health and Nutrition Examination Survey (NHANES I), conducted by the National Center for Health Statistics (NCHS) from 1971 through 1974 (Grossman, Coate, & Arluck, 1987); the second National Health and Nutrition Examination Survey (NHANES II), conducted by NCHS from 1976 through 1980 (Coate & Grossman, 1988); the 1982 and 1989 surveys of high-school seniors conducted by the University of Michigan's Institute for Social Research as part of the Monitoring the Future (MTF) project (our research with these two surveys is reported for the first time in this article); and the 1985 National Health Interview Survey (NHIS) conducted by NCHS (Kenkel, 1993a). The research on youth motor vehicle accident mortality is based on time series of state cross sections for the periods 1975–1981 (Saffer & Grossman, 1987) and 1982–1988 (Chaloupka, Saffer, & Grossman, 1993). The study of alcohol consumption and college completion uses the National Longitudinal Survey of Youth (NLSY), which was begun in 1979 by Ohio State University's Human Resource Research Center and the U.S. Department of Labor (Cook & Moore, 1993).

Much of this research focuses on the cost of beer and the consumption of beer (where possible) because beer is the most popular alcoholic beverage among young people. It capitalizes on substantial differences

---

[2]This assumes that the alcohol beverage industry is competitive and has a perfectly elastic supply function. These conditions are necessary for all of the increase in the tax to be shifted from producers to consumers. Grossman's preliminary research on the determinants of beer prices in the Chamber of Commerce Researchers Association quarterly survey suggests that a 10¢ increase in the state excise tax rate on beer raises the price of beer approximately 10¢. Cook (1981) estimated that a 10¢ increase in the state excise tax rate on distilled spirits raises the prices of distilled spirits 12¢.

in legal drinking ages among states and substantial differences in alcoholic beverage prices among states primarily due to differences in state excise tax rates on these beverages. During the period from 1974 through 1989, for example, state legal drinking ages ranged from 18 to 21 years. In the same period, state excise tax rates on a case of twenty-four 12-oz cans of beer ranged from 4.5¢ in Wyoming to $2.28 in Georgia.

We add beer prices, taxes, and legal drinking ages to the NHANES I and II, the 1982 and 1989 MTF, the 1985 NHIS, and the NLSY on the basis of a given youth's place of residence. Variants of multiple regression methods for categorical dependent variables are used to examine the effects of changes in beer prices or taxes and minimum legal drinking ages on the outcomes at issue while holding constant other determinants of these outcomes, including age, sex, race, and parental characteristics. The beer price and the state beer excise tax are used as alternative measures of the cost of beer because consistent beer-price series are not available for all years in the survey periods. Results with these alternative measures are very similar.

In NHANES I, the outcome pertains to whether persons 16 to 21 years of age consume more than five cans of beer on a typical drinking day in the previous year, three to five cans of beer on a typical drinking day, one to two cans of beer on a typical drinking day, or abstain from beer consumption. The NHANES II outcome identifies persons 16 to 21 years of age who consume beer four to seven times per week in the previous 3 months, one to three times a week, less than once a week, or never. Three alternative measures of alcohol consumption by high-school seniors are employed in the 1982 and 1989 MTF. The first pertains to drinking in the previous year, and it categorizes youths as frequent drinkers (i.e., reporting more than 39 drinking occasions), fairly frequent drinkers (i.e., reporting 10 to 39 drinking occasions), infrequent drinkers (reporting 1 to 9 drinking occasions), and abstainers. The second measure of alcohol consumption focuses on drinking during the month before the survey, and it again defines youths as frequent drinkers (i.e., reporting more than 9 occasions), fairly frequent drinkers (i.e., reporting 6 to 9 occasions), infrequent drinkers (i.e., reporting 1 to 5 occasions), and abstainers. The third measure focuses on heavy drinking, as defined by at least one drinking episode in which five or more drinks were consumed in the 2 weeks before the survey. These data differ from the NHANES I and II data in that the type of alcoholic beverage consumed is unknown. The outcome in the 1985 NHIS is the number of days in the previous year on which a person between the ages of 18 and 21 had five or more drinks of any alcoholic beverage. The outcome in NLSY is college completion by persons between the ages of 14 and 15 at baseline.

In the motor vehicle accident mortality research, logit regressions are estimated for persons between the ages of 18 and 20 in two time series of state cross sections (1975–1981 and 1982–1988). In addition to the real beer excise tax rate (the sum of the federal and state excise tax rate divided by the Consumer Price Index), other determinants of alcohol consumption and fatality rates are held constant. These include: real income; measures of traffic, roadway, and vehicle conditions; driver characteristics; religious participation; and the fraction of the state population residing in counties prohibiting the sale of alcoholic beverages. In the 1982–1988 data set, the effects of recent state legislation discouraging drinking and driving by raising the probability of arrest and conviction for driving under the influence of alcohol (DUI) and increasing the severity of the penalties associated with a DUI conviction also are examined. In this data set, three different fatality rates for both the overall population and youths ages 18 to 20 are examined. The first of these is the total motor vehicle accident fatality rate for each age group. In an attempt to focus on alcohol involvement in these fatalities, two additional, driver-specific, fatality rates are defined. The first is limited to drivers killed between 12:00 a.m. and 3:59 a.m., and it is called the night-time driver fatality rate. The National Highway Traffic Safety Administration (1986) estimated that 75% to 90% of these drivers had been drinking. The second driver-specific fatality rate uses information on the blood alcohol concentration of drivers killed in traffic accidents, and it is called the alcohol involved driver fatality rate.

RESULTS

The measures of alcohol use and motor vehicle accident mortality described previously are negatively related to the cost of alcohol and the legal drinking age. College completion rates are positively related to these two variables. All the estimated effects are statistically significant.

With regard to the magnitudes of the effects at issue, consider the beer consumption effects in NHANES II. A federal policy that increases the tax on beer to offset the effects of inflation since 1951 would have reduced the percentage of youths who drink beer frequently (i.e., four to seven times per week) in NHANES II, from 11% of the sample to

10.2% of the sample. Thus, the policy would have reduced the number of frequent beer drinkers by 7.3%. At the same time, it would have reduced the percentage of fairly frequent (i.e., one to three times a week) beer drinkers from 28% to 26.5%, a total reduction of 5.2%. If this policy were combined with one that raises the tax on the pure alcohol in beer to the same level as that on the pure alcohol in distilled spirits, the reductions in consumption would have been much sharper: a 32% reduction in the number of frequent youth drinkers and a 24% fall in the number of fairly frequent drinkers. The reductions predicted from this combined tax policy are greater than those associated with an alternative policy simulation: a uniform legal drinking age of 21 years. The latter policy would have reduced the number of frequent drinkers by 28% and the number of fairly frequent drinkers by 11%.

In Table 11.1, we use our estimates from the 1982 MTF high-school senior survey to simulate the effects of a policy under which the legal drinking age is 21 in all states in that year and the federal excise tax is indexed to the rate of inflation since 1951. The inflation tax policy would have reduced the number of high-school seniors who drank frequently (i.e., more than 39 times) in the previous year (21% of all seniors) by 45%, the number who drank frequently (i.e., more than nine times) in the previous month (16% of all seniors) by 43%, and the number with at least one heavy drinking episode (i.e., consumption of five or more drinks) in the previous 2 weeks (40% of all seniors) by 18%. These declines are quite large in relation to the drinking-age policy. Under the latter policy, the number of frequent drinkers in the previous year would have declined by 8%, the number of frequent drinkers in the previous month would have dropped by 9%, and the number of high-school seniors with at least one heavy drinking episode in the previous 2 weeks would have dropped by 4%.

Table 11.2 contains an inflation excise tax policy simulation based on our estimates for the 1989 MTF high-school senior survey. The drinking-age policy was not simulated because all states had a drinking age of 21 in that year.[3] The predicted declines in the number of high-school seniors who drank frequently in the previous year or in the previous month, or who drank heavily in the previous 2 weeks associated with the excise tax policy are smaller in Table 11.2 than in Table 11.1. On the basis of the 1989 survey, the tax policy would have caused a 20% decline in the number of youths who drank frequently in

---

[3]Because some state drinking laws enacted in the late 1980s contained grandfather clauses, the effective legal drinking age was not 21 in all states until the middle of 1990. There was, however, little variation in effective legal drinking ages in 1989.

TABLE 11.1
High-School Senior Alcohol Use, Legal Drinking Ages, and Beer Excise Taxes, 1982

Outcome	Actual Distribution (Percentage)	Drinking-Age Policy[a]	Inflation Tax Policy[b]
Panel A: Drinking in previous year			
Abstainers (no drinking occasions)	12.8	+10.6	+80.1
Infrequent drinkers (1 to 9 drinking occasions)	36.3	+3.2	+15.8
Fairly frequent drinkers (10 to 39 drinking occasions)	30.1	−2.5	−19.7
Frequent drinkers (more than 39 drinking occasions)	20.8	−8.3	−45.2
Panel B: Drinking in previous month			
Abstainers (no drinking occasions)	30.1	+7.6	+42.0
Infrequent drinkers (1 to 5 drinking occasions)	41.4	−0.3	−5.4
Fairly frequent drinkers (6 to 9 drinking occasions)	13.0	−5.2	−27.7
Frequent drinkers (more than 9 drinking occasions)	15.5	−9.2	−43.0
Panel C: Heavy drinking in previous 2 weeks (one or more episodes of consumption of at least five drinks in a row)			
No heavy drinking episodes	59.7	+2.6	+12.0
At least one heavy drinking episode	40.3	−4.1	−18.4

[a]The drinking age policy pertains to a minimum legal purchasing age of 21 in all states. Figures represent the percentage change in the number of youths in each category.
[b]Indexing the federal beer excise tax to inflation since 1951 implies a tax of approximately 59¢ per six-pack in 1982. Figures represent the percentage change in the number of youths in each category.

the previous year (i.e., 13% of the 1989 sample), an 11% drop in the number of youths who drank frequently in the previous month (i.e., 10% of the sample), and a 7% fall in the number who drank heavily in the previous two weeks (i.e., 32% of the sample). Thus, the 1982 declines are between two and four times larger than the corresponding 1989 declines.

One explanation of this result is that high-school seniors faced a higher indirect cost of obtaining alcohol in 1989 compared to 1982 because of the upward trend in the legal drinking age. Hence, the same percentage increase in the monetary price of beer in the 2 years represented a smaller percentage increase in the full price of this good in 1989. If the drinking-age policy effectively prohibited alcohol consumption by all persons below the age of 21, for example, an increase in the monetary price would have no impact on the full price. Clearly, because the declines associated with the inflation excise tax policy in Table 11.2 are bigger than those associated with the drinking-age policy in Table 11.1, the upward trend in the drinking age has not prohibited alcohol consumption by high-school seniors.

Kenkel's (1993a) research with the 1985 NHIS indicates that a legal drinking age of 21 in that year would have caused approximately the same 18% reduction in the number of days in the previous year on which a person between the ages of 18 and 21 had five or more drinks of alcohol as a federal excise tax hike large enough to raise the price of beer by 14%. The inflation tax policies in Tables 11.1 and 11.2 would have raised the price of beer by approximately this percentage. Thus, Kenkel's (1993a) estimates of the sensitivity of youth alcohol use to price in relation to its sensitivity to the drinking age are somewhat smaller than ours. In part, this divergence is due to the differences in his outcome measures compared to ours. In particular, our heavy-drinking measure pertains to the previous 2 weeks, and it simply identifies high-school seniors with at least one heavy drinking occasion in that period of time.

TABLE 11.2
High-School Senior Alcohol Use and Beer Excise Taxes, 1989

Outcome	Actual Distribution (Percentage)	Inflation Tax Policy[a]
Panel A: Drinking in previous year		
Abstainers (no drinking occasions)	15.3	+21.5
Infrequent drinkers (1 to 9 drinking occasions)	44.4	+3.8
Fairly frequent drinkers (10 to 39 drinking occasions)	27.1	−8.8
Frequent drinkers (more than 39 drinking occasions)	13.2	−19.6
Panel B: Drinking in previous month		
Abstainers (no drinking occasions)	39.2	+6.2
Infrequent drinkers (1 to 5 drinking occasions)	41.2	−1.8
Fairly frequent drinkers (6 to 9 drinking occasions)	6.9	−6.6
Frequent drinkers (more than 9 drinking occasions)	10.1	−10.1
Panel C: Heavy drinking in previous 2 weeks (one or more episodes of consumption of at least five drinks in a row)		
No heavy drinking episodes	68.1	+3.1
At least one heavy drinking episode	31.9	−6.5

[a]Indexing the federal beer excise tax to inflation since 1951 implies a tax of approximately 76¢ per six-pack in 1989. Figures represent the percentage change in the number of youths in each category.

The main message of the research on youth alcohol use is that the incidence of frequent consumption and the incidence of heavy consumption are inversely related to the price of alcohol in nationally representative surveys. It is particularly notable that these effects emerge in three surveys in the 1980s: the 1982 MTF, the 1985 NHIS, and the 1989 MTF. This is because predictions of the effects of future tax hikes are on firmer ground if they are based on recent data. The research suggests that the negative price effects in the research with the two surveys in the 1970—NHANES I and NHANES II—have not been diluted over time. If reductions in youth alcohol consumption and heavy consumption are desired, therefore, the research indicates that an increase in the federal excise tax on beer is effective in accomplishing this goal. These findings are particularly important because discouraging youth alcohol abuse is likely to lead to substantial future reductions in alcohol abuse among all individuals (recall the positive relationship between alcohol abuse in adolescence and alcohol abuse in later life reported by Rachal et al., 1980) and because frequent and/or heavier drinkers are likely to be responsible for a large percentage of youth motor vehicle crashes and deaths. Indeed, Kenkel (1993a) reported a strong positive association between the number of days youths consumed five or more drinks of alcohol in the previous year and the reported number of occasions of drunk driving in the previous year.

With regard to the magnitudes of the motor vehicle accident mortality effects, Saffer and Grossman (1987) simulated the policies just described for 18- to 20-year-olds in the period from 1975–1981. The enactment of a minimum uniform drinking age of 21 years in all states would have reduced the number of 18- to 20-year-olds killed in motor vehicle crashes by 8% in that period. A policy that fixed the federal excise tax on beer in real terms since 1951 would have reduced the number of lives lost in fatal crashes by 15%, and a policy that taxed the alcohol in beer at the same rate as the alcohol in distilled spirits would have lowered the number of lives lost by 21%. A combination of the two tax policies would have caused a 54% decline in the number of youths killed. These reductions should be compared to the roughly 7,000 persons per year in this age category who died in motor vehicle crashes in the period at issue.

Table 11.3 shows simulated effects of tax and drinking-age policies for 18- to 20-year-olds based on the regression results in Chaloupka et al. (1993). The numbers in each cell give the absolute change in the number of youths killed in fatal crashes in a typical year in the period from 1982–1988 due to the policies identified in the first column. The figures in parentheses are percentage changes in fatality rates due to these policies. For comparative purposes, note that Saffer and Grossman's (1987) computations reveal that the lives of 1,022 youths ages 18 to 20 would have been saved in a typical year in the 1975–1981 period if the federal excise tax on beer had been indexed to the rate of inflation since 1951. In addition, the lives of 555 youths ages 18 to 20 per year would have been saved if the drinking age had been 21 in all states of the United States.

The figures in Table 11.3 indicate that the impact of beer tax increases on youth motor vehicle fatalities in the mid 1980s should not be understated. If anything, these effects are greater than those obtained by Saffer and Grossman (1987) for fatalities in the late 1970s. The inflation excise tax policy, for instance, would have saved 1,660 lives per year in the 1982–1988 period, or more than one and a half times the number of lives per year saved by the same policy in the 1975–1981 period. This policy also would have cut the number of nighttime driver fatalities and the number of alcohol-involved driver fatalities by 40% in each case. Initially, the Bush Administration proposed a tax of 25¢ per ounce of pure alcohol in beer or 81¢ per six-pack. According to our estimates, this policy would have saved 527 more lives per year in the middle and late 1980s than the inflation tax policy would have.

The 1991 increase in the federal excise tax on beer from 16¢ per

TABLE 11.3
Motor Vehicle Accident Mortality Simulations, 18- to 20-Year-Olds, 1982–1988[a]

Simulation	Total Fatalities	Nighttime Driver Fatalities	Alcohol-Involved Driver Fatalities
Real beer tax maintains 1951 value — increase nominal tax with CPI (71.6¢ per six-pack in 1988)	− 1,660 − 32.1%	− 379 − 39.1%	− 739 − 40.3%
Impose a tax of 25¢ per ounce of pure alcohol in beer (81¢ per six-pack)	− 2,187 − 42.2%	− 491 − 50.7%	− 957 − 52.3%
Deficit reduction tax increase — doubling of the beer tax to 32¢ per six-pack	− 611 − 11.8%	− 145 − 14.9%	− 285 − 15.6%
Minimum legal purchase age of 21 years in all states	− 166 − 3.2%	− 42 − 4.4%	− 138 − 7.5%
Minimum legal purchase age of 18 years in all states	+ 498 + 9.6%	+ 118 + 12.1%	+ 389 + 21.3%

[a]Each cell contains estimates of the absolute change in fatalities per year, on average, of the simulated policy (first row) and the percentage change in the fatality rate resulting from the policy simulation (second row).

six-pack to 32¢ would have reduced the number of youths killed in fatal crashes by 611 per year if it had been enacted 9 years earlier. Although this saving in lives is much smaller than the saving under either of the two tax policies discussed previously, it is larger than the 166 additional lives saved per year under a minimum legal purchase age of 21 in all states in the period 1982–1988 or the 498 additional lives lost under a minimum purchase age of 18 in all states in the same period. Put differently, the gain in lives from going to a purchasing age of 18 in all states to a purchasing age of 21 in all states amounts to 664 lives. This is approximately equal to the life-saving impact of a doubling in the beer tax and only two fifths as large as the life-saving effect of a policy that indexes the beer tax to the rate of inflation since 1951. As in the case of the youth alcohol use studies, the basic conclusion to be drawn from the research on motor vehicle accident fatalities is that increases in alcoholic beverage taxes are an effective means of accomplishing the goal of reductions in drunk driving and related deaths in traffic crashes among youth.

DISCUSSION

Can one compute the appropriate or optimal tax on alcohol on the basis of the studies summarized in this chapter? The answer is a qualified *yes*, once the results of other studies are considered. In the language of economics, alcohol use and abuse impose significant external costs. That is, at least part of the costs associated with alcohol abuse are borne by those other than the abuser. These include the loss of life, injuries, and property damage associated with drunk driving and other accidents; loss of life from violent crime; increased health care and insurance costs; and lost productivity costs. Pogue and Sgontz (1989) and Manning, Keeler, Newhouse, Sloss, and Wasserman (1989) reported these external abuse costs as approximately $175 per gallon of pure alcohol, in 1991 prices.[4]

To determine the optimal excise tax on alcohol, the reduction in external costs due to tax hikes must be weighed against the increase in

---

[4]The classification of the costs that abusers impose on themselves is not clear. These are not external costs if the abusers are fully informed about the consequences of their actions, but they are external costs in the case of completely uninformed abusers. In intermediate cases, some portion of these costs should be included in the benefits from reductions in abuse. The studies cited previously present ranges of estimates based on alternative classifications of the costs that abusers impose on themselves.

costs imposed on society by the tax (i.e., the welfare costs of the tax). The imposition of an alcohol excise tax or an increase in its rate results in a loss of consumer surplus—defined as the difference between the value of alcohol to consumers and the amount that they pay for it. Consumer surplus arises because each unit of a good is sold at the same price. This price equals the value of the marginal or last unit purchased by the consumer. Other units are more highly valued than the marginal unit. The welfare costs of the tax equal the loss in consumer surplus minus the revenue generated from the tax. The increase in tax revenue, which is always smaller than the loss in consumer surplus, represents a gain for members of society and must be subtracted from the loss in consumer surplus to obtain the welfare cost of the tax.

On the basis of these notions, Pogue and Sgontz (1989), Manning et al. (1989), and Saffer and Chaloupka (1994) estimated the optimal tax on alcohol in 1991 at $73, $78, and $79 per gallon of pure alcohol, respectively. In 1991, the actual average tax on a gallon of pure alcohol was approximately $35. This suggests that alcohol taxes could be more than doubled before the costs of the increased taxes would begin to exceed their benefits.[5]

The studies cited previously determine optimal tax rates in the context of alcohol abuse among all segments of the population. In a study limited to abuse among teenagers and young adults, Phelps (1988) made use of estimates of the effects of beer taxes on youth alcohol abuse and motor vehicle accident mortality provided by Grossman et al. (1987) and Saffer and Grossman (1987) to compute the optimal tax of beer. His optimal tax lies in the range of 25% to 40% or more of the price of beer. The 1991 rate of approximately 16% (inclusive of federal and state beer taxes) is much smaller than this range. Moreover, Phelps excludes the value of the higher college completion rates due to excise tax hikes reported by Cook and Moore (1993).

To highlight the effectiveness of the tax policy, suppose that one had to choose between this policy and a policy to discourage youth alcohol abuse by raising the minimum legal drinking age from 18 to 21 years. The drinking age is unlikely to fall to 18 in the near future, and we are not necessarily advocating a choice between these two policies. This hypothetical choice involves a similar comparison to the one made

---

[5]To maintain the optimal tax in real terms after 1991, it would have to be indexed to the rate of inflation. The same objective could be accomplished by converting to an *ad valorem* alcoholic beverage excise tax system. Under this system, the tax rate is expressed as a fixed percentage of price.

previously of the welfare costs and benefits (i.e., reductions in external costs) of the two policies. One factor that favors the drinking-age policy in this comparison is that excise tax hikes impose welfare costs on all segments of the population, but minimum-age laws are targeted at the group in the population that accounts for a disproportionate share of motor vehicle accidents and deaths. Two factors, however, point in the opposite direction. First, the enforcement and administrative costs associated with a uniform drinking age of 21 are likely to be much higher than those associated with the tax policy. Second, as emphasized by Kenkel (1993b), the loss in consumer surplus due to a rise in the drinking age cannot in this case be partially offset by an increase in tax revenue because there is no increase in revenue.

Kenkel (1993b) focused on the welfare cost aspect of the previously mentioned choice by comparing policies with the same benefits in terms of reductions in youth alcohol abuse. He considered two specific options: a uniform drinking age of 21, as opposed to 18, and an excise tax hike large enough to raise the price of alcohol by approximately 14%. The 1991 federal beer tax rate of 84¢ per six-pack required to fully adjust for inflation since 1951 would have raised the price of a six-pack by roughly 14%. Using an estimate of the price elasticity of demand for alcohol (i.e., the percentage reduction in consumption caused by a 1% increase in price) of −.7, he found that the welfare costs of the drinking-age policy were approximately one and a half times larger than the welfare costs of the tax policy because the reduction in consumer surplus cannot be offset by an increase in tax revenue when the drinking age rises. This finding does not take into account the costs of enforcing a minimum purchasing age of 21 years.

In conclusion, the research we have summarized suggests that if reductions in youth alcohol consumption, heavy alcohol consumption, and alcohol-related injuries and deaths are desired, an increase in federal taxes on alcoholic beverages is an effective policy to accomplish these goals. Furthermore, current estimates of the external costs associated with alcohol abuse indicate that the appropriate taxes on alcohol should be substantially higher than current taxes. The tax policy appears to be more potent than a uniform drinking age of 21, and the welfare costs of the former appear to be smaller than those of the latter. Combined with Kenkel's (1993a) conclusion that the welfare costs of policies to deter drunk driving exceed those of tax or drinking-age initiatives, the evidence in this article highlights the extremely favorable cost-benefit ratio of tax policy as a vehicle to reduce drunk driving and other negative consequences of excessive alcohol consumption.

ACKNOWLEDGMENTS

Research for this chapter was supported by Grant 5 R01 AA08359 from the National Institute on Alcohol Abuse and Alcoholism to the National Bureau of Economic Research (NBER).

We are indebted to Patrick M. O'Malley and Jerome J. Hiniker of the University of Michigan's Institute for Social Research (ISR) for providing us with restricted data sets from the Monitoring the Future surveys of 1982 and 1989, containing county identifiers. We also are indebted to Jan Howard and three anonymous referees for helpful comments on an earlier draft.

This chapter has not undergone the review accorded official NBER publications; in particular, it has not been submitted for approval by the board of directors.

REFERENCES

Becker, G. S., Grossman, M., & Murphy, K. M. (1991). Rational addiction and the effect of price on consumption. *American Economic Review, 81,* 237–241.

Chaloupka, F. J., Saffer, H., & Grossman, M. (1993). Alcohol-control policies and motor-vehicle fatalities. *Journal of Legal Studies, 22,* 161–186.

Coate, D., & Grossman, M. (1988). Effects of alcoholic beverage prices and legal drinking ages on youth alcohol use. *Journal of Law and Economics, 31*(1), 145–171.

Cook, P. J. (1981). The effect of liquor taxes on drinking, cirrhosis, and auto fatalities. In M. H. Moore & D. R. Gerstein (Eds.), *Alcohol and public policy: Beyond the shadow of prohibition* (pp. 255–285). Washington, DC: National Academy.

Cook, P. J., & Moore, M. J. (1993). Drinking and schooling. *Journal of Health Economics, 12,* 411–430.

Grant, B. F., Hartford, T. C., Chou, P., Pickering, R., Dawson, D. A., Stinson, F. S., & Noble, J. (1991). Prevalence of DSM–III–R alcohol abuse and dependence. *Alcohol Health & Research World, 15,* 91–96.

Grossman, M., Coate, D., & Arluck, G. M. (1987). Price sensitivity of alcoholic beverages in the United States. In H. D. Holder (Ed.), *Control issues in alcohol abuse prevention: Strategies for states and communities* (pp. 169–198). Greenwich, CT: JAI.

Kenkel, D. S. (1993a). Drinking, driving, and deterrence: The social costs of alternative policies. *Journal of Law and Economics, 36,* 877–914.

Kenkel, D. S. (1993b). Prohibition versus taxation: reconsidering the legal drinking age. *Contemporary Policy Issues, 11*(3), 48–57.

Leung, S. F., & Phelps, C. E. (1993). "My kingdom for a drink...?" A review of the price sensitivity of demand for alcoholic beverages. In G. Bloss & M. Hilton (Eds.), *Economic and socioeconomic issues in the prevention of alcohol-related problems* (pp. 1–31). Washington, DC: U.S. Government Printing Office.

Manning, W. G., Blumberg, L., & Moulton, L. H. (1992, May). *The demand for alcohol: The differential response to price.* Paper presented at the Third Annual Health Economics Workshop at Johns Hopkins University, Baltimore, MD.

Manning, W. G., Keeler, E. B., Newhouse, J. P., Sloss, E. M., & Wasserman, J. (1989). The taxes of sin: Do smokers and drinkers pay their way? *Journal of the American Medical Association, 261,* 1604–1609.

National Highway Traffic Safety Administration. (1986). *Fatal accident reporting system, 1984.* (DOT HS Rep. No. 806 919). Washington, DC: U.S. Department of Transportation.

O'Malley, P. M., & Wagenaar, A. C. (1991). Effects of minimum drinking age laws on alcohol use, related behaviors and traffic crash involvement among American youth: 1976–1987. *Journal of Studies on Alcohol, 52, 478–491.*

Phelps, C. E. (1988). Death and taxes: An opportunity for substitution. *Journal of Health Economics, 7,* 1–24.

Pogue, T. F., & Sgontz, L. G. (1989). Taxing to control social costs: The case of alcohol. *American Economic Review, 79,* 235–243.

Rachal, J. V., Guess, L. L., Hubbard, R. L., Maisto, S. A., Cavanaugh, E. R., Waddell, R., & Benrud, C. H. (1980). *The extent and nature of adolescent alcohol abuse: The 1974 and 1978 national sample surveys* (NTIS No. PB81–199267). Springfield, VA: U.S. National Technical Information Service.

Ross, H. L. (1990). Deterring drunken driving: An analysis of current efforts. *Alcohol Health and Research World, 14,* 58–62.

Saffer, H., & Chaloupka, F. J. (1994). Alcohol tax equalization and social costs. *Eastern Economic Journal, 20,* 33–43.

Saffer, H., & Grossman, M. (1987). Beer taxes, the legal drinking age, and youth motor vehicle fatalities. *Journal of Legal Studies, 16*(2), 351–374.

Voas, R. B., & Moulden, J. (1980). Historical trends in alcohol use and driving by young Americans. In H. Wechsler (Ed.), *Minimum drinking age laws: An evaluation* (pp. 59–72). Lexington, MA: Heath.

Author Index

Subject Index